LOVE-CENTERED
MARRIAGE
IN A
SELF-CENTERED
WORLD

LOVE-CENTERED MARRIAGE IN A SELF-CENTERED WORLD

IRVING SARNOFF and SUZANNE SARNOFF
New York University

⬤ HEMISPHERE PUBLISHING CORPORATION
A member of the Taylor & Francis Group
New York   Philadelphia   Washington   London

LOVE–CENTERED MARRIAGE IN A SELF–CENTERED WORLD

1 2 3 4 5 6 7 8 9 0   B R B R   8 9 8 7 6 5 4 3 2 1 0 9

This book was set in Century by Hemisphere Publishing
Corporation. The editors were Sandra Tamburrino and
John P. Rowan; the managing editor was Ralph Eubanks;
and the typesetter was Shirley J. McNett.
Braun-Brumfield, Inc. was printer and binder.

Library of Congress Cataloging-in-Publication Data

Sarnoff, Irving, date.
    Love-centered marriage in a self-centered world /
Irving Sarnoff and Suzanne Sarnoff.
        p.   cm.
    Includes bibliographies and index.

    1. Marriage. 2. Love. I. Sarnoff, Suzanne. II. Title.
    HQ734.S264   1989
    306.81——dc20   89-32933
                                                           CIP

ISBN 0-89116-927-X (cloth)
ISBN 0-89116-939-3 (paper)

To our grandchildren

CONTENTS

PART II: LOVING FOR LIFE

PREFACE

Intuitively, people sense that marriage can be the best medium for satisfying their most profound yearning: the need to love and be loved. However, their intuition is shaken severely by a destructively self-centered world that incites everyone to compete unceasingly for economic and occupational superiority over others. Today, men and women are very uncertain about where to place love in their scale of values, and they are extremely susceptible to the divisive pressures of their individualistic pursuits. They also lack the knowledge essential to assure their gratification and to resolve the conflicts that inevitably arise between spouses. Burdened by such doubts and confusion, how is it possible for husbands and wives to preserve and deepen the fulfillments of the love for which they married?

Our answer to this question has emerged from a long and intensive study. Naturally, we familiarized ourselves with the extensive literature on love and marriage. We also drew on relevant writings in social philosophy, human sexuality, intimate relationships, personality development, and family systems theory. In addition, we interviewed couples who had been married for varying lengths of time, taking them step by step through an open-ended questionnaire we designed for that purpose. But the most unusual aspect of our investigation evolved from our decision to do everything possible to resolve whatever philosophical and psychological conflicts we needed to work through in order to maximize the sharing of our love.

Sometimes, in the course of our marriage, we succeeded in feeling better than we ever dared to believe people could feel. Those glorious experiences convinced us how wonderful married love could be. However, we frequently let ourselves drift into a maintenance operation, stoking the fire of our love just enough to keep it from going out. We also suffered through dreadful periods when we passed like floundering ships on a dark and stormy sea or when we collided, head-on, in outbursts of accumulated misery that we could neither comprehend nor quickly shed.

Thus, from the outset of our project, we directed our energies toward discovering what we were thinking, feeling, and doing when we gave love to each other and when we withheld it. We were already acquainted with existing attempts to account for happiness and dissatisfaction in marriage, but we also knew that none of those theories had explicitly focused on loving as the central phenomenon to be understood in the relationship between spouses.

In adopting that focus, we took on an intellectual challenge that had never been met before. Over time, we saw that our emerging conceptions applied just as cogently to other couples as to us. At that point, we committed ourselves wholeheartedly to the aim of constructing a valid formulation of how *all* spouses could keep love and marriage together for a lifetime.

Having transformed our interpersonal quest into a professional pursuit, we often felt we had trapped ourselves in an overwhelming task. Surely, we would be crushed by its ambiguity and difficulty, which exceeded our stamina and talents and which would make a mockery of our presumption to cope with it. Still, viewing our creative commitment as an expression of our marital one, we refused to let each other down.

To guide our efforts, we employed a dialectical method of exploration: learning by doing and changing what we did in the light of what we learned. Thus, we integrated theory with practice, putting our growing awareness into beneficial action.

However, our constructive changes often led us into new relational dilemmas that aroused old trepidations while demanding
fresh observations and interpretations. Sometimes we had to
remain suspended in anxiety and puzzlement for weeks or
months before we could make sense out of a particular difficulty or, having made such sense, before we could act consistently and effectively to remedy it.

Little by little, our gropings began to coalesce into overarching themes. Finally, we melded our ongoing writings into
an original model of marriage. In this book, therefore, we
present a new perspective on the unique potentials of marriage
for optimal fulfillment in lifelong loving. Addressing every couple's ambivalence about basic goals, we explain how crucial it
is for spouses to make the cultivation of their loving relationship the highest priority in their lives. Yet we fully acknowledge the actual difficulties of adhering to this position, and we
suggest ways for mates to safeguard the primacy of their
relationship—even as members of a society that breeds marital
disharmony.

By contrast, many previous books on marriage ignore the
fact that couples function within the constraints of society and
that they need to deal with the impact of this social context in
conducting their married lives. Besides, these works often advise a husband and wife to look for the origins of their marital
problems in the vicissitudes of their individual upbringing.
Mates are led into separate analyses of their personal histories,
resulting in the kind of solitary introspection and self-
preoccupation that is a barrier to communication and cooperation.

Our book does not perpetuate such deficiencies and mis-
conceptions. We do not imply that spouses are magically immune to the societal forces surrounding them, or that they can
thrive as a loving couple without a strategy to counteract the
corrosive inroads of the socioeconomic system. Instead, we
propose a secure foundation of love-centered values on which
to build a lifelong marriage, and we discuss how husbands and
wives can prevent the havoc of becoming too enmeshed in material acquisition and other forms of self-aggrandizement. Likewise, we point out viable alternatives to help couples harmonize their working lives and childrearing practices with the

cultivation of their own loving relationship. Extending the implications of equality between the sexes into marriage, we discuss how spouses enhance their common pleasure by accepting their intrinsic gender differences and by rejecting the gender-role stereotypes of their cultural conditioning.

Throughout the book we combine this social philosophy with a relational psychology, treating marriage with the depth of consideration its importance deserves. Yet we reduce the bewildering complexity of a marital relationship to manageable proportions, spelling out the essential knowledge mates need to gratify their love and to overcome their terrors of intimacy. In Part I we present the values and dynamics of a love-centered marriage. Articulating the promises and threats inherent in married loving, we describe how all spouses jointly construct the basic relational ingredients for sharing love and for defending against their fear of it.

Unlike traditional viewpoints, we do not treat love and sex as entirely separate motives. Taking a holistic view of the nature of love, we bring out its sexual and affectionate components. We devote equal attention to both facets, showing how satisfaction in each has a synergistic effect on a couple's well-being and, conversely, how suppression of either component is detrimental to their health and morale. But while love arises as an involuntary need, its fulfillment or frustration is contingent on human volition. Consequently, we amply cover the many initiatives spouses can take to increase their romantic involvement.

Departing from simplistic notions of marital discord, we do not portray love as the opposite of either combat or withdrawal. Rather, we uncover the interpersonal links between those defensive tactics and the fear of loving that all couples are bound to experience. With this illumination, spouses can expose the deceitful binds they tie around each other and release the reciprocal flow of their love.

Therefore, our relational psychology is a theoretical breakthrough of major importance. It provides a workable basis for understanding how mates are jointly and equally responsible for creating all aspects of their relationship in the here and now of their interactions. This knowledge permits a husband and wife to talk meaningfully about what they are doing together in the present rather than becoming bogged down in divisive and irrelevant explorations of their individual backgrounds and personalities.

In Part II we apply these dynamics to the process of relational development, setting forth a series of six marital stages that are based on desirable objectives for a lifetime of gratification and growth. In meeting each objective, a couple experiences the promises and threats of love in new ways. Accordingly, in portraying the essence of each stage, we describe in detail how spouses help each other to progress in their ability to love and surmount their predictable fear and defensiveness.

Our theory of relational development is also a novel and significant contribution to the literature on marriage. In keeping with the philosophical ideal of living for love, the desirable objectives we propose are attainable with the psychological insights we provide. Other authors have depicted the crucial junctures encountered by couples who marry in young adulthood, have children, and spend the rest of their lives together. But those accounts do not present a *plan* by which mates could approach each turning point as an opportunity to develop their full capacities for loving. By contrast, we regard this development as the central purpose of marriage, and we envision how a couple can channel all of their other activities and aspirations into it. At the same time, we show how a husband and wife actualize their finest human potentials in the process of developing their loving relationship. Highlighting the compatibility between relational and personal growth, we note the ways in which mates carry this improvement into more humane and honest relations with their children and other people.

Consistent with our goals in writing this book, we have made it accessible to both general and specialized readers. Our exposition facilitates the direct application of our ideas by spouses wishing to repair and enrich their relationships. It also speaks to the needs of engaged couples, as well as unattached and never-married adults who are looking for a balanced account of what a loving marriage is and could be. Similarly, our work gives divorced men and women a chance to see their past difficulties in a new light and to face the prospect of remarriage with greater insight and confidence.

Simultaneously, we offer a host of conceptual innovations

that practitioners can translate readily into effective interventions with distressed couples and families. Moreover, our theoretical framework may suggest fruitful lines of research for scholars in the areas of love and close relationships. Finally, our book is appropriate for adoption as a main or supplementary text in college courses on marriage, intimate relationships, and the family. Indeed, we have already used the manuscript in our own undergraduate classes on the psychology of marriage at New York University. Students responded enthusiastically, finding it intellectually stimulating and enjoyable to read. Many also reported that it helped them to understand and improve their relationships with spouses and fiancés.

Irving Sarnoff
Suzanne Sarnoff

Part I

LIVING FOR LOVE

1

LOVE-CENTERED MARRIAGE IN A SELF-CENTERED WORLD

As a loving relationship intended to last a lifetime, marriage has never been in greater trouble. Broken marriages are leaving more and more adults inwardly crushed—feeling like dismal failures in the one relationship they had chosen and counted on as their essential source of love. Divorce is also burdening a steadily rising number of children with chronic feelings of loneliness and depression, and it is depriving them of suitable models for learning how to function as loving mates when they grow up.

Among the couples who remain married for a lifetime, few are sterling examples of fulfillment in loving. The typical husband and wife quickly abandon the vibrant happiness they enjoyed as newlyweds. Often, they reluctantly decide to stay together "for the sake of the children." Sometimes they drop their original interest in loving and define themselves, quite literally, as partners in the business of guaranteeing their individual existences in a ruthlessly competitive society. Or they plod along hopelessly, resigned to their common despair.

Despite these appalling outcomes, over 90% of Americans continue to get married, and, among those who have been divorced once, about 80% are willing to marry again. Of course, all of these men and women are free to choose other lifestyles. But the magnetic allure of marriage is deeply rooted in the human psyche.

Intuitively, people sense that marriage can be the ideal relationship for gratifying all facets of their innate and enduring need for love: for giving and receiving affection, sexual pleasure, emotional security, and validation—a mutuality that makes everyone feel good about being alive. Besides, in married love men and women can find release from the oppressive confines of their psychological and physical separateness, while harmonizing the stirrings of their spirit with the goadings of their flesh. Both mates can satisfy their hunger for a wholeness of body and soul, and in conceiving and rearing children, they can attain the ultimate in creativity.

These are the longings that turn people toward marriage. Not a marriage of convenience; not an "open" or group marriage; not a two-timing or swinging marriage; not an easy-come, easy-go marriage. When a man and a woman take their wedding vows, they envision a lifetime of ever-increasing intimacy. They yearn to be a couple in the world, yet out of it—entranced by the unending magic of their desire to be together, individuals growing through their relationship yet merging more fully over time—the two who can be as one.

On making the unconditional and monogamous commitment of marriage, both partners pledge to pour all of their love into each other. Not a little or a lot, but all. Seen in this light, monogamy is desirable because it enables a man and a woman to become as deeply involved with each other as it is possible for any two people to be. Under such circumstances the sharing of their love can evoke the most profound feelings of spiritual communion between them; it can surpass every other pleasure in the exquisiteness of its sensual bliss, and it can leave a couple with a more healing state of inner well-being than anything else they could do individually or together. Thus, the emotional and erotic fulfillment of each spouse is compatible with a couple's fidelity, showing that the fullest gratification of love in marriage also happens to be consistent with the highest standards of morality.

If it is theoretically possible for marriage to be so fulfilling, why are so many couples either mired in chronic discontent or getting divorced?

Of course, lifelong loving requires mates to give much more of themselves than they have ever given to anyone before. It tests to the utmost their courage, empathy, patience, and ability to tolerate psychological ambiguity and stress. It draws without limit on their capacity for insight and their willingness to change. It confronts them with the challenge of constantly finding new ways of augmenting their intimacy—while earning a living, raising children, relating to other people, and absorbing the rapid shifts in social expectations about the roles men and women are supposed to enact in marriage.

Today, overshadowing all of these difficulties, a heavy cloud of existential uncertainty is afflicting spouses with anguished doubts about where to place love in their scale of values. At the same time spouses are extremely susceptible to the divisive pressures of separate careers and individualistic pursuits. In fact, given the destructively self-centered thrust of the contemporary world, it is a great accomplishment for *any* couple to create and develop a loving relationship.

Every country on earth—whether capitalistic or socialistic—is strongly committed to national ends and means that are diametrically opposed to love. All societies are primarily devoted to their own aggrandizement, enacted as the limitless striving to augment their wealth, power, and prestige.[1] Within each society, individual success is defined by how much one is "above" or "below" everyone else in income, occupational status, and the ability to control the lives of others. Between societies, progress is measured in terms of a country's "gross national product," "technological sophistication," and "defense capability"—in short, by the ability to buy, impress, and annihilate competitors.

People everywhere have become blindly concerned about making themselves invulnerable through self-glorification. Yet, in the process they have produced the most imminent dangers to their own lives, and to all human existence, by raping the earth, polluting the environment, and setting the stage for a nuclear holocaust. Even in western democracies, people continue to elect leaders who routinely rationalize the homicidal and suicidal implications of these policies: chiefs of state who piously assert, with the demented logic of a Dr. Strangelove, that military and ecological threats to survival on this planet are absolutely essential for maintaining their nations' "standard of living" and "way of life."

Unfortunately, the outlook for living and loving is no more promising among people in the "underdeveloped" countries. They aspire to precisely the same aggrandizing goals as those of their technological superiors. As they get modern equipment and scientific expertise, they employ it in the same destructive ways. So their "development" is also having the effect of hastening the headlong rush toward global devastation.

At elegant dinner parties in New York, London, Moscow, and Peking, educated men and women chat knowledgeably about these mortal and macabre questions: How is life going to end for us—in a whimper of slow suffocation or in the sudden bang of The Bomb? Which impending catastrophe is likely to kill more people—the melting of the polar icecaps or the meltdown of nuclear reactors?

Guests at these gatherings often voice useful ideas about what could be done to prevent such catastrophies. But, after the parties are over, they return to "business as usual." For how could they carry out their ordinary activities if they were constantly preoccupied with—and did nothing to stem—the appalling dangers that are enveloping them? Besides, wouldn't becoming a "success" before doomsday mean that one's life had not been lived in vain?

Of course, some people are responding appropriately to their dire predicament. On an international scale, many are pressing for an end to nuclear weaponry and power plants. Others have been forming networks of mutual help on a wide range of human needs: cooperatively producing and distributing organically grown foods; using renewable sources of energy; making socially responsible investments; and taking better care of their physical and mental health, as well as their interpersonal relationships.[2]

Still, the great majority of people go about their daily rounds with seeming confidence that all will be well for them as long as they follow the dictates and diversions of the societal status quo. When some dramatic harbinger of the Apocalypse, like the disaster at Chernobyl, pierces their facade of equanimity, they falsely deny that the same horror can befall them. The technocrats and bureaucrats of *their* nation, they convince themselves, would never be *so* fallible. Thus, they take immediate comfort in the delusion that such a calamity will always strike in some other place, far away, permitting them to watch its gruesome unfolding as televised entertainment in the coziness of their own homes.

Politically, whole populations are resorting to a similar mode of magical thinking. With the petulance of helpless children in distress, they regress into paroxysms of patriotism. "Take us to a strong leader," they demand, "someone who is tough enough to assume all the responsibility for sheltering us from any source of harm." Then, attributing their dreadful malaise to the presumably hostile designs of other nations, they give their own governments more money for armaments. So, they increase the likelihood of an international conflagration.

Simultaneously, large numbers of people are searching for deliverance through membership in religious institutions. Many of these congregants are only intensifying their long-standing reliance on the authority of their churches, synagogues, and mosques. But others are "born-again" religionists, who are scurrying back into these "folds" like panicky sheep and who are eagerly submitting to doctrines and rituals they had previously discarded as undemocratic and meaningless. Some have even joined fundamentalist sects, hypnotizing themselves into unquestioning obedience and zealously striving to spread the rigid tenets of their fanatical faith.

These fruitless patterns of "adjustment" show how far most human beings have gone in refusing to deal honestly with the horrifying situation they have brought upon themselves. Inevitably, this refusal is also being expressed in outright decadence—the ultimate in false consciousness—for decadence is knowing better but doing worse, and it is apparent that increasing numbers of people are deciding to do exactly what they know is bound to worsen not only the quality of their own lives but also that of their society.

In this cynical capitulation love is likely to be the first casualty. If people can no longer believe that life will go on beyond the span of their own existence, why should they worry about anyone's welfare, including their own? Why bother to sustain the life-enhancing qualities of a loving relationship—enduring involvement, effort, and care—when the endurance of life itself is so besieged? If one cannot stop the universal dance of death, why not join it? And join it they do, grabbing for as many transient "kicks" as they can get, from cocaine to craps, from one more drink to one-night stands.

The plight of love in the contemporary world is nowhere more poignant than it is in the United States. America does present couples with various societal supports that could be put to excellent use in securing the gratifications of marriage. The national creed of everyone's "inalienable right to life, liberty, and the pursuit of happiness" gives Americans a strong philosophical backing for choosing any lifestyle they believe will make them happy. Parents, schools, religious organizations, and the mass media also place considerable emphasis on the desirability of love, as well as on humanitarian, equalitarian, esthetic, and intellectual values, which can bring out the most socially constructive and intrinsically gratifying potentials of human nature. In addition, Americans have used some of their environmental riches and scientific inventiveness to nurture and improve the quality of life by creating an abundance of goods and services, by providing protection for health and conveniences for comfort, by increasing longevity, and by vastly expanding the range of cultural possibilities for human realization.

Theoretically, therefore, American men and women have an ideological and material base for founding a loving marriage. However, because the values of aggrandizement have become so firmly entrenched, most people tend to believe that happiness can best be secured through the accumulation of wealth, primarily, and, secondarily, through the power and prestige that money can buy.

Having individually embraced these self-centered values as their most revered goals in living, most people avidly pursue them throughout adulthood, and they frequently find it difficult to see that it may be impossible, through no fault of their own, to make much headway in climbing up "the ladder of success." In fact, the stratification of American society by economic class and racial caste provides some groups in the population with much less access to the coveted criteria of aggrandizement than it does to others. Besides, within the past few years, the gulf between the upper and lower classes has widened sharply, and corporate mergers have placed more and more of the nation's wealth in the hands of a shrinking circle of monopolists.

Still, most couples enter marriage with the illusion of being able to "have it all ways"—a continually increasing amount of money, status, influence, *and* fulfillment in love. Very soon, however, both mates are obliged to make a host of choices, testing the basic values that motivate them. Typically, they become more and more involved in pursuing the values of aggrandizement that are reinforced all around them by friends, family, neighbors, colleagues, and employers and that pop straight into their brains in the electronic showers they take every night while watching television.

Harboring more ambitions than they can possibly attain—even if they are members of socially advantaged groups—husband and wife become wrapped up in separate fantasies of personal glorification. In these private daydreams they may spend hours visualizing how to advance in their jobs, increase their income, get "one up" on their colleagues, receive more recognition in their communities, and exert more influence on their relatives. Similarly, if they feel they made a mistake or missed an opportunity in the process of aggrandizing themselves in any of these ways, they may inwardly "run the reel" over and over, imagining what they "could" or "should" have done to be perfect achievers.

Mates also bring a posture of social warfare into their marriage. After all, in the battle zone of daily work, each contestant is pitted against everyone else, and each is poised to drive himself or herself mercilessly in competing against others. Crazed from this combat, a husband and wife trample on one another while ignoring their own needs for the rest, relaxation, and peace of mind that are so essential for the cultivation of their love.

The American economy seems almost designed to keep couples in constant turmoil. Having become addicted to materialism, mates may feel that they never have "enough" money.

So they strap themselves to obtain it, often disregarding whether or not they are doing work that is harmful to themselves or others. Easy marks for easy credit, they may dig themselves into a bottomless financial hole from the first days of their marriage. Given such a situation, most of the reported arguments between mates hinge on the issue of money—who earns it, who makes the most, and who spends how much and for what.[3]

Of course, poverty can be extremely stressful for a couple's relationship. However, research studies have shown that size of income by itself does not accurately predict marital strife and instability.[4] Nor does wealth guarantee marital satisfaction. Rather, above the level of subsistence, a couple's economic contentment is most affected by how *relatively deprived* they feel. Thus, even affluent mates can see themselves as paupers in comparison to the *very* rich and famous. As their income goes up, they may feel an even greater desire for the material acquisitions that signify a higher social status, and they can wind up mutually shattered by their own insatiability. Consequently, many couples are leaving their loving relationships in ruins as they frenetically grasp for more.

THE QUEST FOR A LIFE DEVOTED TO LOVE

Ironically, many of these same people were deeply moved by the exhilarating wave of consciousness that began to sweep across the affluent nations of the West in the 1960s. It carried the inspiring message that human beings finally had on hand all the material resources, scientific knowledge, and technological capacity to produce abundance, health, and peace for everyone.

This insight was extremely momentous in both its personal and social implications. Most fundamentally, it meant that people no longer had any *practical* reason to remain abjectly subservient to mammoth and centralized socioeconomic structures, which *deliberately* create and enforce scarcity, generate not only the ravages of poverty but also those of war and pollution, and subject employees to competitive, impersonal, unhealthy, and authoritarian conditions of work. Indeed, with the nonexploitative use of miniaturized technology, as advo-

cated by Murray Bookchin, people could set up small, cooperative, and equalitarian communities that would also be economically viable, ecologically sound, and self-governing.[5]

Of course, only a few people dedicated themselves to such
radically different and liberatory forms of communal life. But
millions of men and women—especially young ones—explored
a variety of ways to nurture their raised consciousness. In effect, they began to turn away from the age-old competition to
become successful in aggrandizement, and they turned toward
being fulfilled in loving and in living peacefully with others.

In line with this change, these youthful explorers sought
greater personal access to a spiritual endowment that Carl
Jung had identified as unique to human beings.[6] This precious
gift is ordinarily called *wisdom*—an innate capacity for knowing how to live in optimal harmony with oneself, with other
people, and with the rest of nature.

To make more direct contact with this "spark of the divine" within themselves, these youths experimented, often simultaneously, with yoga, meditation, and psychedelic drugs.
Meanwhile, they effectively adapted their shift in values to the
politics of mass protest. Taking to the streets with the antibat-
tle cry of "Make Love Not War," they led a national drive that
finally pushed the American government into a withdrawal
from its invasion of Vietnam.

Regarding marital relationships, the organized movements
for female and male liberation gave couples a great impetus to
loosen the shackles of their social conditioning in the maintenance of gender inequality. Unfortunately, the resulting reactions of husbands and wives often were dolefully divisive.
Some mates interpreted such liberation as freedom from the
commitments they had made to be faithful to each other. So
they leapt into promiscuity, with predictably disastrous consequences for their mutual trust and relational solidarity. Other
spouses broke up their relationships because they were per-
suaded, erroneously, to view marriage as intrinsically and irre-
mediably unjust to women.

Among the persuaders, Kate Millett, echoing an opinion
popular with many feminists at the time, denounced monogamy as a patriarchal contrivance designed to perpetuate the
domination of men over women.[7] Yet while she invoked a clas-

sic work by Frederick Engels, *The Origins of the Family, Private Property, and the State,* to bolster her argument, she omitted a key element in his position. True, as she says, he believed that monogamy was invented to serve the male prerogatives of patriarchy, and he also saw marriage in existing societies as reflecting the sexism built into the stratification of socioeconomic class, with the husband accorded more status and power than the wife. However, Millett ignored Engels' explicitly stated conviction that a loving marriage is by nature monogamous, since "sexual love is by its nature exclusive. . . ."[8]

Certainly, while retaining a heartfelt fidelity to each other, countless spouses of the 1960s and 1970s did succeed in reducing their adherence to stereotypical gender roles. Many husbands unwrapped their sensitivity and tenderness, feeling free at last to talk about the nuances of their emotions and to participate more actively in rearing their children. At the same time, wives freely voiced anger over every facet of their social subjugation. They asserted their inherent right to the same work and pay as men and openly expressed their erotic desires. So, in their loving relationships, many spouses grew more comfortable about displaying the whole spectrum of feelings, abilities, and traits that characterize the common humanity of both sexes.

However, the reigning oligarchs of the Establishment mobilized their awesome powers of coercion to stop the momentum of the "counterculture." For example, in the spring of 1970 the Ohio National Guard shot and killed several students at Kent State University in the midst of an antiwar demonstration, and universities later set up severe penalties for students and faculty who might continue to use strikes and other kinds of civil disobedience that had erupted on college campuses across the country.

Naturally, feeling the full crunch of this oppression, erstwhile dissenters grew very wary about taking action that could cost them their livelihood—or even their lives. Moreover, dedicated to political means congruent with their philosophical ends, they had renounced the use of violence as a tactic for contending with the organized and legalized violence of the State.

Although these men and women had shown admirable

courage in their peaceful forms of protest, they had also been masking their inevitable fear under the false consciousness of a magical belief that a "new age" was already dawning—that they could bring their "love consciousness" securely into the world without endlessly struggling against the entrenched social opposition to it. Besides, most of these people were more "hooked" on individualism than they had thought themselves to be. Typically, even at the height of their transient rebellion, they endorsed the fallacy of equating freedom and fulfillment with the ability to do "one's own thing." So, after dropping back into the "mainstream," they frequently rationalized their hard-driving careerism as the pursuit of "self-actualization."

In the 1980s the reactionary policies of the federal government have been discouraging the development of any broad movement aimed at liberating human energies for a life based on loving. Of course, individual men and women still fall in love and get married, and they generally reject the old-fashioned sexism that rigidly assigned wives to "homemaking" and husbands to "breadwinning." But they have been reverting to the traditional norms of marriage that define it as a familial *institution* for preserving the economic, political, and religious institutions dominating the entire society.

Now, reflecting the conservative climate of the times, many couples are staging their weddings as extravaganzas of social conformity and conspicuous consumption—all precisely preprogrammed to the specifications of a Miss Manners.[9] Then, after a honeymoon trip to the "right" place in the "proper" attire, they "settle down," as if encased in cement, to a pragmatic arrangement. Thus, they hope to provide each other with companionship, largely as an emotional buffer against the stress of their jobs; to have children; to accumulate wealth and possessions; to gain social approval; and to maintain a religious affiliation.

Recently, however, some mates, who had participated in the counterculture, have been expressing discontent with this relatively loveless type of marriage. Having become successful "yuppies," these people are starting to wonder whether or not they are doing themselves, their children, or anyone else a favor by keeping up a lifestyle that enslaves them to the System.[10]

Indeed, as George Orwell said in his prophetic novel, *1984*, true liberation is the freedom to love.[11] Exercising this freedom, lovers find joys infinitely more transporting than any to be found in the service of Big Business or its political twin, Big Brother, and they are not eager to forfeit their lives and their happiness—or their beloved children—to bolster the power of military, corporate, and governmental elites.

On the other hand, these ruling groups maintain their domination by promoting policies that foster a high level of international tension with its concomitant threat of cataclysmic warfare and that create enough unemployment to worry people about their economic security. Simultaneously, the rulers direct the energy held back from loving relationships into militarism, imperialism, and consumerism—activities that tighten the control of the Establishment while increasing the frustration and socioeconomic submission of the general population.

On the most fundamental level, therefore, a husband and a wife liberate themselves by liberating each other through the fulfillment of their common need to love. In the interest of their mutual liberation, they would also wish to see it extended as broadly as possible to others. Surely, all couples will be forever unfree as long as they waste their lives in doing things that prevent them from loving *and* that lend support to the societal subversion of loving relationships.

Of course, the State does not *forbid* lovers to marry, but it does bring marriage under the control of its laws. Historically, too, the Church has imposed its own authority on couples by getting them to marry under its institutional auspices. By doing so, formal religions extend their influence, acquire considerable income, and recruit a steady supply of adherents.

Admittedly, the Church does disseminate principles, such as the virtues of lifelong commitment, loyalty, and devotion that help to bring out the loving potentials of marital relationships. Organized religion also does a lot of other good work in behalf of human welfare, sometimes even mobilizing congregants to oppose political and economic injustice. At the same time, however, it functions as an ideological prop for the State. For example, as chaplains, clergy of various denominations bestow the blessings of God on the Armed Forces, whose deadly missions are far from spiritual. Meanwhile, in abiding by some religious teachings on marriage, couples place undesirable crimps on the governance of their relationship and on the amount of erotic pleasure they experience.

Long mystified into viewing marriage as a social and religious institution, any pair of mates may quickly lose sight of *why* they married and *for whom*. Besides, every couple has to put forth a concerted effort in assuming total and exclusive responsibility for defining the terms of their own loving relationship, and they are bound to wander into many impasses of fearful confusion during the course of a lifelong marriage. So, it is understandable that husbands and wives would wish to clutch onto a highly legitimized notion of marriage in order to clamp a fixed structure on their relational ambiguities.

THE INHERENT FEAR OF LOVING

The barriers that impede every couple's ability to love are not entirely cultural in origin. On the contrary, a basic inhibition against loving is rooted in human nature. Even if the socioeconomic system gave more support to love as the central goal in living, men and women would still have to overcome the opposition to loving that exists within the very fabric of their beings. For the unique gratifications of marriage come from opening oneself as completely as possible to another person. But *nobody* can make such an offering of his or her *entire life*—one's body and soul—without feeling threatened at the core of existence.

As vulnerable, flesh-and-blood creatures, spouses are easily upset by involuntary concerns about their personal safety, and they are highly vigilant about protecting their individual lives. Yet they wish to expose their vulnerability to the utmost in making good on their marital commitment. So they are continually caught up in an existential paradox: the very process of loving evokes the fear that their survival is in jeopardy.

Ironically, this fear does not originate in any physical source of imminent danger that stands outside of mates and impinges upon them. Rather, it erupts as a reaction to the *psychological threats* they inevitably sense, from *within* themselves, as they act to fulfill the promises of their love. Thus, along with their innate need to love and be loved, all mates have an equally inherent fear of giving and receiving love.

Love impels people to get together and relate harmoni-
ously. But the fear of loving inclines them toward self-
centeredness and interpersonal strife. Consequently, these opposing motivations continually stir up conflict within and
between all husbands and wives.

Never free from their fear of loving, spouses jointly create
and employ an array of defensive tactics as they relate to one
another. For example, to defend against the terror of increasing
their intimacy, they may throw sarcastic barbs at one another,
argue heatedly, or even engage in physical violence. Alternatively, they may resort to diverse forms of mutual withdrawal:
avoiding each other's company, limiting their sexual contacts, or
even dissolving their marriage. Similarly, mates tie binds of deception and dishonesty around each other in fearfully reacting
against a common yearning to deepen their interpersonal union.
At the same time, they may lapse into cheating, manipulation,
and exploitation.

People have implicitly yielded to their fear of loving in establishing societies of aggrandizement throughout the world.
Certainly, it is neither necessary nor desirable for men and
women to love everyone with the sexual and affectionate
wholeness they put into marriage. But people could relate to
one another with the fundamental attitudes of helpfulness and
concern that characterize the interpersonal orientation of a loving relationship. Instead, they have been choosing greediness
and competition—behaviors indicative of the apprehension that,
by being generous and cooperative, they might endanger their
own lives.

Focusing on the United States, Christopher Lasch has at-
tempted to trace the proliferation of this phenomenon to the
ongoing decline of capitalism, which he believes is inducing the
kind of parental neglect that makes children grow up narcissis-
tic.[12] But his analysis fails to take note of the facts that point to
a crosscultural reality—namely, that every nation, whether in
the American orbit, the Soviet bloc, or nonaligned, is opting for
blatant self-centeredness *and* is expressing that option in *basically identical* values, aspirations, and socioeconomic hierar-
chies.

This sameness suggests that what is happening universally
reflects the intrinsic nature of human beings rather than the

transient effects of a certain kind of society and childrearing. Thus, if clinical pathology is to be ascribed to self-centeredness that is stimulated by fear, every person on earth would qualify for the diagnosis of "latently insane."

Having set into place the societal apparatus for accelerating this kind of lunacy, people are severely oppressed by it. Indeed, the existing social system reinforces the very fear that stimulated its establishment in the first place. Moreover, everyone's social oppression is now all the more acute since human beings can enact their fearfulness with technologies lethal enough to exterminate the entire species.

So, to assure their long-range welfare, people eventually will have to make the collective changes required to elevate love over the fear of loving as the guiding principle of social organization and functioning. Meanwhile, they will constantly need to quell their natural tendency to use the formidable power of the mind to "overkill" in their fear-driven zeal to be invincible against the vulnerability of sharing.

Similarly, to actualize the loving potentials of their marriage, a couple has to become involved in two never-ending struggles: a struggle to affirm and nurture their relationship in the midst of a self-centered society and a struggle to choose consistently in favor of expressing their inherent capacity to love instead of reacting with self-centered defensiveness to their equally inherent fear of loving.

LOVE-CENTERED MARRIAGE: A HOLISTIC MODEL

In this book, we articulate the ramifications of this double struggle, offering a new concept of marriage as the optimal medium for developing the lifelong capacity to love. Our formulation spells out what is realistically required to succeed in taking this pathway to human realization. We call our approach "love-centered" because it assumes love is the supremely desirable value in living and in marriage. Accordingly, we subscribe to the holistic ideal of integrating what is best for married people with what is best for humanity in general.

Scientifically, the word "holistic" was coined to describe an orientation to the study of biological organisms. In this perspective the living creature as a *totality,* is the focus of research, and its constituent parts and external surroundings are seen in relation to the organism's overall functioning.[13]

Holistic investigators aim to discover how people can harmonize the various aspects of their own functioning—and relate to their environment—for the explicit purpose of advancing their well-being. Holistic health is concerned with the bodily and mental processes a person can planfully coordinate to serve the goal of enhancing his or her wellness.[14] Likewise, a holistic view of ecology covers the natural and social phenomena that people have to integrate to maintain an environment conducive to their maximal welfare as a species, while minimally harmful to other forms of life.[15]

In applying this holistic viewpoint, we combine a *social philosophy* with a *relational psychology*, describing how a man and a woman can pool their physical and emotional resources to build a lifelong relationship for their mutual well-being. In essence, our model of marriage explains how mates can maximize their ability to love and minimize the negative effects of their fear of loving. We also take into consideration how couples are affected by their environment and, reciprocally, how they can counteract its destructive features while exerting an increasingly positive impact on their children, their work, and on society.

A SOCIAL PHILOSOPHY OF MARRIAGE

Most mates get married because they fall in love and want to be together for the rest of their lives. However, they may fail to clarify just how important loving is for them as compared to other goals they cherish. If a husband and a wife are unclear on this bedrock philosophical issue, they have no firm anchorage for what they are really and truly doing as a couple over time. They cannot hold themselves or each other to account for evading responsibility in carrying out a jointly espoused lifeplan, and they are very susceptible to disagreements about how to cope with the debilitating pressures of society.

In contrast, a love-centered marriage is founded, by definition, on a social philosophy in which mates explicitly decide to uphold love as the highest of their values. Committed to this position, they are motivated to make the cultivation of their loving relationship their top priority in living, placing it above *all* other pursuits. They then can deal consciously with everything else they do—their work, their childrearing, their recreations, and their community activities—as an opportunity to enrich the sharing of their love. Thus, they set into place a coherent and common focus for their energies.

Whenever spouses deviate from this agreement, they can harken back to it and confront any attempt they may be making to displace love as their chief objective. Consequently, their philosophical commitment gives them a lasting basis for keeping their personal ambitions under control *and* subordinate to the best interests of their relationship.

Of course, with their cultural saturation in aggrandizement, all couples will find it very difficult to relegate the pursuit of money, prestige, and power to a secondary position in their lives. In fact, they can expect to remain ambivalent about their priorities for a lifetime, feeling continually tempted to give up opportunities for nurturing their love in favor of chances to promote their individual careers—to give up time for making love in order to spend time in making money.

Undoubtedly, centering their marriage on love requires mates to be very serious about affirming their own values and equally resolved about passing up chances to make more money or to become more influential and well-known. These renunciations are bound to arouse their apprehensions. They are likely to worry about what they may be missing socially and vocationally or how they may be jeopardizing their financial security, even though they sincerely feel, in their heart of hearts, that they have everything they need and want when they are in each other's arms.

It *is* difficult for couples to follow the wisdom of their hearts when their heads are assailed on all sides with contrary guidance—when their love is challenged by the alarmingly high rates of marital unhappiness, infidelity, and divorce. But spouses are not automatons who must conform to the social system. They *do* have the ability to live by the values of loving, even if they are fearful of doing so and even if they have to depart from what the majority of married couples are doing.

Indeed, love is the most revolutionary of social motives since it inspires people to treat one another very differently from the ways in which the present society induces them to interact. Carrying this message throughout the book, we emphasize the desirability of approaching marriage *not* as a fixed institution but as a loving relationship that can be conducted as a potent force for personal and social transformation.

True, spouses are only a twosome—the smallest of all possible groupings. But from the standpoint of humanity's future, their dyad is the most essential of all social units. Representing both sexes of the human species, a husband and a wife conceive and rear children, without whom there would be no population to organize into societies of any kind.

Within the scope of their own loving relationship, mates are free to discard the premises of scarcity and hierarchy that now sow contention and exploitation throughout the world. Between the two of them, they have the opportunity to cooperate in establishing a classless utopia of social equality, holding and sharing all of their possessions in common. And, since there are no limits on the untapped abundance of their mutual love, they never have to worry about depleting the sexual and affectionate wellsprings of their own happiness.

By cultivating this kind of relationship, mates help each other to realize their capacities for honesty, cooperation, generosity, and reliability. At the same time, they acquire the ability to recognize and tame their equally human tendencies to be deceitful, rivalrous, greedy, and untrustworthy.

As they manifest these positive changes in daily contacts with others, a husband and a wife improve their social interactions. In fact, what it takes in essential decency to be loving and equal with a mate is *exactly* what it takes to be a sane, balanced, and mature adult. So, as they learn to love each other more deeply, mates also learn how to relate to friends, colleagues, and acquaintances in a more genuinely caring manner. In addition, by seeing a couple uphold the primacy of their own relationship, other people know where they stand and feel more comfortable in relating to them.

Consequently, love-centered mates do not wish to retreat from meaningful work and social activities. On the contrary, they have a philosophical incentive to help each other in finding occupations congenial to their values and their talents, and they have a vital stake in joining with other people to press for economic and political programs aimed at making society more hospitable to loving relationships.

In the process of actualizing this philosophy of marriage, mates can deepen their emotional and erotic satisfactions, grow to the fullest in personal strength, and overcome the thorniest of interpersonal problems. As a result, they sustain the incomparable joys of the love for which they married, and they experience the best that life has to offer anyone—at any time or place. Then, even if the world does not reverse its fatal course, their lives will have been worthwhile.

Surely, a husband and a wife do not have to wait for a societal revolution to turn themselves around. Rather, by centering their marriage on love—and by raising children who grow up with the same commitment to loving—mates serve, in their own exemplary fashion, as contributors to change for a better world.

NOTES

1. Sarnoff, I. *Society with tears*. New York: Citadel, 1966.
2. Ferguson, M. *The Aquarian conspiracy*. Los Angeles: Tarcher, 1980.
3. Coleman, J. C. *Intimate relationships, marriage, and family*. Indianapolis: Bobbs-Merrill, 1984, p. 376.
4. Ibid., p. 378.
5. Bookchin, M. *Post-scarcity anarchism*. Berkeley: Ramparts, 1971.
6. Jung, C. G. *Two essays on analytical psychology*. Princeton, N.J.: Princeton University Press, 1972.
7. Millett, K. *Sexual politics*. New York: Doubleday, 1970.
8. Engels, F. *The origins of the family, private property, and the state*. New York: International Publishers, 1942, p. 72.
9. Martin, J. *Miss Manners' guide to excruciatingly correct behavior*. New York: Warner, 1982.
10. Schwartz, T. Second thoughts on having it all. *New York Magazine*, July 15, 1985, pp. 32–41.
11. Orwell, G. *1984*. New York: New American Library, 1961.
12. Lasch, C. *The culture of narcissism*. New York: Norton, 1978.
13. Goldstein, K. *The organism*. Boston: Beacon, 1963.
14. Pelletier, K. *Mind as healer/mind as slayer*. New York: Delta, 1977; and *Holistic medicine*. New York: Delta, 1979.
15. Disch, R. (Ed.). *The ecological conscience*. Englewood Cliffs, N.J.: Prentice-Hall, 1970.

2

MARRIAGE AS A LOVING RELATIONSHIP

Essential as it is, a philosophy of marriage does not give a couple the knowledge to put their loving values into practice. They still face the challenge of translating their ideals into realities. So they also need a *psychology* adequate to their philosophy. For while a philosophy is a set of values defining what people want in life, a psychology is a set of ideas about how to attain those goals.

Countless couples marry without having faced the psychological complexities of marriage. Most newlyweds have only vague and simplistic notions about what is necessary to sustain and augment the rewards of their relationship. New mates often believe the power of their love is sufficient, by itself, to carry them through all the relational difficulties they will encounter over the span of a lifetime. But a loving marriage cannot be taken for granted and still retain its original vitality. After all, before they married, lovers generated their zest precisely because they were so actively delighting one another—and so concerned about discovering whatever they needed to know in order to feel sanguine about making their individual decisions to marry.

Once married, however, many spouses put the conduct of their relationship on some sort of remote control, assuming it will automatically resolve whatever problems crop up between them and it will make whatever choices are required to insure their mutual gratification. Soon, they act as if neither of them is responsible for nourishing the love for which they decided to marry. As a result, millions of spouses drift into relating to each other like lifeless robots, slowly burying themselves alive in their very own marriage beds.

In conceptualizing the psychological bases of marital success or failure, theorists used to concentrate on *individual* motives and behavior and on how the similarities and differences between people affect their interactions. Naturally, this orientation led many counselors and therapists to attribute the outcome of a marriage to the backgrounds and personalities of the particular partners within it.

Couples influenced by this viewpoint are inclined to blame their marital dissatisfactions on each other. When mired in a sticky morass of alienation, these mates may feel, like the characters in Sartre's *No Exit*, that "Hell is the other."[1] Alternatively, husband and wife may share the blame, ascribing their lack of harmony to a mismatch of their personalities or to unresolved "hang-ups" from each one's past. But such an assessment only drives them into dead ends of solitary introspection and mutual recrimination—and away from the constructive task of cooperating to repair what they have actually *created in unison.*

As reported by Daniel Goleman, psychology editor of *The New York Times,* the past trend in marital research, which looked for the personality profiles of compatible individuals, has largely been abandoned. Apparently, those studies found no compelling connection between personality traits and marital happiness. Goleman observes "the consensus among most marital researchers is that personality is less crucial to marital success than is the nature of the relationship itself. As the late Nathan Ackerman, a pioneering family therapist put it, even two neurotics can have a happy marriage."[2]

In line with Goleman's remark, professionals interested in couples are increasingly acknowledging the futility of trying to understand a relationship in terms of theories that were originally created to explain what goes on within an individual. Now, a growing body of knowledge is based on the assumption that the relationship between spouses is the crucial entity for investigation and remediation.

A RELATIONAL PSYCHOLOGY OF MARRIAGE

According to Martin Buber, the capacity to relate lovingly is the finest and most unusual of all human potentials for creativity.[3] But it is a potential that nobody actualizes in social isolation; it is only brought out by two people in their direct encounters.

For Buber, the prototype of all relationships is the connection between a mother and the fetus in her womb.[4] While they are separate organisms, their beings are vitally interrelated. Each of their lives is part of a collective wholeness. Their basic union is represented in the way their separateness is joined, and their individual well-being is contingent upon the nature of their relatedness.

After being born, people retain a profound feeling for this unbroken harmony of existing with and through another. Besides, if left alone after their entry into the world, they could neither survive nor develop the potentials of their species. Thus, people make the interpersonal connections required for the satisfaction of their needs. These social arrangements are defined in and through the relationships they create with one another.

A marital relationship is a creation that a man and a woman produce for the purpose of gratifying their common need for love. Through that relationship they have the opportunity to become the best it is possible for people to be; a becoming whose actuality is realizable by neither one nor the other alone—no matter how gifted each may be—but *only* in what they *create together.* Consequently, the communion of lovers elevates both of them to the highest plane of human realization, even if each one, separately, demonstrates little artistic or intellectual talent. Conversely, the most accomplished artists and scientists remain creatively deficient as long as they do not become full and active participants in a loving relationship.

However, unlike a painting or a scientific report, a relationship is intangible. It is not a palpable organism, as are the individuals who participate in its construction; its fluidity cannot be fixed, for leisurely examination, as is a butterfly pinned to a mat. In fact, it is quite a task to make sense of the elusive and evanescent happenings that occur when people relate to one another. Consequently, relationships are extraordinarily difficult to conceptualize and to study.

Attempting to overcome this difficulty, Harold Kelley and eight coauthors state, in their encyclopedic volume *Close Relationships,* that "two people are in a relationship with one another if they have an impact on each other, if they are 'interdependent' in the sense that a change in one person causes a change in the other."[5] This definition is congenial to academically trained social psychologists since it permits them to apply the conventional logic of the scientific method in which effect is assumed to follow cause in a linear chain of events. Such investigators have produced a lot of informative data and generalizations by using standardized techniques of observation and statistical analysis to sort out how Michael affects Mary—and vice versa—in a series of actions and reactions that move sequentially over time.

Confined to this definition, however, nobody could deal with the fact that people in relationships interact within a nexus of meaning to which they already subscribe. To be sure, Mary may respond to something said or done by Michael. Then the response of Mary may be followed by another action on the part of Michael, and they may go on acting and reacting in a readily observable and temporally punctuated fashion. However, in a given sequence, *none* of their behaviors may reflect any *change* that each is *causing* the other to make. Instead, as Ronald Laing has illustrated so poetically in *Knots,*[6] *both* people may be behaving in accordance with the *same set of internalized rules* they had devised as a couple. Neither of them is actually exerting *any* new or genuine impact on the other. Indeed, Michael and Mary may periodically re-enact a virtually identical script, *cued by it* to deliver their respective lines and gestures.

Gregory Bateson and his colleagues began to uncover such systemic transactions in the 1950s.[7] Subsequently, more and more theorists, particularly in the fields of family and marital therapy, have been viewing relationships as interpersonal systems in which each participant is behaving within a commonly agreed upon network of assumptions and expectations. Many of these arrangements are made silently and kept hidden in a maze of mystification. Moreover, each person may play quite different roles in carrying out the system of communication they have created in unison. But the participants coordinate their role playing to maintain a shared scenario.

Leading proponents of this school, as represented by Maria Palazzoli and her coworkers,[8] do believe that an interpersonal system can be changed by altering its underlying premises. However, such a change is difficult to make since each person in the system has to agree on it. Besides, all people are presumed to have a psychologically vested interest in preserving the intactness of their ongoing systems: an inertia that borders on sheer absurdity.

As applied to marriage, this theory regards every couple as inventing their own idiosyncratic system, which they are inclined to perpetuate as an end in itself—even if it has very damaging effects on both mates. Meanwhile, husband and wife may compete for the power to control their marital system. But if either one appears ready to quit their "game," the other quickly tries to entice him or her back into it. Thus, unbroken homeostasis in the established system is held to be the motivating aim for both of them.

OUR DEFINITION OF A RELATIONSHIP

Informed by these theorists, we view a marital relationship as a shared conception that is created equally and simultaneously by both a husband and a wife. However, we believe that mates have a very *meaningful* motivational basis for forming and sustaining their relationship: it is absolutely essential for the fulfillment of their need to give and receive love. Thus, they overtly create the interpersonal agreements that enable them to satisfy that common need. Yet, as we have noted previously, mates are inevitably struck by the fear of loving. As a result, they also make covert agreements to defend themselves against that fear.

Therefore, our relational psychology addresses the elemental conflict between love and fear that confronts *all* husbands and wives, *regardless of how alike or different they may be in background or personality.* By understanding how they represent this conflict in their relational ingredients, mates penetrate the otherwise bewildering complexities of their interactions. Attaining such cognitive clarity, they can act purposefully to prevent their sharing of love from being usurped by their fear of loving.

Two persons form their relationship by communicating what is going on inside and between them. Often, the flow of their communication is so rapid and spontaneous they do not even notice the initiatives each is taking. They may easily feel caught up in a process that by-passes their personal volition and responsibility. Nevertheless, both are *deciding* what to say and what to keep secret; what to do, see, hear, and comment upon; and what to ignore, deny, or remain silent about. Out of this constant stream of decisions, people distill the contents of their relational consensus.

Thus, through the interlocking simultaneity of their face to face communication, prospective mates *jointly* abstract the same configuration of meaning. This shared conception is comprised of representations, in each person's mind, about the thoughts and feelings they are communicating—verbally and nonverbally. In their mental construction, both partners include ideas and pictures of themselves and one another; of how the two of them are getting along; and of the agreements they make about ways to interact in the future. As a result, they start to perceive themselves as a collective entity—as a "we." Then they maintain that perception of their "we-ness" along with their self-images as separate individuals.

People take the complex totality of their relational concept with them when they are apart, preserving all of its elements inside their heads. Whenever they are together, they rely on this common cognition as a guide for their direct contacts. However, as they continue to interact, they disclose new thoughts, feelings, and behaviors that they use *implicitly* to elaborate the mental representations they have already begun to share. A man and a woman also alter their relationship by *explicitly agreeing* to change specific elements of its content.

Subsequently, they bring both kinds of modifications into their encounters.

Many spouses do not realize that they, themselves, determine all aspects of their relationship. They therefore refer to their marriage as "it," as if their relationship were an alien object imposed on them by an unfathomable and capricious source beyond their control—a "thing" they had no part in creating and have no further personal responsibility for directing.

Such mates may say, "*It* is working;" "*It* isn't working;" or, "Hopefully, *it* will work out" when they are actually talking about the quality and outcome of their own interpersonal creation. Naturally, this inanimate and depersonalized view lightens the load of responsibility each one would otherwise feel in contemplating how both of them have been and are relating to one another. But such a disavowal of responsibility also prevents them from doing what only they can do—as individuals within the context of their relationship—to improve their marital happiness.

However, by regarding their relationship as a jointly created *and* changeable concept, mates give themselves the motivation to keep on changing it for their progressive satisfaction. Thus, as we will show, they make the specific agreements for building their "romance"—the relational ingredient they use to represent and enhance the sharing of their love. On the other hand, resistance to such positive change stems from the need to maintain their "complicities"—the relational ingredients they construct to defend themselves against the fear of loving. To release the loving energy tied up in those defenses, mates can also take more responsibility for identifying and breaking their protective pacts.

Clearly, a loving relationship is more than the mere summation of each person's input. Through the intertwining of their consciousness, a man and a woman meld their separate contributions into a novel and unique conception that neither could create or enact without the other—just as nobody can converse, make love, or conceive a child without the participation of someone else. It is this collective creativity that enlivens and empowers a husband and wife, providing them with a dynamo of energy they draw upon throughout their married lives to multiply the fruitfulness of their tangible productivity and their pleasure in being together. Ideally, each spouse can openly acknowledge the other as indispensable for actualizing his or her individual potentials for loving. It is just as desirable for both of them to cherish their relationship as the interpersonal reality each one needs to become personally fulfilled. Indeed, *the relationship between self and other provides the medium of fulfillment for both of them.*

THE HOLISTIC NATURE OF LOVE

Since ancient times philosophers and poets have speculated inconclusively on the nature of love. But psychologists have made no attempts to theorize systematically about love until quite recently; and they are not even close to any consensus on how to define it.

Nevertheless, we evolved our own conceptualization from familiarity with the wealth of writings on the possible meanings of love. In putting together our holistic view, we were especially stimulated by the work of Sigmund Freud and Alfred Adler. Actually, these seminal theorists regarded love very differently, and as arch rivals, they did not hesitate to belittle each other's concepts. Still, we found solid virtues in their intellectual differences.

Freud brilliantly and daringly called the world's attention to the significance of sexuality in human behavior and psychological development. Inventing psychoanalytic therapy, he also sought to apply his ideas about sex toward the goal of helping people to fulfill their capacities for love and work. However, in his concept of libido,[9] Freud saw love as merely a sublimation of a physiological drive that people have in common with other animals. He also considered human sexuality intrinsically rapacious. He argued it must be curbed—repressed—to a great extent in order to permit social cooperation and cultural evolution.[10]

Given these assumptions, Freud concluded that affectionate feelings arise from efforts to release libidinal tension.[11] Of course, people are socialized to disguise the real character of their intentions from themselves and those—called "objects" by Freud—from whom they wish to obtain relief. Having learned to regard their animalistic aims as personally and socially unacceptable, people mentally transmute their sexual urges into affection.

Freud believed people are involuntarily impelled to act on their sexual drives in a myriad of ways, although they may have no awareness of the connection between their manifest behavior and their underlying impulses. In fact, Freud was thoroughly deterministic in his scientific outlook. True, as a therapist, he said that a patient's improvement depends largely on his or her willingness to change. "But as a psychological theorist, Freud proposed no concepts to deal with the behavioral and experiential effects of willful decisions."[12]

In striking contrast, Adler[13] postulated the existence of an innate need for affection that people can gratify only in reciprocal relationships. In due course, this need becomes linked with a person's equally innate potential for social interest, by which Adler means the distinctively human capacity to care for, empathize with, and act in cooperative solidarity with other people.

Adler did not deny the instinctive basis of sexuality. But from his standpoint a person's sexual behavior reflects how much he or she has developed social interest. Therefore, a desire for sexual contact may be selfish and greedy or it may be altruistic and generous. For Adler, then, the hallmark of loving is the ability of people to be authentically concerned about one another whether or not sexual relations occur between them.

Adler also felt that human beings were highly capable of volition. Indeed, he credited them with the ability to *create* their own lifestyles for coping with their sexuality, need for affection, capacity for social interest, and everything else that impinges involuntarily on them, including their particular physiques and parental pressures.

We agree with Freud that an involuntary yearning for sexual contact is always a component of love, even when it is split off from consciousness. Consistent with Adler's idea of social interest, however, we see this desire as connoting a mutuality of pleasure. In this respect, our position coincides with the observations made by Laing, who remarked that the lack of responsiveness and gratification in a sexual partner is a source of extreme frustration, nullifying any relief a person may experience in an orgasm.[14] Finally, we see merit in Adler's concept of affection, regarding it as no less instinctive, urgent, or gratifying to fulfill than is the desire for sexual satisfaction.

In our view, people always function as psychophysical totalities. So, as an innate need, love is a blend of sexual and affectionate components, representing the bodily and mental characteristics of human beings. Moreover, as Ashley Montagu has written, "It is impossible to want to be loved without wanting to love others."[15] When a man and a woman love each other, they experience it as an involuntary craving for union with all facets of themselves. Yet they voluntarily choose how to give and receive this wholeness of loving.

The Involuntary and Voluntary Aspects of Loving

In fable and in fancy, love has often been portrayed as a divine but hypnotic urge, driving everyone to do its bidding. People delight in the fantasy of Cupid shooting arrows of irresistible involvement into their hearts; of men and women being smitten by glancing unexpectedly into each other's eyes; and of loving marriages that are made in heaven and bestowed upon lucky couples as a gift of Heavenly Grace.

These images are appealing because they omit the element of volition that is, in fact, an integral part of the processes of falling in love, making love, and developing a loving marriage. Why carry the burden of responsibility that freedom of choice imposes on all the activities of loving? Isn't it easier and far less upsetting for people to see themselves as innocent beneficiaries—or victims—of their involuntary impulses to love?

Surely, all men and women are impelled by an innate need to love and be loved, a need that is as painful to contain as it is pleasurable to fulfill. But the times, ways, and circumstances in which human beings express love are *not* determined by biological inheritance. There is always a *dynamic interplay* between the involuntary emergence of a loving impulse and a person's ability to exert voluntary control over the expression of it. Thus, people are capable of deciding to relate lovingly whenever, with whom, and in any way they choose.

Because of its crucial and lifelong implications, deciding on a mate is not merely an act of choice but also the most important of all choices a person can make. So, on their way to marriage, a man and a woman often postpone the finality of their mutual commitment. Meanwhile, they wait until their deepest feelings crystallize involuntarily in the forefront of their consciousness. Gradually, they evolve a "gut-level" conviction that both of them have found, in each other, the one person they want to be with more than anyone else in the world—that their love is too true to deny and too precious to lose. Still, they have to take *the responsibility to act on* what they truly feel, and they have to use their *volition* to affirm the unwavering desire of their hearts.

Nevertheless, even the most impassioned lovers are dismayed by the heavy sense of responsibility that goes along with their freedom of choice. First of all, this heaviness intrudes on their awareness by leading them to attend to "where they are coming from" and "where they want to go." Secondly, people are a puzzlement to themselves as they try to sort out their motives, values, and possible courses of action, seeking to discern truth from falsity and expediency from wholeheartedness. Third, no one is perfect in predicting the outcome of his or her decisions. Rather than accept that imperfection, however, people may balk at choosing among viable alternatives, or they may appear to make a choice when, in fact, they inwardly perceive it as tentative and still to be made. Moreover, they are reluctant to *limit* themselves to the constraints implied in making *any* particular choice. They therefore vacillate about decision making, unreasonably hoping to secure all possible alternatives without having to renounce any of them.

While a man and a woman are selecting each other for marriage, they also feel the full weight of the fear of loving. Paralyzing the will to love, this fear is a constant impediment to the making of their decision, and it fills them with ambivalence and hesitation. They hold back and withdraw, even as their minds and bodies are going out to each other.

Like love itself, the fear of loving arises involuntarily. However, as is true of love, people do have the capacity to impose voluntary control over their reactions to the involuntary eruption of that fear. When they are "going together," a man and a woman use their volition to tolerate their common fear of loving and prevent it from crippling their ability to marry.

Once married, they can overtly make all the decisions required to translate their loving desires into gratifying actions. Simultaneously, they can bring to light the covert links between their defensive tactics and their fear of loving—an ongoing process of mutual revelation necessary to prevent their fear from undermining the success of their relationship.

Still, there are limits to the amount of control any couple is capable of exercising over the multitude of circumstances that impinge on their lives. For example, although they can choose to have a child and decide how to rear it, they do not have the power to determine the exact time of conception; the precise course of the wife's pregnancy and delivery; or the condition of their newborn infant. However, they *can* use their volition to *relate lovingly* throughout the entire reproductive process *and* to cope reliably with whatever unexpected crises occur after making their fateful choice to conceive. Similarly, while mates cannot forestall the debilitation of their aging, they can decide to respond to each other with maximal acceptance, compassion, and emotional support.

Surely, a husband and a wife are free to establish any pattern of lovemaking they consider desirable. As they interact, they decide how, when, and where to make love. Of course, they do not always make their agreements explicit on a verbal level. Feeling spontaneously aroused by one another, they may agree, without saying a word, to engage in sexual intercourse.

Then, to intensify their involuntary arousal, they must choose how and where to fondle each other's flesh, and they stimulate their ongoing physiological reactions as they voluntarily unleash and communicate their mutual affection. By choice, they gaze into each other's eyes, letting their innermost tenderness shine through them. Deliberately, they draw their fingertips teasingly over their groins, already churning with irrepressible waves of desire. Together, they willfully mount the peak of their rising passion, deciding at last to surrender to its overflowing urgency. Finally, in the aftermath of their orgasm—in the calm that involuntarily suffuses them—mates may choose to turn away from one another or to remain entwined in an intimate embrace.

Expressing the Sexual and Affectionate Components of Love

A husband and a wife cultivate the wholeness of their love when they offer, receive, and enjoy sexual pleasure *and* when they relate to one another with as much care, concern, and consideration as they give to themselves. When they speak and act tenderly, honestly, and cooperatively, they "turn each other on," thereby enhancing the eroticism they feel and want to express. Conversely, they derive the fullest pleasure from communication when they speak and listen with the warmth of passion in their voices and the sparkle of sensuality in their eyes. As they allow themselves more sexual intimacy, they increase their joy in being together and heighten their motivation for sharing affection in other ways.

When they separate eroticism from affection, mates drastically diminish the richness of their potential fulfillment. By neglecting either component, both deprive themselves of the energy they are withholding in blocking the expression of that aspect of their love. If they perpetuate this deprivation, they become chronically frustrated.

It makes no difference which component of love is being unexpressed. If mates have a lot of sexual interaction without putting much affection into it, they are holding back the element of love that gives their intercourse genuine passion and that permits them to experience the ecstasies of merging both mentally and physically. They tend to remain emotionally dissatisfied, and their disaffection is bound to show up as a weakening of their fervor and enthusiasm in lovemaking.

If mates usually are tender and affectionate but hold back their erotic feelings, the psychological quality of their relationship will suffer eventually. Regardless of how loyal and devoted they may be, they are likely to become physically tense and sensually starved without the release and relaxation of regular sexual contact, and their erotic deprivation will be reflected in a corresponding deadening of their emotional vitality.

Empirical studies have documented the dismal results of this marital pattern of separating sex from affection. Evidently, as Robert Blood found, American marriages "start out

hot but grow cold."[16] Therefore, many writers on loving relationships have declared that mates can be expected to change
from "passionate" to "companionate" within a few years after
they marry. Presumably, from then on the sexual excitement of
most couples slides "down the tubes" to virtual nothingness.

But the "companionship" these couples supposedly retain
is likely to be equally blighted, since it lacks the spark that is
struck only when a husband and wife are sharing their minds
and their bodies. Naturally, in the course of their daily interactions, these mates give each other some of the psychological
benefits of close association. Still, the original intensity of their
marriage withers in direct proportion to their erotic and emotional stagnation.

A couple's ability to maintain—and to increase—the holistic satisfactions of their love depends, to a great extent, on
what they believe is possible. In this respect spouses have been
misled seriously by those who have mistakenly equated frequency with destiny. Elaine and G. William Walster,[17] among
many others, tend to present the widespread marital decline
from passionate to companionate as foreordained by fate, as if
mates had neither the will nor the competence to prevent such
a loss in the quality of their relationship; indeed, as if the only
thing a couple can do is submit to its inexorable unfolding.
Accordingly, these psychologists do not offer any insights that
might help mates to develop both the passionate and the companionate aspects of their love.

Like so many lay persons, these professionals have failed
to grasp the basic fact that a husband and a wife jointly create
everything included in their relationship. This means that they
make the splits between the passionate and companionate
facets of their loving feelings. It also means they can *prevent
and repair* those splits. Consequently, mates do not have to
resign themselves to a passionless marriage.

DEVELOPING A LOVING RELATIONSHIP

Even the most joyous of newlyweds have only begun to
savor the rewards of their relationship. But how can they arrange to develop their mutual satisfactions to the fullest?

In this respect, the available descriptions of relational development also offer couples little encouragement. In a comprehensive review and commentary on this subject, George Levinger actually postulated *deterioration* as a *stage* in marital development.[18] Although he notes, in passing, that such an impairment is not inevitable, he has found it to be so commonplace as to warrant inclusion as a modal occurrence in marriage.

However, this bleak outlook does not consider what marriage could be—if mates decided to make it the "main event" of their lives *and* if they planfully brought out the loving potentials of their relationship. Indeed, by viewing deterioration as a foregone conclusion, newlyweds may feel hopeless about their future. Likewise, older mates already wrestling with interpersonal problems that beset *every* couple, including the most loving, may be deprived of any incentive to improve their relationship.

By contrast, we emphasize the genuine prospects for *continuous and lifelong* relational development. Of course, it is impossible for a couple to anticipate all the strokes of fortune or misfortune that may befall them from forces beyond their control. But it is possible for mates to agree on a long-range plan for developing their own relationship, and they have it completely in their power to determine how they will relate to each other in the course of implementing the way they want to go through life together.

With this use of their volition, couples choose how to remain loving in the face of unwanted adversity. They also decide what initiatives to take toward creating relational changes that would increase their ability to love. Over the course of their lifelong relationship, mates are called upon to make both kinds of decisions repeatedly. Otherwise, they may become embittered by the traumatic events that inevitably distress them, or they may miss out on the chances they do have for determining the conditions of their own happiness.

In Part II of this book, we integrate our concepts of relational dynamics and development, visualizing the optimal course of a marriage. Thus, we set forth a series of desirable objectives that provide a couple with specific channels for progressively increasing the loving quality of their relationship at successive intervals of time. These objectives are consistent with the social philosophy of living for love, and they are real-istically attainable, given the possibilities for change embedded in all relationships.

As mates meet each objective in its temporal order, they move from one stage of a love-centered marriage to the next. However, as they make progress in cultivating their love, they also stimulate their common fear of loving, and they contrive new defenses against that fear at every developmental stage. Consequently, the development of a couple's relationship is not an "either/or" proposition, not either loving *or* defending against the fear of it. Rather, mates are simultaneously increas-ing their ability to love *and* defending themselves against their fear of loving. Paradoxically, therefore, in the very process of developing their marriage for the better, they also develop it for the worse.

Accepting this dialectic of relational development permits a husband and wife to be more at peace with the progress they *do* make in loving. They also become less harsh with them-selves about having to suffer the stressful tensions that go along with their defensiveness. This mutuality of understand-ing and compassion gives them the emotional strength to coop-erate in maintaining the supremacy of their love over their fear of loving at every period in their marriage.

Thus, motivated to practice the holism of love—and to ful-fill its promises—mates can "go the distance" without losing their initial pleasure and zest. They do *not* have to forgo the uplifting excitement of passion for the bland comfort of sexless companionship. Instead, while remaining *passionate compan-ions*, they can go on, for a lifetime, developing the relationship they began as ardent lovers *and* best friends.

NOTES

1. Sartre, J. P. *No exit and three other plays.* New York: Vintage, 1955.
2. Goleman, D. Marriage research reveals ingredients of happiness. *The New York Times,* April 16, 1985, p. C1.
3. Buber, M. *I and thou.* New York: Scribner's, 1970.
4. Ibid.
5. Speaking for themselves and their coauthors, Ellen Berscheid

and Letitia Anne Peplau make this statement in Chapter 1, The emerging science of relationships. In H. H. Kelley, E. Berscheid, A. Christensen, J. H. Harvey, T. L. Huston, G. Levinger, E. McClintock, L. A. Peplau, & D. R. Peterson, *Close relationships.* San Francisco: Freeman, 1983, p. 12.

6. Laing, R. D. *Knots.* New York: Pantheon, 1970.
7. Bateson, G. *Steps to an ecology of mind.* New York: Ballantine, 1972. pp. 201–227.
8. Palazzoli, M., Cecchin, G., Prata, G., & Boscola, L. *Paradox and counterparadox.* New York: Jason Aronson, 1978.
9. Freud, S. Three contributions to the theory of sex. In A. A. Brill (Ed.), *The basic writings of Sigmund Freud.* Book III. New York: Random House, 1938.
10. Freud, S. *Civilization and its discontents.* New York: Norton, 1961.
11. Freud, S. Two encyclopaedia articles. A. Psychoanalysis. B. The libido theory. In J. Strachey (Ed.), *Collected papers of Sigmund Freud.* London: Hogarth, 1950, Vol. V., p. 134.
12. Sarnoff, I. *Testing Freudian concepts: An experimental social approach.* New York: Springer, 1971, p. 263.
13. Ansbacher, H. L., & Ansbacher, R. R. (Eds.). *The individual psychology of Alfred Adler.* New York: Harper & Row, 1967.
14. Laing, R. D. *Self and others.* Middlesex, England: Penguin, 1969, pp. 84–85.
15. Montagu, A. *On being human.* New York: Hawthorn, 1966, p. 93.
16. Blood, R. *Love match and arranged marriage.* New York: Free Press, 1967, p. 86.
17. Walster, E., & Walster, G. W. *A new look at love.* Reading, Mass.: Addison-Wesley, 1978.
18. Levinger, G. Development and change. In Kelley et al., op. cit., pp. 315–359.

3

THE PROMISES AND THREATS
OF LOVE

The sexual and affectionate wholeness of love contains four intrinsic promises that a man and a woman can fulfill throughout their married life. As they voluntarily actualize these promises, mates delve deeper and deeper into four realms of psychophysical enrichment. In plumbing these depths, they realize the finest of their human potentials and develop the strengths of their relationship.

However, in relating as openly and unreservedly as is necessary to redeem the promises of love, a husband and a wife make themselves as vulnerable as people can become, and they put the entirety of their relationship to the most severe tests. Consequently, in the process of making good on each promise, they are assailed by a basic existential threat.

As we will explain in subsequent chapters, mates build their lifelong romance by continuing to fulfill the promises of love. Reciprocally, they use their romance to augment those spheres of gratification. On the other hand, they also experience the threat that accompanies each of the four promises, and every threat evokes the fear of loving. So spouses contrive complicities to keep that fear from obliterating their ability to love, and each complicity reflects the specific threat that originally spurred them into forming it.

Thus, mates activate not only the promises but also the threats of love through their ongoing interactions. They fully share in every interpersonal behavior that is involved in fulfilling each promise. Likewise, they feel the threats in common and jointly agree on how to cope with their consequent fear of loving.

EXPANDING THE BOUNDARIES OF INDIVIDUALITY

People perceive their lives as being contained inside a relatively stable set of psychophysical boundaries. Within those boundaries, they identify themselves as possessing particular capacities, traits of personality, bodily characteristics, skills, interests, and values. Taken as a whole, this configuration of attributes is the person's awareness of being an individual with a mind and body of one's own—a human being who is recognizable over time and distinguishable from everyone else.

From early childhood, people rely on that sense of themselves to interact with others in society and to cope with the challenges of living. They associate the intactness of their individuality with the perpetuation and success of their lives. People may welcome the prospect of continuing to extend the range of their experiences and to develop their talents. But they regard these changes as occurring within, not as opening up, the boundaries of their individuality.

Eventually, however, those boundaries imprison everyone's need to love and be loved, a need that cannot be appeased unless a person is willing to expand his or her sense of individuality to include another. In fact, it is precisely this mutual inclusion that gives the concept of a relationship its basic meaning.

In a *love-centered* marriage, spouses make a fundamental shift in orientation toward their own identities. As single persons, they had regarded their organismic separateness as the grounding for their concepts of themselves. Once married, however, they *voluntarily agree* to place their individual selves under the primacy of their relationship, and each conceives of himself and herself—*first and foremost*—as a member of a couple.

A husband and a wife create their collective identity in unison, equally claiming its ownership and partaking in its effects. Neither one feels their relational "we" to be contained solely inside the perimeter of his or her separate being. Rather, they perceive it as existing within, and enacted between, both of them.

Spouses feel personally enlarged by what they give one another. They are not diminished, as individuals, by uniting more deeply, nor are they deprived of the gratifications they could get from doing whatever their personal endowments permit. Since each spouse is motivated to bring out the best in the other, they can cooperate in facilitating the expression of their individual talents and abilities. By fostering their mutual intellectual and emotional growth, husbands and wives function better in all respects than they could if they did not have each other's psychological support.

Mates yearn to unite at the *inner core* of their separate beings—not merely at the periphery. They want to open wide the gates of their solitariness; to flow forth and become an ever-increasing part of each other's life. Through this mutual flowing, each of them feels "alive in ways he or she has not previously experienced."[1]

This melding and enlivening is superbly exemplified in sexual intercourse, when each mate includes and is included by the other in a physical and psychological union. Approaching each other, they begin to experience an overlapping of their individual boundaries. In posture they incline gently toward one another, moving to close the physical distance between them, and their rapid breathing echoes the excitement of their growing intimacy. Revealing the contents of their consciousness in a spontaneous exchange of affection, they communicate their wish for interpenetration on a mental level.

Surrendering to this merger, their "hearts go out" to one another. Like ramparts of sand, the usual perimeters of their self-consciousness are washed away by the rising tide of their passion. Uplifted by the "rush" of that tide, both soar with erotic desire. Making contact with their eyes, their pupils dilate, the better to "take each other in" *and* to let themselves out.

A simultaneous dilation—with similar intent—occurs in the blood vessels of their genitals. The husband's penis, engorged, enlarged, and hardened, anticipates penetration. Reciprocally, the opening of the wife's vagina widens, becoming moist and soft, ready to receive and envelop him. While interpenetrated, they take less and less notice of where one of them ends and the other begins. As they let themselves "melt" into each other, their ecstasy increases. Ultimately, their expansiveness grows to the bursting point of orgasm, when their merger is so transforming that it temporarily dissolves the last traces of their feelings of separateness.

By disclosing their inner lives to one another, mates also dissolve the boundaries between their psyches. When they engage in a truthful conversation, they open the windows of their hearts and souls. Love is *not* blind as the old adage claims. Through the eyes of unconditional love, mates actually can see each other more clearly than anyone else can see them, and they have an incomparable opportunity for reciprocal evaluation. Both of them have been naked in each other's arms, displaying beauty *and* blemishes, power *and* frailties. Each knows *exactly* when the other is serene or upset, elated or depressed, involved or detached. Thus, they become the world's experts on the subject of one another's assets *and* liabilities.

Another overlapping of their individualities occurs when mates cooperate to select a dwelling place. The walls of their domicile are the *literal boundaries* that encompass *both of them.* Within this common space they share the most intimate aspects of their relationship. Whatever home they choose to inhabit symbolizes the reality of their couplehood. So, while looking for a house or an apartment, husbands and wives constantly are reminded of the fact that they are "in" their marriage together.

Their home, humble as it may be, is the place where they completely sequester themselves from others and revel in their intimacy. Every bit of furniture they put in its place, every little trinket they display, and every color they paint on the walls is a symbol of their interpersonal blending. As they get into the task of selecting a home and creating their own special ambience within it, they get deeper "into" one another.

Ideally, mates also can combine their individual abilities and sensibilities by working together to make a living. Obviously, if they run their own enterprise, they have to discuss every aspect of its functioning, welding their separateness into joint decisions. By carrying out these decisions, they amplify their "we-ness," and each identifies his or her "me" with the commonality of their expanded individualities.

However, many spouses cannot arrange such ideal conditions of work. Still, it is possible for them to confide in each other about all of their occupational satisfactions and frustrations, offering and accepting suggestions for improving the effectiveness of their individual work. At the end of their daily routines, and on weekends and vacations, they can also participate in avocations and recreations of interest to *both* of them. Through this participation they regularly devote themselves to the same activity at the same time. Thus, they narrow the psychological gap induced by their pursuit of separate vocations.

Finally, by conceiving a child, mates expand the boundaries of their individuality to the utmost. In procreation a husband and a wife literally fuse the separate cells of their sperm and egg, and their composite strands of genetic material tie their individual contributions into the totality of their common creation.

Of course, each mate may be very pleased to see some of his and her characteristics in the child. But a loving couple greatly appreciates the miraculous way in which their individualities have merged in the child's unmistakable uniqueness as a person. For the child, like their relationship, is more than a mere summation of their separate selves. Rather, their offspring is a novel fruition and personification of their union in loving.

Seeking the benefits of a loving relationship, men and women leave the safe but limiting confines of their singleness and enter the risky but liberating mutuality of a marriage. Still, they are very hesitant to give up that safety and take the risk involved in sharing the totality of their individual existences— their bodies and their minds. Describing this hazard in the technical vocabulary of psychoanalysis, Freud wrote, "At the height of being in love, the boundary between ego and object threatens to melt away."[2]

Consequently, becoming a married couple is inevitably threatening to both spouses. It makes them feel as if they could lose their long-held sense of being separate persons. If they lost that, how could they do *anything*, even survive, on their own? What if they merged so much that they could not function apart from each other?

When smitten by the threat of losing their individuality, neither husband nor wife is likely to recall the benefits they have gained in uniting. Instead, they are inclined to slam shut the gates of their accessibility and to displace "we-ness" with "me-ness," closing the boundaries of their individuality around their separate selves.

Feeling mutually menaced, mates become psychologically *and* physically "uptight." Avoiding eye contact, their pupils narrow to pinpoints; their facial and bodily muscles become taut as armor; and the fibers of their blood vessels constrict, preventing the flow of life-infusing blood that prepares the genitals for the interpenetration of lovemaking. Indeed, neither one is in the mood, or the physical state, for making love. The husband feels too "turned off" to get an erection. The wife has an analogous reaction: her vagina remains dry inside and its entrance closes in a spasm.

Along with such episodes, every couple suffers through periods when they vacillate between the promise and the threat of including each other inside the boundaries of their individuality. These are the times when they realize that, to increase the sharing of their love, they have to merge more completely as a couple than they ever did before.

Even after husbands and wives have been married for years, they feel threatened about losing their individuality. Ironically, as they succeed in becoming more intimate as a couple, they feel even more concerned about their interpersonal merger. As mortal creatures, they are always motivated to protect their personal existence. No matter how love-centered their marriage may be, they need to feel they are capable of taking care of themselves as individuals. So they retain a self-centered concern for their own welfare, "just in case" something goes wrong with their relationship. They realize that one of them is destined to die before the other, and they worry about their ability to function separately if they outlive their mate.

The lifelong threat of expanding the boundaries of individuality is increased greatly by the emphasis America places on individualism. This philosophy, as Jacob Burckhardt says,[3] emerged in full force during the Renaissance, holding that there can be no higher virtue in life than developing one's uniqueness and being recognized for it—especially through activities that elevate one's standing in the socioeconomic system. As a result, people have been led to equate all of their individuality with only a small part of it—their egoistic aspirations.

When mates fail in self-aggrandizement, they are likely to perceive themselves as worthless "nothings" and insignificant "nobodies." They often believe their personal chances of becoming a "something"—or a "somebody"—would be jeopardized if they merged their individualities too deeply. Yet in resisting an ever-deepening merger, they necessarily weaken their sense of individuality, which is more strengthened by the giving and receiving of love than by any degree of individualistic success they can achieve.

INCREASING INTERDEPENDENCE

Interdependence is such an evident feature of relational interaction that some theorists, for example Kelley et al., have made it *the* defining characteristic of a relationship.[4] While regarding it as only one among the four promises and threats of love, we have no doubt about its importance for any couple.

Surely, in getting married a man and a woman gain an incomparable sense of emotional security from knowing they are wedded to a person whose love is special and wholehearted: someone who can be counted on always and for anything; a person for whom one is irreplaceable and infinitely precious. It is just as reassuring to feel indispensable to one's mate—to know that one's love is essential to a mate's happiness and well-being—and that one is prepared, at any time, to respond to a mate's distress with loving care, willing to do whatever has to be done to help. Thus, a husband and a wife become equally *dependent on* and *dependable for* one another.

As a couple, they are motivated to help each other in meeting all their physical and psychological needs. Each is interested in preserving the health of the other, and in remaining healthy for the other. In addition, they depend upon each other to follow through in handling their economic, parental, and social responsibilities while also sustaining the priorities of their loving relationship.

Through their mutual support both mates flourish individually, as compared with unattached persons. Married people, research has shown, are happier and freer of mental illness. "They are also less vulnerable to physical illness, have fewer psychosomatic symptoms, and have lower mortality rates."[5] Similarly, by depending on and being dependable for one another, mates develop psychological maturity. Each becomes a more trusting and trustworthy person. Spouses also grow in humility by repeatedly turning to each other for assistance and finding the other's ideas and support an aid in coping with problems that stumped them as individuals.

While increasing their interdependence, mates develop a view of themselves as a competent and reliable team. Getting a mental feedback from this positive image, both draw courage from "replaying" their joint accomplishments and from cheering each other on toward what they want to accomplish in the future.

A similar development takes place as they "team up" in making love. Even before getting started, each is *dependent on* the other for assessing and communicating the mutuality of their desire. Then, during foreplay and continuing through orgasm, each is *dependable for* the other, giving as much consideration to his or her wishes as to one's own. Through this interdependence mates guarantee the mutuality of their sexual satisfaction, making it difficult for them to imagine experiencing the same degree of fulfillment with any other partner.

A husband and a wife who feel so gratified may regard each other as "a good lay." But this description is incorrect since it excludes the crucial element—interdependence—that gives their lovemaking its goodness for both of them. Actually, it would be more accurate, and more supportive of their marriage, for a couple to characterize the quality of their sexual intercourse in relational terms as *"we're* a good lay."

However, all mates feel threatened by the truth of their interdependence, which drives home the fact that they are not—and can never be—individually sufficient unto themselves for the fulfillment of their need for love. This awareness alarms them because it means that, no matter how individually proficient they become in attending to their own vital needs, they still have to put themselves in the position of depending totally on someone else in order to love *and* be loved.

Of course, it is threatening to recognize that another person's love cannot be secured simply by offering one's own love or by the imposition of one's own will. Love can only come freely from another, as a gift; within a loving relationship, one runs the risk of being hurt, exploited, rejected, or abandoned by one's beloved.

This threat of *dependence on* a loved one is reinforced throughout a person's upbringing. Children in every society are bound to learn that nobody, not even their own parents, can be depended on to respond to them in an unequivocally loving way at all times.

Moreover, the ethos of American society leads people to believe they are not supposed to need or to rely on other people for anything. Instead, one is supposed to be a "rugged individualist," a bulwark of self-sufficiency in everything one does. Yet, in contradiction to this ideology, *the fact of social interdependence* is what makes it possible for everyone to live. Despite the virtual religion that prevails about the desirability of independence, the entire economy rests on the reliability of all the people who work together in it. Don't people routinely entrust their lives to complete strangers—pilots, bus drivers, train engineers, and all the motorists on the road—every time they travel from one place to another? Don't they expect their urgent letters to be carried across continents and oceans by people they never see?

On the other side of interdependence, people are as threatened by being *dependable for* a mate as they are about being dependent on one. The willingness to be dependable in a loving relationship requires a self-imposed and permanent constraint on one's freedom of action—an open-ended commitment to go on being lovingly available no matter what personal inclinations may tempt one to hurt, exploit, reject, or abandon one's partner. People resist being so dependable, thinking it will deprive them of the ability to be spontaneous and to stay fully "in charge" of their own lives.

Like the threat of being dependent, the threat of being dependable is fed by a lot of childhood experience. One cannot grow up without realizing, even if never admitting it to anyone, that one has often let others down; that one has led people to have expectations of honesty, trust, and unwavering affection that one did not consistently uphold—indeed, that one willfully violated in the interest of some self-centered desire.

Just as it deprecates people for depending on each other, American society tends to undermine the value of dependability in a loving relationship. The socioeconomic system rewards those who are ready to put opportunities for occupational advancement and personal achievement above their marital interdependence. People often make disparaging remarks about individuals who deliberately pass up chances for more status, power, and money just to be available for their mates. Husbands and wives who trust each other completely may be considered foolishly naive, and those who spend a lot of time together, preferring each other's company to being with anyone else, may be regarded as weak, immature, or "neurotically dependent."

TRANSCENDING DIFFERENCES IN GENDER

Marriage offers mates the opportunity to transcend their biologically rooted *and* their socially conditioned differences in gender. In this twin transcendence, they can rid themselves of the inadequacy feelings they have harbored about the intrinsic limitations of their own sex and shed the inequities of their gender-role stereotypes. At the same time, they acquire higher levels of mutual acceptance and appreciation for one another's physical and psychological characteristics, permitting them to be loving with greater flexibility and genuineness.

By welcoming familiarity with their differences in anatomy and physiological functioning, husbands and wives develop an understanding and appreciation for what it is to be a member of the opposite sex. A husband empathizes with the plump and swaying fullness of his wife's breasts; with her nipples going from soft to taut to soft again; with the curve and bounce of her buttocks; with the sensitivity of her clitoris and the almost painful intensity of pleasure it gives her when he stimulates it; with the lush warmth of her vagina and its amazing elasticity; with the mixture of delicacy and firmness running through her body; with the quickening of her breath when she reaches a climax, its rippling rings of release seeming to turn her belly inside out.

Using her empathic abilities, a wife learns about the tapering contours of her husband's hairy chest; the square set of his shoulders and the flexing muscles of his arms; the sloping shallowness of his hips; the texture of his testicles and the way they rise up when she fondles them; the wonderful responsiveness of his penis and the exact spots on its shaft and head that drive him wild when touched; the strength of his impassioned grip on her shoulders; and the throbbing pulsations of his ejaculation filling her up as he abandons himself to the frenzy of his thrusts.

To supplement this experiential learning, mates can tell each other about the sensations and emotions that occur within them while they are making love. As a result, they give each other more sexual pleasure, which provides both of them with a greater sense of personal adequacy and makes each one feel more complete as a human being. This feeling of completion enables them to be more accepting of their own and each other's sex. Such personal and mutual acceptance frees them to become more familiar with the "mystery" they are to one another. Although they will never fathom that mystery completely, mates continue to explore it for a lifetime, getting to know each other better and better in the Biblical sense of knowing.

Love-centered mates also broaden their relational equality by flexibly sharing *all* the roles and responsibilities that insure the welfare of their marriage. As they discard the oppression of sexism, they also experience the excitement and satisfaction of doing things that they had avoided because it was supposed to be a "woman's" or a "man's" work.

For example, in the process of furnishing their first apartment, newlyweds may discover that the husband has more talent than the wife for interior decoration. His greater perceptiveness in visualizing how things will fit into their rooms enables him to make better choices about what to purchase. Soon, they decide to let him take on the role of leadership in this domain, which both of them had considered "forbidden" to men.

Meanwhile, the same couple learns that the husband is quite inept at keeping their financial records. By contrast, the wife has more mathematical and organizational ability for doing the banking, filling out tax forms, and managing their expenditures. They therefore agree to let her "take over" in this area of role playing, which they had stereotypically assumed to be "inappropriate" for women.

While becoming more egalitarian, both mates actualize personal potentials they had always felt too inhibited to express. They also become more authentic and relaxed with each other since neither has to feign a nonexistent competence. As a couple, they benefit by having a more attractive home and a more effective system of accounting. In addition, they gain the confidence to explore similar changes in other areas of role playing.

Of course, even if both mates are employed in different fields, they play the same *marital* role of making a living. But neither of them is capable of doing the other's job, and, while at work, each of them has to deal individually with the strains of their positions. However, when they get home at the end of a day, they interact as equals by airing their tensions and agreeing on solutions to their occupational problems.

In their own home, mates are in the place where their cultivation of equality is not opposed or mediated by the hierarchical arrangements of their daily employment. Here they are completely free to combine their energies in doing the routine chores of housekeeping for which no special talent is required in either mate.

Of all domestic activities, however, the rearing of their children is the most important for a couple to share in every respect—from feeding, diapering, and playing with them to making the myriad of decisions about their health and education. Indeed, parenting is not a "chore" for mates, despite its undoubtedly wearing demands, but a unique chance for them to develop their capacity to love in equal measure; to enjoy the process and results of that development; and to impart the same loving and egalitarian values to their children that they display toward each other.

However, a husband and a wife invariably feel threatened as they act to transcend their gender differences. Regarding their inherent differences, they are naturally wary about what is unfamiliar to them. They cannot help but experience some apprehension about the mystery each is to the other. Besides, the intimate interactions of a heterosexual relationship continually remind each spouse of the limitations of his and her particular gender. Both are well aware that the other possesses physical attributes lacking in themselves, and they feel limited in comparison to one another.

A wife can never acquire a penis, nor can she attain her husband's lifelong capacity to sire children. A husband can never bear, give birth to, and breast-feed a baby, nor can he experience the multiple orgasms his wife is capable of having. Consequently, each mate is threatened about being essentially "flawed" as a human being.

The possibility of equalizing their roles is just as threatening to mates. As a result of having absorbed the social stereotypes of how they *should* feel and behave, both worry about becoming too much alike. A husband may hesitate to cultivate such human characteristics as gentleness and sensitivity that the culture labels "feminine," afraid of becoming—or being taken for—an unmanly "wimp" or a homosexual. Reciprocally, a wife may be reluctant to develop such "masculine" traits as physical strength and assertiveness lest she turn into—or be regarded as—an unappealing "ball breaker" or lesbian.

Unfortunately, too, the values of the socioeconomic system, with its glorification of occupational achievement above everything else, make members of both sexes feel as if they are frittering away their lives if they become too involved in anything except their careers. Of course, cultural bias continues to define childrearing and housekeeping as female activities, even if a woman is employed full time at a demanding job. As Philip Blumstein and Pepper Schwartz reported in their survey *American Couples,* working wives still perform those marital functions with relatively little help from their husbands.[6] Many of these women are concerned about their adequacy to handle all of these diverse responsibilities with the same effectiveness. On the other hand, a wife may grow uneasy at the thought of losing her one-sided prerogatives at home, and she may never encourage her husband to develop her degree of interest and skill in parenting.

Conversely, a husband may resist a wife's invitation to participate equally in childrearing and in housework, for he may perceive such participation as a menace to his ability to go "all out" in advancing his career. A husband may also feel gravely threatened if he sees his wife surpass him in earning power. In fact, as Caroline Bird reported in *The Two-Paycheck Marriage,* the likelihood of a couple getting divorced increases when a wife's income exceeds that of her husband.[7] In her interviews Bird also found that a husband may become very upset if his wife's success leads her to devote less attention to him and more to her own strivings.[8]

IMMERSION IN THE PLEASURE OF LOVEMAKING

For infants, pleasurable immersion in the wholeness of loving is not an exceptional event. Babies are expected and encouraged to steep themselves in the happiness of sensual contact with a loving person. Held by a parent, they regularly luxuriate in the joys of rubbing and nuzzling; of clinging and touching; of being petted and kissed. Like puppies or kittens, they have no built-in inhibitions about acting on their impulses, and they freely express their pleasure in grunts, squeals, and gurgles. In fact, they are doted on all the more for their irrepressibility, which adults find cute and adorable. Thus, infants generally are allowed to spend countless hours in a mindless bubble of bliss.

This bubble is soon destined to be broken forever. As children develop their minds, they lose the innocence of an unknowing indulgence in the sensuality that accompanies the physical expression of love. Of course, their developing mental abilities permit them to enter a veritable universe of symbolic enjoyment. The same development also makes it possible for them to know what they are doing and why they are doing it.

From the time they first acquire self-awareness, people cannot help but think about whatever they do, and they can no longer escape the challenge of deciding how, when, where, and with whom to fulfill their innate need for love.

In a love-centered marriage, husband and wife can most happily use their volition for deepening their immersion in the pleasure of lovemaking. Since they are capable of directing their consciousness, they can decide to rid their minds of extraneous thoughts and fantasies from the moment they step into bed. Then, by focusing awareness precisely on their shifting points of bodily contact, they pick up and stir the currents of desire that swirl between them. As they embrace, they linger here, there, and everywhere, sculpting their innermost feelings of affection onto each other's flesh. They float lingeringly on the river of sensuality each feels rushing in from the other's hands, mouth, and genitals. Meanwhile, from the beginning of their arousal through the aftermath of their climax, they spontaneously give voice to their rising passion—in murmurs, gasps, and groans.

By using their minds as the most sophisticated of sex organs, mates return, as often and as fully as they wish, to the idyllic Land of Love. Yet to get there, they employ the most primitive modality of sensation in the human repertoire: the sense of touch. This is what they relied on primarily, as babies, for expressing and gratifying their loving inclinations; and touch remains the indispensable vehicle for their subsequent trips into the Eden of eroticism.

What mates are hungry to recapture, as an extraordinary alteration in their experience of living, was quite ordinary to them as infants. In appeasing this hunger again and again, they feel virtually reborn. Even a stern school teacher and a commanding executive tend to drop their occupational roles and personal pretentions as they disrobe. Acting as playful as little children, they may even lapse into baby talk. With the magic of their touch, they reawaken the holistic quality of their primordial experience of love, and they transport each other into the altered state of consciousness that characterizes sexual intercourse. This alteration begins at arousal, intensifies through foreplay, and peaks to a crescendo of dissolution at orgasm. Ultimately, as a couple rides the orgasmic waves of mental oblivion, they leave their adult preoccupations on some far-off shore of forgetfulness.

While moving toward the mindlessness of orgasm, mates can choose to dawdle on tantalizing detours along the way. In making these choices they stimulate their sexual-affectionate responses, which suffuse them with the "rush" of passion that courses involuntarily through their bodies. By evoking these involuntary reactions, they liberate themselves from their usual psychological and behavioral restraints, and temporarily they feel more akin to babies and animals than to their usual selves.

In fantasy, every couple can imagine being perpetually immersed in an untroubled realm of erotic pleasure. In actuality, however, couples practice this immersion less than they could—if they were more capable of tolerating its inherent threat. In fact, all grown-ups are threatened as they sense themselves "regress" and become "animalistic." What if they become as helpless as infants? What if their contortions, grimaces, and cries of sensual satisfaction were to unleash "the beast" in them, never to be tamed again? What if they dally so uncontrollably in the pleasure of lovemaking that they become unable to do anything else?

All of these concerns are natural and understandable. Adults do need their mature minds to function in a complex society. So they are menaced when they feel their mental controls slipping away from them, even though they are the ones who decide to use their minds for that very purpose.

The threat of mindlessness is most acute as lovers approach orgasm, the zenith of their altered state of consciousness. To attain orgasmic release, they have to relinquish *all* the control they had been mentally exerting to heighten and prolong the pleasure of their foreplay. Only through such a complete surrender can they be swept away by the surging forces of their involuntary orgasmic reflexes. Yet if they relinquish mental control, how can they be sure of regaining it again? Thus, while crossing the threshold into the most exquisite of human pleasures, people are worried that their imminent ecstasy—as the word literally implies—will drive them totally out of their minds.

Naturally, through repeated experience of orgasmic gratification, a husband and a wife increasingly welcome such a transient "loss" of their minds. They also learn to recognize and tolerate their apprehensions about getting involved in the sensuality of foreplay. Still, because the enjoyment of lovemaking occurs by using the mind to "lose it," the pleasure of sexual intercourse continues to be threatening, even to the most sexually active mates. For this reason all couples place self-imposed restrictions on how much time and energy they devote to lovemaking, and they also limit the extent to which they "let themselves go" when they do make love.

Society does not make it easy for mates to cope with this threat. On the contrary, America is not a Temple of Love. In paradoxical fashion, its methods of socialization and its economy combine to buttress the inherent existential barriers against immersion in the pleasure of lovemaking.

One side of this paradox is represented by the practices of childrearing, which coerce boys and girls into repressing the sexual component of their feelings of love. This repression may later fill them with "pleasure anxiety," a phrase coined by Wilhelm Reich[9] to describe the apprehension that many adults feel about the anticipation of orgasmic release. Extremely repressed men and women may even conjure up expectations of literally bursting or exploding. They therefore chronically prevent themselves from experiencing a sexual climax.

However, as Reich noted,[10] everyone engages in some sexual repression in the course of growing up. Consequently, all adults have some degree of pleasure anxiety, and this anxiety can make it all the more difficult for mates to let themselves be propelled into the mindless bliss of an orgasm.

Another by-product of sexual repression is guilt, which derives from the punishment that parents widely employ to induce antierotic attitudes in their children. Over time, children learn to indict themselves for having erotic inclinations, and they make this notion of "badness" an integral part of their conscience. Subsequently, as adults they feel guilty for displaying or even for fantasizing about the sexuality of loving, and they punish themselves to expiate their guilt in a variety of ways, including rigidly self-enforced abstinence from erotic enjoyment.

Parents and educators further instill this syndrome in the

minds of children by remaining silent about the pleasurable aspects of sexual behavior. Mothers and fathers usually make *no* reference to their children's erotic feelings. In their study on patterns of childrearing, Robert Sears, Eleanor Maccoby, and Harry Levin "did not encounter anyone who helped the children identify the *emotional* states related to sex"[11]; they added, speaking about parents, "none, . . . as far as we could tell, said: 'You're feeling sexy, that's why you're acting like that.' "[12] Yet these investigators learned that many parents explicitly remark on a child's feelings of anger when he or she is behaving aggressively.

Thus, the same parents who teach their children to identify and cope with their hostility are unwilling to help them in dealing with their sexual sensations and desires. These mothers and fathers may also feel obliged to instruct their offspring in the mechanics of reproduction, but generally they make no mention of how enjoyable sexual intercourse can be. Similarly, formal courses on sex education carefully avoid any allusion to the connections between the functional and the pleasurable dimensions of sexuality.

This avoidance implicitly communicates a very negative and invalidating social message about the actual nature of erotic stimulation that children and adolescents personally experience as pleasurable within themselves. Indeed, these youths are led to believe that what they spontaneously feel is good is "really" bad, precisely because it is so pleasurable. So they learn to regard their own erotic sensations as "dirty" and to perceive themselves as unclean for having those sensations.

Naturally, this grotesque training in "morality" can only exert destructive effects on an adult couple. It predisposes them to refrain from showing their "dirtiness" to each other, and it causes them remorse for experiencing the pleasure that goes along with their sexual relations. Besides, in the wholeness of loving, affection is expressed in and through physical contact between a man and a woman. But if mates believe that sexual interaction is "wrong" *because of* its pleasure, they may feel it is necessary to limit the amount of affection they exchange. Thus, in recoiling from eroticism, mates actually dilute the true morality of their relationship, which is centered on the greatest possible sharing of their love.

But while American culture diminishes the pleasure of loving through the inculcation of antierotic anxiety and guilt, it promotes exactly the same diminution by encouraging the loveless pursuit of sexuality. To this end, the contemporary ideology of consumerism emphasizes an acquisitive grasping for erotic stimulation as an end in itself, disconnected from the holistic sharing of love.

The mass media incite people to do whatever "turns them on"; to go out and *get* whatever sexual thrills they can take from others, whether from a prostitute or a casual affair. Likewise, people are constantly exhorted to use their money for conspicuous consumption—instead of for purchasing the time, privacy, and conditions to enhance their loving relationships and their lovemaking. Many couples invest heavily in buying things they do not need but can display to others as signs of their economic success: a "showplace" of a house, a "whopper" of a swimming pool, objects of art that are "conversation pieces," clothes and furs that "drip" with money, and automobiles that make others "green with envy."

Swayed by cultural commandments to consume, a husband and a wife may treat each other as mere articles of consumption and approach their lovemaking purely as an act of self-indulgence. They may even speak of their intercourse, to quote Rollo May, as "having sex"[13]—not as making love.

This popular colloquialism—having sex—evokes the image of a decidedly acquisitive act, like "having lunch." It implies that a person is primarily motivated to *obtain* pleasure by using someone for the relief of a physiological appetite. It refers neither to love nor to its affectionate component. Instead, it separates the relational aspects of sexual intercourse from its physical effects.

By adopting this attitude toward lovemaking, each mate tries to take more and more from the other—and to give less and less. Eventually, they lapse into an ironic self-consumption in which they literally devour their time and energy in a futile striving for the completeness of satisfaction that can only be attained through a caring communion between them.

Because of their conditioning in aggrandizement, Americans have become very dependent on social approval and tangible rewards as incentives for anything they do. But when a husband and wife make love, without making babies, they are rewarded only by the intangible gratifications of their privately created delights. No one else sees their exquisite pleasure. Society does not pin a medal on them for their success in enjoyment. They have no diplomas, degrees, promotions, investibles, or collectibles to show for their experience, no matter how fantastic it may be for them.

Thus, while putting their bodies through the mechanics of sexual interpenetration, both mates may be thinking of projects to further their separate ambitions. Or, as solace for their difficulties in acquiring the trappings of self-aggrandizement, they may imagine themselves as "having sex" with a famous Hollywood star or television personality, trying to derive a much bigger boost to their vanity than they can get from one another.

These splits between inner thought and outward action show how adherence to the values of aggrandizement leads spouses to forgo their potential pleasure. Under such circumstances, couples can hardly fail to be disappointed by making love, and they may well wonder whether it is worth the bother of going through the motions of doing it.

NOTES

1. Levenson, H., & Harris, C. N. Love and the search for identity. In K. S. Pope & associates, *On love and loving*. San Francisco: Jossey-Bass, 1980, p. 268.
2. Freud, *Civilization and its discontents*, p. 13.
3. Burckhardt, J. *The civilization of the Renaissance in Italy*. New York: Mentor, 1960.
4. Speaking for themselves and their coauthors, Ellen Berscheid and Letitia Anne Peplau make this statement in Chapter 1, The emerging science of relationships. In H. H. Kelley, E. Berscheid, A. Christensen, J. H. Harvey, T. L. Huston, G. Levinger, E. McClintock, L. A. Peplau, & D. R. Peterson, *Close relationships*. San Francisco: Freeman, 1983, p. 12.
5. Kelley, H. H. Epilogue: An essential science. In Kelley et al., *Close relationships*, p. 493.
6. Blumstein, P., & Schwartz, P. *American couples*. New York: Morrow, 1983.

7. Bird, C. *The two-paycheck marriage.* New York: Rawson, Wade, 1979, p. 13.
8. Ibid., p. 61.
9. Reich, W. *The function of the orgasm.* New York: Farrar, Straus, & Giroux, 1971, pp. xv–xxxii.
10. Ibid.
11. Sears, R. R., Maccoby, E. E., & Levin, H. *Patterns of childrearing.* Evanston, Ill.: Row, Peterson, 1957, p. 190.
12. Ibid.
13. May, R. *Love and will.* New York: Delta, 1969, p. 47.

4

BUILDING THE ROMANCE

The romance is the *most invigorating* ingredient in a couple's relationship—the part of their relational construct they use solely for the purpose of representing and enhancing the love they actually share. Both spouses mentally depict the sexual and affectionate strands of their loving thoughts, feelings, and behavior. Acting on these fond images, they blend those two components in symbolic and tactile communication, integrating their psychological and physical functioning as loving persons. Increasingly, they cultivate a common perception of being inside the same enchanted chamber of intimacy and desire.

Contrary to the opinion of some authorities,[1] a couple's romance is not a trivial or misleading fantasy that interferes with their ability to accept the realities of married life—and that they should renounce quickly for their own good. Rather, a couple's romance is the *dynamic stimulant* of their relationship: a common source of energy they can always activate to move toward an ever-deepening gratification in the wholeness of their love. Romance vastly augments their individual reservoirs of energy when they are together and when they are apart; reinforces their relational solidarity and gives them a common sense of purpose for their future, which they can contemplate enjoyably and work toward enthusiastically; and it serves as a permanent repository of exhilarating memories and aspirations that they draw upon for encouragement and inspiration.

Mates intensify this romantic commonality as they fulfill the four promises of love throughout their marriage. Reciprocally, as they elaborate their romance, adding new cognitions to it from their progress in loving, they improve their ability to redeem those promises. For example, as newlyweds immerse themselves in the pleasure of lovemaking, they gain a keen appreciation for their good fortune—and good judgment—in having chosen each other as lifelong mates. As they mentally incorporate this gratitude into their romance, they bring its energizing effects into their sexual relations, treating each other more tenderly and exchanging more affection. Thus, they deepen their pleasure in making love.

Building up the romance involves a great outpouring of the love that mates had bottled up as unattached individuals. When single, they felt they were living only for themselves. They had nobody to evoke and to share the untapped power of their capacity for loving. However, by creating their marital relationship, they liberate and direct that power, living not only for themselves but also for one another.

Becoming coauthors of their very own love story, mates collaborate in portraying their evolving relationship; how wonderful they feel together; the marvelous experiences they have already shared; and how happy they are to be facing the future as a married couple. Cherishing their romance as a rare work of art, they want to embellish its beauty, and the material for their artistry comes from many sources.

Sometimes, a husband and wife are inspired by a particular song, hearing in its lyrics and melody a perfect expression of their loving feelings. Struck by this representation of what is going on between them, they make it the musical theme of their lifelong romance. For us, "Venezuela" was the haunting song that played in the background when we made love for the first time. Instantly, it conjured images of torrid sensuality, of daring adventure, and of meeting any challenge that confronted us. So it assumed a spine-tingling significance as the overture to our dramatic "zap!"

Some mates may see themes of their romance in a film.

Holding hands in a darkened theater, they become enthralled in watching a courageous couple surmount obstacles to their relationship in a foreign and forbidding land. They interpret the movie as portraying their own determination to prevail as lovers while exploring the depths and hazards of life together.

Spouses also enlarge their romance by going places and doing things: finding ambiences and experiences that bring new insights into their shared feelings. While riding horses along the ridge of a mountain, their eyes may meet in a lightning flash of recognition. "Here we are, sitting on top of the world, with prospects for happiness as vast as the vistas out there." Or, walking through a blossoming park in springtime, they may suddenly stop and kiss to convey what both are thinking: "Isn't it amazing to feel this good about being together?"

Indeed, as the hero and heroine of their own romance, mates make their pairing an incomparable and irreplaceable one. Over the years, they become increasingly aware of what they are putting into their love story, and they take great pleasure in adding new chapters to it.

Even when they are apart, each spouse can "get high" by thinking about the other and by invoking romantic images of their interactions. These remembrances provide a charge of vitality that brightens the experience of whatever they happen to be doing on their own, giving them pleasurable anticipations of being together as soon as possible. Again face to face, they further multiply the amount of energy they generate from within themselves. These currents crackle between them, leaving no doubt in their minds about how uniquely vitalized they are by their relationship.

COMMUNICATION AND MARITAL UNITY

Mates bring to marriage an infinite storehouse of love that is always available for them, and they passively experience the presence of this treasure when its emanations light up their individual selves. But they cannot extract its mine of riches unless they *actively communicate* their love to each other.

Husband and wife satisfy much of their yearning for interpenetration in verbal intercourse, each striving to penetrate and be penetrated by the sharing of consciousness. By speaking and listening in a dialogue of mutual disclosure, they can merge as they do when making love. If they willingly reveal whatever is on their minds, they obtain the pleasurable release that comes from unblocking their pent-up emotions, and they discover depths of feeling and psychological insight they never knew before.

In this kind of communication, mates make love mentally. Their dialogue is what Shakespeare called "a marriage of true minds." Talking openly is often erotically stimulating—even when a couple is not directly discussing sexual matters. In public places, conversations between husband and wife are sometimes so ardent that a casual listener easily picks up the sexual overtones of the love flowing between them. In the midst of a delightful discussion, walking arm in arm along a street, an elderly couple is as romantic as newlyweds. From their twinkling eyes and smiling faces, people see they are "getting off" on whatever they happen to be saying.

Animated mates are equally involved in *every* feature of their conversations, including the nonverbal expressions that accompany their speech. Naturally, they create the pleasures of such "love talk" by participating with full reciprocity and openness—equally willing to give, receive, and keep their lovelights turned on during their interactions. In fact, the greatest enjoyments of a marital conversation arise when each mate is the undivided focus of the other's rapt attention; when each is seeking to know and be known completely, as a whole and unique person.

Romantic mates periodically review the manifold nuances of their love: how precious they are to each other, how much fun they have as a couple, how much more they enjoy being together than with anyone else in the world, and how much each inhabits the other's thoughts, fantasies, and dreams. Cynics may regard such declarations as "mushy," "sentimental," and "unrealistic." Yet the loving couple knows full well that these expressions are among their most sustaining realities.

Actually, most couples place good verbal communication, along with gratifying sexual relations, very high on the list of factors accounting for marital satisfaction. One study of happily married spouses found that they relish their conversations, and many of them cannot remember a time in their relationship when they lacked for something interesting or meaningful to talk about. Overall, they regard the well-being of their relationships as "their responsibility, their task, their project."[2] Some of these mates also reported that their joint efforts to communicate honestly produced better understanding of themselves, each other, and human existence in general. Thus, Eric Strauss, the researcher, concluded that their relationships can be viewed as a "laboratory or classroom for this form of discovery or education."[3]

Reflective mates realize that the source of their vitalizing cohesiveness is entirely intangible. This realization is awesome. How can the two of them feel so powerfully united as one? In their amazement a husband and a wife may experience a spiritual enlightenment. At their loving peaks, they may attain the awareness of having tapped into a unifying force that implicitly connects all forms of life. By opening themselves to one another, they have made a joint connection with that same force. So they perceive their own relationship as partaking in the oneness that underlies the order of the universe.

Religious couples often interpret the miraculous effects of their love in authoritarian terms. Even when engaging in sexual intercourse, they may see themselves as obeying the benevolent will of an all-loving God, who lives in, through, and between them. However, we believe that the Spirit can be neither personified nor encompassed by any particular sect and that no denomination has an exclusive pipeline to it. Besides, by insisting on the superiority of their doctrines, competing religions have spread disharmony and bloody warfare, thereby reviling the divine essence all of them profess to share.

Although we do not subscribe to any institutionalized religion, we are moved to have faith in the spirituality of love. We feel deeply grateful for the chance to participate in the transforming spiritual power of our own relational union and humble in the recognition that we are only two sparks of the same fire that produces the light of love for all human beings.

The Common Dream

Before they married, each spouse had been hero or heroine of a solitary romance, a gripping fantasy of how exceptional and lovable he or she would become by means of personal achievements later in life. As Daniel Levinson found,[4] many American men enter marriage with their minds firmly fixed on what he calls "the Dream," imagining themselves in a career that will bring them money, fame, and influence, and they see this success as making them worthy of love in their own eyes and in the eyes of everyone else.

While they see themselves striving upward and onward, these men envision their wives as helpmates, working "behind the scene." Gail Sheehy[5] has reported equivalent fantasies among women, who imagine being socially lauded and rewarded for their personal accomplishments, although they may view their husbands as playing a supportive role in their success.

The projected hopes of youthful spouses generally include the archetypical adult desire to satisfy the need for love directly—in a loving relationship. Still, in the individualistic dreams they bring into marriage, they curry basic benefits of love—approval, acceptance, and validation—from activities that "pay off" in some distant future *and* that take place *outside* the realm of their marital relationship.

Admittedly, personal dreams of conventional success often motivate people to actualize their particular gifts. The lure of social appreciation may also give them an extra incentive to take the risks of competing with others in the same field of work. While falling in love, therefore, many men and women exchange the details of their personal dreams and discuss how they can help one another to realize their creative potentials. But people oriented toward a love-centered marriage can meld their *individual* aspirations into the construction of a *common dream,* making it the cornerstone of their lifelong romance.

Ellen Berscheid, a leading researcher on the psychology of emotion, has emphasized the potential importance of such commonality in dreaming. As she says, ". . . within close relationships, perhaps it is only people who can continue to dream dreams that include their partner who can stay emotionally alive within a relationship."[6]

Assuming mates are in philosophical agreement about the supreme value of their loving relationship, how is it possible for them to pursue lesser priorities in ways that most enhance the quality of their marriage? What is the best way to coordinate what they do, occupationally, with their overarching commitment to merge more lovingly throughout their lives?

By jointly confronting these basic issues, mates increase their creativity. The synergy of their collaboration results in solutions to problems neither of them could have arrived at separately. Simultaneously, they shed their old dreams of being solitary strivers who feel compelled eternally to swim alone toward an ever-receding shore of insatiable self-aggrandizement. In this respect they are shedding nothing but potential trouble. For the more strenuously people have tried to pursue their personal versions of the American Dream, the more surely have they produced a nightmare of seething tension and frustration for themselves and others.

Unfortunately, the present socioeconomic system is not designed for helping couples realize their common dreams of love. On the contrary, the division and the specialization of labor exacerbate the interpersonal divisiveness inherent in society's individualistic values. When husband and wife leave their home and go to work, they are separated automatically. If only one spouse is employed, the other fills his or her day with very unrelated activities. When both work, they rarely find jobs that permit them to spend their time side by side. Still more infrequently are couples hired as a team, sharing all the responsibilities of a particular job. Rather, most mates have separate positions in different locations.

Consequently, husbands and wives typically wind up spending more time during their waking hours with other people than with each other. Those who stay at home gravitate toward relationships with their children or with neighboring peers of their own sex, and they may gradually disclose more thoughts and feelings to friends than they do to their own spouses.

Likewise, employed spouses tend to develop confiding relationships with other workers. Wives may become friendly with other female employees, discussing their marital problems. Husbands may form friendships with fellow workers, airing difficulties they have with their wives. Over time, spouses can become more and more alienated while becoming closer to people at the office or factory.

Since nobody can avoid feeling attracted to some people
with whom they work, spouses also are tempted to get romantically involved with other employees of the opposite sex. Of
course, couples have the ability to restrict the scope of those
attractions and refrain from scuttling their marital fidelity.
Still, a man and a woman who spend day after day in close and
cooperative association, sharing the same activities, challenges, and responsibilities, often begin to relate with camaraderie and affection. In terms of intimacy and emotional significance, these kinds of relationships can rival the ones they
have with their own mates; eventually, it may be very difficult
to keep from "going over the line" that differentiates congenial colleagues from active lovers.

Far from having the freedom to determine the conditions
of their work, employees must submit to the rules and standards established by their employers. Although this conformity
varies in type and extent from job to job, it exerts a noxious
effect on the maintenance of a marital romance.

The backbreaking strain of menial labor, such as mining
and construction, leaves employees with little energy to put
into loving their mates. Monotonous work, requiring the constant repetition of a boring task, as on an assembly line or at a
computer terminal, stupifies people and saps their morale. For
example, in her study *Blue-Collar Marriage*, Mirra Komarovsky quotes a typically dispirited husband on his wife's
attitude toward his work: "I don't take much interest in it my-
self so I wouldn't expect her to if I couldn't."[7] In such jobs men
and women are thwarted severely in their needs for self-
expression, and since their salaries cannot eradicate their suffering, they are prone to feelings of victimization.

Many workers of both sexes use their spouses as scape-
goats for venting the rage they generate in their frustrating
jobs. But even if they refrain from scapegoating, they may feel
unlovable and impotent. When their working day is over, they
often try to drown their troubles in beer and whiskey, blot
themselves out by watching television, or fade into silent stu-
pors of self-pity.

One might suppose things would be much better for couples who have more interesting, less physically exhausting, and
more lucrative jobs. Certainly, executives, managers, or ex-

perts in a profession get a lot of intrinsic satisfaction from their occupations. However, the more employees get paid and the higher their status, the greater the expectations employers have of them—and the more they demand from themselves. These people frequently take work home at night and on weekends. Even if they are not doing some job-related project during their leisure time, they may be thinking about it while ostensibly interacting with their mates. Thus, many husbands and wives may feel—and, indeed, may be—more wedded to their companies and their careers than to each other.

In contrast, by agreeing on a common dream, love-centered mates switch on the beacon light that gives direction to their lifelong romance and guides them safely into the harbor of mutual contentment. As they progress in realizing this dream, they bring out the very best that is in each of them, and as they blend their personal assets, they make the actualization of their individual capacities consonant with the primacy of their relationship. In fact, these mates have the opportunity to *reassess* what they want in *all* aspects of the life they share, not just within the arena of achievement.

For example, on getting married we founded a common dream in which we saw ourselves as talented members of a well-matched and happy pair. We had no doubt about how close we wanted to be nor how much we enjoyed each other's company—in and out of bed. So our hopes for the future included the idea of having a great deal of time to be together.

The wish to have children was always a major element in our common dream. We wanted to become the best parents we could possibly be: to have healthy, happy, and loving children who would be a realization of the love we shared and whose personalities would reflect the psychological sensitivity with which we reared them.

Sharing the same aesthetic sensibilities, we hoped to live in beautiful surroundings. Beginning with our first apartment, we realized how much we loved "playing house." Subsequently, we dreamt of having a home that reflected our common tastes.

We looked forward to earning a decent living through work that would be socially constructive and optimally expressive of our abilities. In whatever vocation we would take up, we also longed to become widely known and admired. But we were determined not to pursue public acclaim just to get it and not to make money just to make it. In our common dream we saw ourselves as being strong enough to resist such temptations, preserving the integrity of our humanitarian values and cultivating our development as creative people.

However, our definition of creativity, at that time, was extremely individualistic: still tied to seeking acclaim for the products of our personal uniqueness. So, in our most outrageous fantasies we portrayed ourselves as the "Renaissance Man and Woman," each striving for one's own greater glory.

Since we had not yet clarified our position about the preeminence of our relationship, we frequently lapsed into tipping the balance of our values in the direction of individual egoism. Still, whenever we felt the noxious effects of that imbalance, we did try to right ourselves again by putting more of our weight on the side of love. Our common dream represented a confused attempt to find a balance between our mutual love and the personal ambitions embedded in our approach to creativity.

Eventually, we stopped our waffling and chose conclusively in favor of loving, but not until we had developed sufficient awareness of the importance and power of our *relationship*. With that insight, we made a fundamental change in the content of our common dream, adding our present concept of working together and dropping our previous fantasies of personal striving. Now we fully utilize our separate talents in jointly producing our lectures and our writing, and the more we unite through our *interpersonal* creativity, the more we bring out our individual capacities for self-expression and improve the quality of our collective productions.

As in our case, mates are capable of changing their common dream as they evolve their relationship. Certainly, it is appropriate for them to eliminate features that are too perfectionistic and demanding for *any* couple to accomplish or that no longer serve the enrichment of their marriage. They are also wise to add elements appropriate to the realistic scope of their growing abilities, their physical condition, and their stages of relational development.

RELATIONAL RELIABILITY AND SOCIAL RESPONSIBILITY

By doing work that is helpful to others, mates express on the public scene the kind of consideration and trustworthiness they privately share with each other, and their occupational involvement in society is consonant with their marital romance. Conversely, if they take jobs that require exploiting or injuring others, they set themselves up for a corrosive conflict between what they do for a living and how they would like to live.

On the other hand, it is essential for mates to *give each other* the time, care, and attention for increasing their interdependence and for keeping their loving relationship the top priority in their lives. Both need to demonstrate—in consistent action—that *no* occupational achievement, either personal or collective, is as important as the welfare of their marriage; that *nothing* they could accumulate in the material realm is worth undermining their ability to love one another.

Otherwise, mates may slip into the practice of subordinating the frequency and quality of their interpersonal contacts to the pursuit of their careers. If that happens, they may also decrease their vocational effectiveness. For by reliably nurturing their marriage, they grow in their ability to relate dependably to others and to utilize their skills most productively.

Unfortunately, "time is money" sums up the self-enslaving equation that Americans have been taught to apply as a formula for exercising reliability. Thus, "speeding" has become a mode of existence for countless American couples who are driven by limitless ambitions into feeling that they are being unreliable and wasting time if they do not "make every minute count" in pursuing some materialistic goal. People do not rely on these inner compulsions alone for their speediness. Instead, they "hop themselves up" by drinking coffee, smoking cigarettes, snorting cocaine, or taking amphetamines, which are aptly known as "speed." Consequently, they neglect their health by becoming workaholics and drug addicts. Many of the same people turn to alcohol, sedatives, and tranquilizers at night—trying to "calm themselves down" enough to fall asleep. But whether or not they use drugs, mates who incessantly strive to make more and more money cannot be adequately interdependent in attending to each other's need for love or in making the intimate contact necessary to build their romance.

With ironic futility some spouses try to make a romance out of "beating the system." Individually, they proceed to "kill themselves" in acquiring affluence. Then they spend the "loot" of their "killings" on sumptuous indulgences and conspicuous consumption, rationalizing that "living well is the best revenge." But what crime are they avenging, if not the disregard of their intuition, which has been trying to tell them all through their loveless acquisitions that baubles and luxuries are pale pleasures compared to those they could have been giving one another? And how well can they be living if they become more devoted to accumulating and displaying material objects than to loving each other?

Other mates try to heighten their interdependence by seeing themselves as "two against the world." This conspiratorial theme for a marital romance is understandably popular. In the jungle of society, where everyone is "one-too-many" as Sartre said,[8] why not become allies in the tooth-and-claw struggle against all others? So, like the notorious Bonnie and Clyde, who robbed banks to finance their relationship, many couples believe they can build their romance by preying on people economically.

Of course, duping people in business is not as damaging as riddling them with bullets. But "conning" others can only be part of a pseudoromance—not a genuine one. In using hostile and exploitative means to maintain a collective image as a dependable couple, mates plant the seeds of mutual suspicion between themselves. For how can they keep from mistrusting one another when they are so ready to mistreat others for their own manipulative ends?

Alternatively, some couples have been adopting economic arrangements that are consonant with the values of a love-centered marriage. These mates fuel their romance by seeing themselves as social innovators whose morale rests *not* on conformity to the existing society but, rather, on their will to resist its destructiveness. They link their relational interdependence with the interdependence extending between themselves and others. As Adler suggested,[9] they bridge their marital and social interests, and they take responsibility for sustaining an amicable connection between themselves and humanity at large.

Some mates are implementing the goal of being coworkers in the same socially useful enterprise, such as a farm, a natural food store, a business devoted to solar energy, or a consultation service for distressed people. Others get jobs in the same department of a university or hospital. Or, if they are in the same profession, they work together in a group practice.

Some of these couples are moving out of large cities and into small towns and rural areas where they enjoy a much more relaxed pace of living and reduce the gulf between their working lives and their married lives. Both spouses are within minutes of their places of work. Even if they have separate jobs, they can travel to work together and meet regularly for lunch. Having easier access to their children, they also function more reliably as parents. In addition, they benefit by being in a community where residents know each other personally, spontaneously offer one another help, and hold each other more directly to account for their behavior than people in urban and suburban areas.

By quitting jobs in defense industries, other spouses are chaneling their skills into work that contributes to peace and human welfare. Likewise, such couples are withdrawing their surplus earnings from banks and companies that support the military-industrial complex, and they are investing in industries that manufacture ecologically sound products. Thus, they integrate reliable investment in their own economic future with what will be good for generations to come. The more these couples make their livelihood and their lifestyle consistent with their social values, the more they raise their morale and enrich their romance.

RELATIONAL EQUALITY AND MUTAL ACCEPTANCE

Many mates now are intent on shaking off the stereotypical gender roles that past generations of husbands and wives felt compelled to play, and their willingness to deviate from sexist norms heightens their romance. Indeed, as they implement the humane ideal of social equality between the sexes, they improve their own relationship, each becoming more capable of interacting with the other on the basis of their essential commonality as human beings.

However, mates need to avoid falling into the trap of judging their *relational* equality by their *individual* standings in the socioeconomic hierarchy of the nation. By definition this structure is unjust. Why bring its injustice into a marriage centered on love?

Yet many supposedly "liberated" couples have eagerly jumped into this very oppression. Bent on advancing limitlessly in their occupations, both of them unleash the same unswerving ambition and singleminded competitiveness that always typified "go-getter" husbands. Sprinting in separate lanes on a "fast track," neither spouse is protected from the stresses that husbands used to bear alone. True, these avid careerists may find it easy to appreciate each other's suffering. But they may also find it very difficult to switch from being "hard-driving" and "hard-nosed" all day at work to being warm, tender, and romantic lovers in their bedroom at night.

However, love-centered mates have a philosophical perspective for preventing such destruction of their marital happiness. Knowing that genuine liberation is the freedom to love, they would want to play their occupational roles in ways that give them the most time and energy for *actually loving* each other, for enjoying the pleasure of *being together* from day to day, and for preserving their health. Therefore, the crucial question to ponder in considering their occupational roles is: How equally are they contributing to their mutual fulfillment?

Naturally, husband and wife are not being equitable, as a couple, if both of them have full-time jobs but only one does the additional work of parenting and housekeeping. On the other hand, they may sustain their overall equality very well by being flexible about their involvements in work. Thus, while one mate works full time, the other, working only part time, does relatively more of the other things vital to their marital welfare, and they may also decide to "take turns" in doing the full-time job. Similarly, they may alternate between working and studying, each becoming the sole source of *their* income for the time the other is preparing for an occupation most suitable to his or her talent.

Assuming they foster their relational equality in these ways, mates still face the challenge of intensifying their romance by transcending their *intrinsic* differences in gender. In this respect, lovemaking is the ideal activity for maximizing their mutual acceptance and appreciation.

Actually, the four stages of the human sexual response *are the same* for both sexes.[10] Men and women have described their orgasms in identically glowing terms: as bolts of electricity surging and streaming through their bodies; as thrilling upheavals propelling them into whirlwinds of delicious oblivion; as being tossed about like a beautiful feather, swirling and soaring in waves of weightless air, untroubled about how they will float down to earth again. When presented with such descriptions, a group of experts was unable to differentiate between the responses of males and females.[11] Clearly, orgasms are equally gratifying to people of both sexes, and by participating equally in all the stages of their lovemaking, a man and a woman can alternate between initiating and receiving erotic advances.

Still, to complete the act of sexual coupling, the husband's penis must enter the wife's vagina. Likewise, to guarantee their common pleasure, it is essential for her to *enjoy yielding to his genital penetration,* just as it is essential for him to *feel pleased about penetrating her.*

For a most relaxing climax, the husband needs to thrust into his wife as wildly and powerfully as he desires. But to feel free to do this kind of thrusting, *he needs her to receive it* with the most ardent welcome. Reciprocally, the releasing quality of her orgasm depends on her freedom to give herself over to his accelerating penetration; to be as eager to accept his thrusts as he is to plunge further and further into her depths—until both have gone as far as they can go; until his pulsating ejaculate fills her with the completion she is as aching to receive as he is to give; until her rippling convulsions bathe him with her gift of consummation, which he wants as much as his own orgasm.

In fact, women have expressed a desire to be "filled up" in order to experience the full sense of merger they crave with their husbands. *The Hite Report* quotes one woman as "wishing his penis could reach clear up to my neck, that he would just crawl inside me."[12] Similarly, Virginia Clower, a psychoanalyst, reported that during deep genital interpenetration, a woman may have the romantic fantasy of her mate's penis reaching up and kissing her cervix at the moment of climax.[13]

Men have voiced a complementary longing to be completely interpenetrated at the moment of orgasm. As one respondent told Karen Shanor in her study of male sexuality, "It kind of blossoms out. That's what it feels like. I can feel it expelled into her and wrapping all around us as we thrust toward each other."[14] Sometimes, before his ejaculation, a husband's desire for merger is felt less as an immediate urge to thrust than as a wish to keep his penis enclosed in his wife's vagina. Similarly, one of Clower's female patients imagined that her mate experienced her vagina as if it were lined with velvet so that it cuddled and comforted him.[15]

These subjective reactions indicate that genital coupling gives each partner the fullest possible experience of knowing the other as a sexual being. Interpenetrated, the man is literally inside the woman's sexual organ, as privy as a male can be to the perception a woman has of her own vaginal functioning. Likewise, by enveloping his penis, by literally surrounding it with the walls of her vagina—which not only adhere to its form but also draw it steadily inward—the woman gets as close as any female can get to knowing how it feels to have the erect and thrusting organ of a male.

Still, total reciprocity between the sexes in their capacity for orgasm is precluded because men need a refractory period before they can go through another orgasmic cycle that includes ejaculation. The length of this period varies with age, becoming longer as men grow older. Of course, a man can get an erection very soon after ejaculating, and he can then resume vaginal interpenetration. He can even work himself up to a climactic sensation that feels similar to an orgasm—without the ejaculate. But even youthful husbands *and* their wives have to tolerate some delay until the man's body has time enough to restore the fluids needed for another ejaculation.

By contrast, women of all ages have the potential to attain *one complete orgasm after another,* without having to wait for any equivalent bodily replenishment, and without any appreciable time between each orgasmic cycle. Some women, especially after a great deal of satisfying sexual experience, can go on and on having orgasms, stopping only because of sheer exhaustion.

Accepting this differential "fact of life," mates transcend it by involving themselves *equally* in a *continuous exchange* of affection while the wife has repeated orgasms, if she is so inclined. The *husband can yield himself to her orgasmic desires* by concentrating his consciousness on being completely with her and by adapting his body to her body, whether she asks him to get on top of her, to give her more manual stimulation, or to let her mount him and press her genitals against his.

With such an orientation a husband does not feel "left out" as his wife gratifies a desire for multiple orgasms, and she does not feel she is having an experience he is not enjoying and helping to create. Instead, they are grateful for her physiological capacity, which allows *both of them* to prolong and intensify the peak experience of loving each other.

SEXUAL SHARING AND CONTACT WITH NATURE

Sexual intercourse is the most complete means mates have for communicating their love. The subtle nuances of tenderness and adoration that cannot be put into words—that words are inadequate to describe—can be communicated in how they touch, how they bring their bodies and their genitals together, how they abandon themselves to their orgasmic release, and how they stay in contact in the aftermath of their lovemaking. Mates remain in blissful communication even when they decide to let a "golden silence" envelop them in the sublimity of their contentment after making love. Thus, communication *through* their sexual relations is essential to a couple's sense of being romantically entwined.

A couple's romance is also enhanced as they communicate *about* their sexual relations. By accepting the fact that lovemaking *is* crucially important to their relationship, mates give themselves a great incentive for discussing ways to increase their mutual pleasure. Indeed, the experiential quality of that pleasure is a valid index of how well they are integrating the sexual and affectionate components of their love.

When spouses tell each other what kind of stimulation is most pleasing, they heighten the level of their erotic arousal and the enjoyment of their foreplay. They derive the same benefits in agreeing to explore new techniques and positions for moving toward the peak of orgasmic release. By making verbal contact after their climax, they continue to express their affection, and when they exchange praise for some special way in which they made love or say how much they value one another's physical attributes, they become more intimate and relaxed.

Diane Pike, widow of the late Bishop James A. Pike, has glowingly described the rewards of this "love talk." She felt the greatest gift to their sexual relations was the fact that "we gave each other verbal feedback in the midst of our lovemaking; . . . So we very quickly came to being very sensitive to what the things were that were extraordinary . . . Which positions, for example, . . . were nice when we were tired, and which ones were great when we were feeling ecstatic."[16] Mrs. Pike and her husband advocated this kind of communication to other couples "because it made so much difference to us. It heightened the experience—observing and saying, WOW, that's fantastic—to have immediate feedback instead of trying two hours later to reflect on what was good and what wasn't good."[17]

Naturally, a couple incorporates such glorious impressions of their sexual relations into the fabric of their romance. These positive representations are a most natural aphrodisiac for them. When they think about themselves as husband and wife, they conjure up a pair of passionate lovers, an image that is intrinsically arousing, and when they say how good they feel about their lovemaking, they further the growth of their romance.

Since lovemaking is an extremely sensual activity, it thrives on a couple's yen for involvement in the experiential nuances of person-to-person contact. However, some of the most widely used technologies lead people into vicarious realms of second-hand experience, blunting their appetite for direct contact with one another. In particular, television provides a vast domain of symbolic substitutes for relating to others. For countless people, as Marie Winn asserts in *The Plug-In Drug*, these electronic pictures have already become captivating to the point of addiction.[18] Many of these viewers have already reversed the significance between actual life and its visual surrogates. Thus, they regard what they see on the "tube" as vividly and ineffably real, and they consign their own day-to-day lives to the order of an inferior fantasy.

Of course, many spouses must use such devices as computers and word processors in order to earn a living. But they need not subvert their free time, at home, by routinely dissolving into a television screen. Rather, they preserve the pleasure of their first-hand experiences by using their privacy to discover fresh ways of opening their bodies and souls to each other.

This kind of opening is facilitated by interaction with a spacious and unspoiled environment—where people have the chance to get in complete touch with the nature of their own beings. "Our inner life is complete," writes D. T. Suzuki, "when it merges into Nature and becomes one with it."[19] Unfortunately, however, many mates now live in cramped, crowded, noisy, and polluted surroundings. Insidiously, these conditions adversely affect a couple's level of energy, dampening the exuberance of their lovemaking.

So, husband and wife strengthen their romance by regularly opening themselves to communion with the natural world. Steeped in the beauties of nature, they are motivated to immerse themselves deeply in the sensuality of lovemaking, and they can recover from the cumulative stresses of their usual environments.

All mates need the winey rush of fresh air passing through their nostrils. They need to feast their eyes on luscious clouds drifting through an azure sky. They need to hear the ocean break upon the shore, filling their souls with the roaring rhythm of its music. They need the buoyancy of soothing waters to yield the gravity of their physiques and psyches. They need the warmth of the sun to melt away their knots of tension.

As the sages of Zen observed, it is possible to discover the greatest ecstasies in living only by giving up self-centered concerns and preoccupations. People can learn to bring an attitude of reverence to the focus of their attention—on whatever it happens to be: the subtle color of *this* flower; the perfect shape of *each* tiny dewdrop glistening on its crisp leaves; the delicate texture and captivating aroma of its petals gently unfolding in the morning light.

This receptive and appreciative participation is necessary for spouses to maximize the quality of their sensual experiences. To enjoy the special "suchness" of any aspect of nature, they have to give their consciousness over to it wholeheartedly, holding nothing back. At the same time, they need to let its uniqueness seep into them. Eventually, they can lose all feeling of separateness between themselves and whatever they are contemplating.

Given the intermeshing synchrony of their minds and their bodies, a husband and wife are stimulated erotically when they let themselves be moved by experiences of beauty, just as they feel beautiful when they let themselves enjoy lovemaking. Indeed, it may be difficult for them to resist the impulse to make love when their skin still tingles from a cool, refreshing dip in the sea. Mates often feel like the most exquisite and romantic pair of lovers in the world as they loll languidly in one another's arms on a summer afternoon while a sweet-scented breeze softly caresses their naked limbs.

Thus, through exposure to the sensuality of a natural setting, mates can intensify the pleasures of their lovemaking. The subsequent signs of consummation emanating from within each partner—as well as from the two of them as a couple— have a very positive impact on those with whom they relate in the course of their daily activities. Requited lovers not only *feel* beautiful themselves but they also *look* beautiful to others. Why else would "all the world love lovers," if not by empathizing with the existential beauty they reveal for all the world to see?

When such fervent mates walk into a social gathering, they appear to raise the level of illumination for everyone, as if their electricity is immediately plugged into all the lamps in the room. Wherever they go, they let the mutuality of their love shine for all to see. One glance into their glowing eyes confirms that each has seen in the other what William Blake has said every couple hopes to find: "The lineaments of Gratified Desire." In fact, they may seem to be surrounded by a common aura, a field of energy similar to those in Kirilian photographs of various organisms, including human beings.[20] So, others find it difficult to think of them as unrelated individuals, and people tend to imagine them as naturally belonging together, testifying to the compelling social impact of a couple's romance.

NOTES

1. See, for example, Coleman, *Intimate relationships, marriage, and family*, p. 195.
2. Strauss, E. S. *Couples in love.* Unpublished doctoral dissertation. University of Massachusetts, Amherst, 1974, p. 124.
3. Ibid., p. 129.
4. Levinson, D. *The seasons of a man's life.* New York: Knopf, 1978.
5. Sheehy, G. *Passages.* New York: Dutton, 1976.
6. Berscheid, E. Emotion. In Kelley et al., *Close relationships*, p. 155.
7. Komarovsky, M. *Blue-collar marriage.* New York: Vintage, 1967.
8. Cited in Laing, R. D., & Cooper, D. G. *Reason and violence.* New York: Vintage, 1971, p. 114.
9. Adler, A. *Social interest.* New York: Capricorn, 1964, Chapter XV.
10. Masters, W. H., & Johnson, V. E. *Human sexual response.* Boston: Little, Brown, 1966.
11. Vance, E. B., & Wagner, N. N. Written descriptions of orgasm: A study of sex differences. *Archives of Sexual Behavior,* 1976, *5*, pp. 87–98.
12. Hite, S. *The Hite report.* New York: Dell, 1976, pp. 200–201.
13. Clower, V. Significance of masturbation in female sexual development and function. In I. M. Marcus & J. F. Francis (Eds.), *Masturbation: From infancy to senescence.* New York: International Universities Press, 1975, p. 139.
14. Shanor, K. *The sexual sensitivity of the American male.* New York: Ballantine, 1978, p. 14.
15. Clower, op. cit., pp. 139–140.
16. Otto, H. A., & Otto, R. *Total sex.* New York: Signet, 1972, pp. 294–295.
17. Ibid., p. 295.
18. Winn, M. *The plug-in drug.* New York: Bantam, 1978.
19. Barrett, W. (Ed.). *Zen Buddhism: Selected writings of D. T. Suzuki.* Garden City, N. Y.: Anchor, 1956, p. 256.
20. See, for example, Mann, W. E. *Orgone, Reich, and eros.* New York: Simon and Schuster, 1973, pp. 299–302.

5

DEFENSES AGAINST THE FEAR
OF LOVING

Like other organisms, human beings are born with a tendency to become fearful in any situation that appears to threaten their lives. People are exceedingly vulnerable creatures whose survival is contingent on continually securing food, air, water, shelter, and protection from every conceivable source of harm. They are very easily frightened, and fear is an omnipresent accompaniment of their existence.

Because fear is a message of the most urgent significance, it plays an indispensable role in adaptation by providing people with warnings about the presence of danger. Fear also leads them to focus their efforts on surmounting the danger. Mobilized by fear, they can struggle in whatever way is necessary for them to survive.

Alarmed by an environmental threat to their common welfare, fear can spur a couple into making excellent use of their mental abilities. Fearing the consequences of a possible drought, food shortage, or other calamity of nature, husbands and wives pool their ideas to guarantee their survival. Similarly, they work cooperatively to obtain a livelihood and to save the income they need to insure their existence against the threats of a competitive socioeconomic system. They are also activated to "move heaven and earth" to save their children from the ravages of a serious illness. In these cases, fear helps mates protect their own lives and those of their loved ones, and since they obviously have to remain alive to go on loving, they can regard their fear as an ally to the preservation of their relationship.

Experienced in its raw intensity, however, fear makes people tremble and sweat; their hearts thump wildly and their heads spin in confusion. If fear becomes sufficiently acute, it can totally incapacitate a person, inducing nausea, a claustrophobic feeling of helplessness, and, finally, a "blackout" or fainting.

By its very nature, therefore, fear is the hardest of all emotions to bear without "freaking out" and yielding automatically to its behavioral dictates for self-preservation. People feel they have to do something to reduce the full force of their fear. Otherwise, with their consciousness drowned, they are entirely at the mercy of whatever external danger is menacing them. They cannot choose—or take—any means to maintain their existence.

In fulfilling the promises of love, mates experience the *internal psychological* threats that are presented by those promises. Each threat arouses the fear of loving. So, just as in the case of confronting some external danger, they are motivated to become preoccupied with provisions for their individual safety, and they are inclined to take actions aimed at protecting themselves—rather than to go on being loving.

Fear generally preempts all other motivational states, including love, in the forefront of people's consciousness. Because the fear of loving emerges as involuntarily as the fear stimulated by an objectively based danger, its emergence leads mates to react as if their lives actually were being threatened. Consequently, they tend to respond immediately and unthinkingly by fleeing and fighting. For in early childhood, they began to rely on those defensive reactions when their fear was provoked by external threats. They learned that, through escape and attack, they could discharge the painful tensions of their fear *and* protect their lives against what was endangering them. So, by the time they get married, men and women are conditioned to use the same methods in reacting to the *internal* threats that arouse their fear of loving. Indeed, when that fear is aroused, they feel impelled to defend themselves not only against what they perceive to be threatening, but also against their experience of fear itself.

Of course, through escape and attack, mates do siphon off some of the intensity of their fear. However, by using those habitual defenses they cannot eliminate or cope constructively with the threats—from within themselves—that provoke their fear of loving. In fact, as long as they resort to those defenses, they are really fleeing from and fighting themselves, although each mate acts as if the *other* is the source of danger. Consequently, they fail to realize that the threats they experience arise inevitably from their own involvement in a loving relationship; they make it even more difficult to understand the subjective origins of those threats; and they cannot benefit from such an understanding by deciding on—and taking—an effective course of action to go on sharing more and more of their love.

EMOTIONAL TRANSFORMATIONS OF THE FEAR OF LOVING

Because the fear of loving stems from *feelings of threat to one's own life,* it is awesomely difficult to handle in a nondefensive manner. Mates try to dilute the disabling effects of that fear by censoring its direct manifestation in their own consciousness, and they transform it into modulated, disguised, and less upsetting emotions—primarily as rivalry, greed, detachment, distrust, envy, spite, and sensual numbness.

The connection between such emotions and fear has also been acknowledged by others, although they do not make this linkage to the fear of loving as such. Thus, Silvano and James Arieti write, "Certainly fear is not the only emotion that separates people or creates distance between them. More complicated feelings bring about a similar effect, for instance, . . . anxiety, anger, hostility, hate. . . . But if we analyze all these negative emotions, we recognize that they are built on a foundation of fear."[1]

Of course, mates feel oppressed by their negative emotions. But they are not as incapacitated as they would be if they let the fear of loving register directly on their consciousness. For example, it is easier to live with unrelenting rivalry than with naked terror.

The twin defenses of "fight" and "flight" also are built into the interpersonal effects of all the emotional transformations of fear. Mates show the defense of fighting as each contends with the presumably threatening other, rather than with the psychological threats, emerging from inside themselves, that are actually stimulating their fear. At the same time, they enact the defense of fleeing in the mutuality of their antagonism, which automatically puts distance between them and prevents them from relating to each other as lovingly as they could without their fear-inspired animosity.

Still, in these emotional transformations, mates discharge some of their fear of loving. But they also use these transformations to *disavow personal responsibility* for the existence of their fear. For instance, by letting the fear enter their minds in the guise of rivalry, each mate can imagine ways of attacking to get "one up" on the other—and of escaping a "put down" from the other. In these fantasies, which can be spun in the absolute safety of utter silence, husbands and wives often attempt to make themselves feel more secure and less afraid.

DISHONEST COMMUNICATION AND THE FEAR OF LOVING

When they are face to face, a husband and wife are constantly motivated to keep from being overwhelmed by the fear they stir up through their exchange of love. They try to obscure the presence of this fear from themselves and from one another. Yet the intimacy of their relationship implicitly invites them to share *whatever* is going on inside themselves. Their dialogues are conducted under the mutual assumption of honest communication since that is the only way they can express their love. So they are torn between their need to disclose themselves honestly and their need to defend themselves against their fear of loving by not disclosing it.

In varying degrees all husbands and wives use both honest *and* dishonest communication. To convey their love and to fulfill its promises, they choose to reveal what they are thinking and feeling, what each has done and plans to do. To defend *themselves* against the fear of loving, they choose to withhold information *from one another,* including many feelings and thoughts, as well as actions taken and anticipated, which they associate with their fear and the threats that give rise to it.

The emotional transformations of the fear of loving have the same intrinsically disturbing qualities that make it difficult for people to tolerate the consciousness of fear itself. Thus, mates also try to defend themselves, through dishonest communication, against their own awareness of those transformations. For example, even when they are extremely suspicious of one another, they may studiously refrain from any mention of their distrust.

Fear and its emotional transformations are widely condemned by cultural prejudices, which further inhibit honest communication. In American society, people often are considered "chicken" even for *experiencing* fear as well as for showing it in any way. People are also disapproved of and disapprove of themselves as "piggish" for experiencing and displaying the self-centeredness embedded in envy, distrust, and every other emotional transformation of the fear of loving.

These negative emotions are just as intrinsic to human functioning as affection, trust, compassion, and similar feelings that society has labeled as "positive." However, the emotional transformations of fear are unflattering to people, making them seem vicious and grasping. Such traits remind them of the animalistic and self-seeking rather than the spiritual and generous side of their nature, and this reminder may be the basis of the social disapproval of such emotions.

PERSONAL DEFENSES AND DISHONEST COMMUNICATION

Historically, Freud invented the mechanisms of ego defense[2] in explaining how individuals avoid a total loss of their adaptive abilities in the face of potentially incapacitating fear. In using these defenses, people give up a portion of their consciousness. But this sacrifice permits them to go on functioning with their usual repertoire of mental skills.

Some of these mechanisms, such as denial, blot out the perception of an external source of danger, for example, the immediate proximity of a nuclear power plant. Consequently, a person can live or work in a nearby location without constantly experiencing the harrowing dread of an accident at the plant.

But most of these Freudian mechanisms aim to prevent the awareness of some *inner* motivational state whose past expression has exposed a person to grave danger. Thus, a child learns to repress sexual inclinations that his or her parents had met with physical punishment or with the threatened withdrawal of their love. Naturally, this repression cuts the child off from conscious contact with those feelings. Yet this very splitting permits him or her to interact with the parents without the omnipresent fear of doing or saying something that will incur their wrath.

Freud assumed that all of these mechanisms operate automatically and unconsciously, that people are not cognizant of when and how they employ their individual defenses. Moreover, he did not include the fear of loving, in the terms defined here, as the focus of such protective measures.

However, people regularly resort to *deliberate and conscious forms of lying* in their efforts to reduce this fear. Indeed, mates defend themselves personally by being dishonest in three different ways while they are presumably communicating with each other. First, they can simply avoid communication altogether. In *lies of omission,* they withhold their individual feelings and thoughts about the threats that arouse their fear of loving. Second, they can engage in *pseudocommunication,* voicing random chitchat and gossip that they realize— without admitting it—is merely a distraction from their underlying agitation. Or they may appear to concentrate intently on some topic, earnestly considering, for example, an entire catalogue of varieties in choosing *the* most appropriate wine to serve with a particular gourmet dish. Meanwhile, they know they are using this elaborate conversation as a dodge to avoid talking about their troublesome feelings and the threatening aspects of their relationship.

Finally, mates can decide to tell deliberate lies about what they think, feel, and do, even when each is asked directly by the other to speak the truth. Through such *lies of commission,* they purposely deceive one another about thoughts, feelings, and behavior that each fears could be damaging to their personal security, self-esteem, and regard by the other.

Although they may succeed in deceiving each other, spouses entrap themselves in their own deceptions. Once they have lied about something they are afraid to accept in themselves, they tend to reinforce their defensiveness in subsequent conversations about the same material, that is, they keep on lying over and over again.

Actually, by the time they reach adulthood, husbands and wives are highly accomplished in the art of lying. In the course of growing up, they have had ample practice in covering up thoughts, feelings, and actions that, if revealed, might lead others to chastise, punish, or disapprove of them. "Most people in our society are not well taught in honest expressions of feeling or direct assertions of personal interest. When we feel sad, we are told to cheer up. . . . When we want something for our own sakes alone, we are told not to be selfish."[3]

Besides, nobody's parents are models of pure truthfulness. Even the most morally upright of mothers and fathers regularly withhold from their children many facets of their own ethical transgressions and relational problems. People also learn that, if they want to get ahead in the socioeconomic system, they can maximize their chances by keeping competitors and supervisors from knowing about many of their personal plans, fears, doubts, and feelings of inadequacy. They also tend to cover up their affection since admitting that feeling may render them vulnerable to manipulations by others who might not feel the same way about them.

COMPLICITIES: INTERPERSONAL DEFENSES AGAINST THE FEAR OF LOVING

In *The Politics of the Family,* Laing put forth the idea that people in close relationships frequently make unspoken agreements to abide by a common set of rules governing their interactions. He characterized these accords as "transpersonal" defenses,[4] reflecting the common need that members of a family have to protect themselves from the chaos of uncertainty that might send all of them into an existential panic unless they upheld the same assumptions about how to relate to one another.

We have drawn upon Laing's formulation to conceive how a man and a woman deal with the paradox of being afraid to share much of the love they actually feel toward each other. Indeed, the fear of loving accompanies every couple's exchange of love from the very beginning of their relationship. Thus, all mates develop *interpersonal defenses* through which they cooperate—*by mutual deception*—in keeping their common fear from overwhelming them. We call these defenses "complicities" since each person is a full, equal, and willing accomplice in their formation and perpetuation.

A man and a woman create their complicities by agreeing to be simultaneously and unwaveringly dishonest about their fear of loving, and about the inner threats that arouse that fear in both of them. Obviously, in creating a complicity they cannot openly and explicitly agree to deceive each other. Verbal articulation about what they are doing would make it impossible for them to act as if they do not know they are lying to themselves and each other. It is amazing how many agreements of this kind can be made in total silence. Spouses are much better at reading one another's minds than they want to admit. Such an admission would make it harder for each to pretend not to know what the other is thinking. So, through their common pretentions of inscrutability, they agree to spare one another from the recognition of their mutual deception.[5]

Complicities are the second of the two basic psychological ingredients of a loving relationship. But, in stark contrast to the romance, complicities are devious and furtive creations. Just as their romance is the most important mental support for the sharing of love, a couple's complicities are the most important mental defense against their fear of loving. Eager to make the evolving contents of their romance an openly shared love story, they are equally motivated to stamp an unbroken seal of secrecy on the existence and meaning of their complicities, and the silence surrounding the pact they are forming shrouds the contents of their agreements in a heavy veil of ambiguity.

A couple's unuttered pledge to avoid *future* scrutiny of how they are defending themselves gives them a powerful incentive to keep the existence of their complicities buried below the surface of their consciousness. However, by vigilantly guarding against truthful acknowledgment of their defensiveness, they cut off the spontaneous flow of honesty between them and stifle their exchange of love. Thus, while their romance is the dynamic stimulant a couple uses to energize themselves, their *complicities function as the dynamic depressant of their energy*—a common blockage by which they thwart the outpouring of their love. And while their romance increases their morale, their complicities necessarily diminish it.

An excessive accumulation of complicities can explain the motivational basis for relational stagnation that has puzzled experts who have described its manifestations and consequences. Thus, one of them remarks: "The outstanding feature of many repetitive conflicts is their rigidity. . . . For whatever motivational reasons, one of the people involved initiates a sequence that evokes complementary behavior from the partner, who then becomes an accomplice in playing out their familiar scenario."[6]

Nevertheless, every couple constructs a variety of complicities to defend themselves against the fear stemming from all four threats of love. When reacting to the fear instigated by a specific threat, each mate transforms it into emotions that are less disturbing than fear itself. These emotional transformations of their fear also indicate the psychological nature of the threat. Simultaneously, a couple silently agrees on a behavioral scenario for acting out these emotional transformations.

For example, when mates are threatened by the possibility of expanding the boundaries of their individuality, they transform the fear aroused by that threat into feelings of intense rivalry and greed. They set up a repetitive and fixed pattern of interaction, expressing their common feelings of rivalry as unabating competition. They greedily strive for their own ambitions and undermine any attempt each makes to prevail over the other. Avoiding communication about the meaning of what they are doing together, they do not acknowledge their rivalrous feelings; they do not discuss the connection between those feelings and their fear of loving; and they do not trace their fear to its origins in the threat that stimulated it. Lastly, in maintaining their falsehoods, they may resort to every method of dishonesty—lying by omission, by commission, and by pseudocommunication.

The interpersonal defense of complicity includes both "fight" *and* "flight." Sometimes, the element of fight is more obvious in a complicity, as in the case of mates who viciously compete. When they are together, they fill their time with constant bickering and arguments about which one should have his or her way in regard to a decision that affects them jointly. Although this couple is interacting directly, their fighting is also a form of flight—a mutual withdrawal. So, while they use fight as their ostensible way of defending themselves, they are also preventing themselves from being as close and tender as they could be.

By contrast, the element of flight may be the most apparent characteristic of a couple's complicity, demonstrated by mates whose fear is stimulated by the threat of immersion in the pleasure of lovemaking. Through their unacknowledged agreement to spend most of their time in separate pursuits, these mates avoid the possibility of sexual contact. By using this avoidance as the manifest method of dealing with their fear, they forgo the gratifications of making love. However, by constantly frustrating each other, they are expressing mutual hostility. Their perpetual evasiveness thus also reflects a fight reaction to their fear.

Like the romance, complicities are anchored in mental representations of how spouses view themselves, each other, and the two of them as an interacting pair. However, while their romantic images portray the love they share and the truthful ways in which they are relating, the images representing their complicities reflect the emotional transformations of their fear of loving and the deceitful manner in which they are relating to reduce that fear.

In a competitive complicity, for example, both spouses "bring themselves down" by thinking of one another as rivals. When they are apart, the husband sees his wife as an enemy who is deliberately pushing herself to surpass him. In her symmetrical perception, he is intent on becoming victorious over her. They also imagine how to mask their plans for conquering one another, and they fantasize about how they will cagily interact when they are together.

So, in their mind's eye, they become repellent to themselves and to one another. The wife sees herself as looking haggard and distraught from contending so relentlessly with her husband, and she has just as unappealing a picture of his face, tight-lipped and taut as he hides his thoughts and feelings from her. The husband has similar images of his own strained appearance and the corresponding signs of stress in his wife. In visualizing their anticipated interactions, she views him as just waiting to rub her nose in any failure of her individualistic strivings. And he sees her as poised to pounce on any chance for disparaging his personal abilities.

Bringing these hostile cogitations into their face to face interactions, both mates are continually on edge—each monitoring himself and herself against giving the other any advantage in their covert contest. Under these conditions, they can hardly derive any pleasure in each other's company. Rather, they can only become much more tense together than they would be if they were alone.

COMPLICITIES AND THE THREAT OF EXPANDING THE BOUNDARIES OF INDIVIDUALITY

Married for 12 years, Richard and Marsha Crane had lived in several different apartments. As a childless couple, they had been very satisfied with a one-bedroom place near their respective offices. Before having their first child, they had no trouble in agreeing to move into a two-bedroom garden apartment located in a more residential neighborhood. When their second child was born, they easily shifted to a three-bedroom apartment in the same housing complex. Now, they could finally afford to buy a spacious and comfortable house.

However, their decision to acquire a *permanent* home of their own involved a deeper relational merger than they had ever made before. Suddenly, Marsha and Richard were acutely reminded of the depth of their interpersonal union—and that they were heading for an even more extensive overlapping of their personal boundaries. They also knew it would be necessary for them to stake a large portion of their *combined savings* and *future income* on this one purchase, a fact that underscored the seriousness of their common choice. So, their decision severely threatened each one's sense of self.

In a similar situation, some mates soon tolerate the fear of loving triggered by this threat, and they promptly succeed in buying a house that is pleasing to both of them. However, Richard and Marsha were so shaken by the threat of losing their individuality that they formed a complicity to stave off its incapacitating effects. Transforming their fear into rivalry and greed, they tacitly agreed to enact those emotions in such a way as to resist the outcome of what they had seemingly decided, at long last, to do. While doggedly continuing to look for a house, they prevented each other from buying one.

Going through the motions of searching for their dream house, the Cranes gave each other the impression of having a unified vision of what they wanted. But, when they were actively considering a *particular* house, they became absorbed in separate fantasies about what the place would do for their own self-images. Then, they persisted in trying to gratify their egoistic wishes, with total disregard for one another. Both evaluated every house as a private possession, as a means of self-aggrandizement, and not as a step toward actualizing a common dream.

As a result, they did not approach their task as a *joint* venture, emphasizing what "*we* would love to have in *our* house; the number of rooms *we* need for *our mutual* comfort; and the setting that would be pleasing to *both of us.*" Instead, Richard and Marsha were preoccupied with individual desires to "get mine." Each greedily refused to give up "the special features that *I must have* in *my* house; the particular style that *I* find fitting to *my* way of life; the amount of space I need for *my personal* pleasure; and the location that is most convenient for *me.*"

Sometimes, when they saw an attractive possibility, both of them managed to find some irreparable fault with it. If the neighborhood and school district were good, they disliked the layout, or they complained about the high cost of maintenance.

On the other hand, if Richard reacted in a positive manner, Marsha prowled around critically until she found an unacceptable imperfection. She rejected the kitchen as too old-fashioned or thought the living room was too cramped for the cocktail parties she saw herself giving for colleagues in her department. Reciprocally, when she admired a house that had everything for her, Richard became petulant, sneering at the inferior quality of the building materials and workmanship. He dismissed it as inadequate for a person of his status and taste.

The Cranes often diverted attention from what was really going on between them by engaging in hours of pseudocommunication. They would go into great detail about why they liked or disliked a specific place and how they could have decorated and furnished it—if only this or that hadn't been wrong with it. But these fruitless conversations were just a part of their game, and in their self-centered defensiveness, they went on frustrating each other by passing up one good prospect after another.

Despite themselves, the Cranes would occasionally see a house that did meet the requirements each of them had stipulated. However, terrified to join forces at last and buy it, they would either delay in submitting their bid or they offered too low a price. Thus, they would invariably lose out, "by chance," on the deal.

COMPLICITIES AND THE THREAT
OF INCREASING INTERDEPENDENCE

Reacting fearfully to the threat of increasing their interdependence, mates transform that fear into feelings of detachment and distrust. Of course, these emotional transformations induce a sense of psychological distance between them, an alienation that is expressive of flight and fight. Detachment has the specific effect of discouraging the possibility of being *dependable for* one's mate—of being accountable and "all there," ready and willing to help in meeting the needs he or she may express. Emotionally detached mates convey a clear message to one another: "Don't count on me." At the same time, they experience themselves as being sealed off from one another and sealed up inside themselves.

Conversely, the emotion of distrust is specifically directed against the possibility of being *dependent on* a mate. Obviously, when they feel mutually distrustful, mates shy away from relying on one another, and each is bound to see, in the other's distrust, a hostile lack of confidence in oneself.

Mates threatened by increasing their interdependence blend detachment and distrust into their complicities. Although their scenarios may be very diverse, all of these complicities have the same interpersonal objective: to demonstrate the couple's shared falsehood about *how independent they are—how little they need each other.*

When they were single, Tony and Marie Furillo had been extremely sought after by other potential mates. In fact, at the time they met, Tony was in the process of breaking up with his current girlfriend, while Marie was doing the same with her live-in lover. But they were so attracted to one another that they had no doubt about their willingness to stop playing the field forever.

For about a year after their honeymoon, the Furillos were virtually inseparable. Both experienced a great new charge of happiness in presenting themselves as mates wherever they went. Besides, they quickly set up an easygoing pattern of depending on each other for help in their careers. Spontaneously, Marie would call Tony from her law office during the day, getting his reactions to courtroom strategies she was preparing. Just as freely, Tony telephoned her from his real estate agency to hear what she would do if she had to handle one of his vacillating clients.

Nevertheless, their rapid increase in interdependence began to threaten them unbearably, and they formed a complicity to quell the fear evoked by that threat. First, they stopped their consultations on professional matters. But then they extended their defensive scenario to include a repetitive demonstration of how little they needed each other in the very heart of their relationship—their connection as husband and wife.

Now, when they go to parties, the Furillos blatantly flaunt their emotional detachment by going off to have separate flirtations. Inwardly, each is very apprehensive about the other's seductive behavior, which arouses their mutual terror of being abandoned. However, following their covert script, they mask all outward signs of their worries.

Marie is appalled to see how warmly women respond to Tony, who turns on the charm to attract them. Because of her intention to deny any dependence on him, however, she pretends not to see what he is doing. But she continues, quite brazenly, to invite the advances of other men—and to put Tony on notice that he cannot count on her fidelity. Yet she cannot shake off her agitation over how he is carrying on, and she is fuming beneath her "come hither" smiles because her flirtations do not seem to get a rise out of him.

Tony is equally troubled by Marie, who is encouraging men to regard her as sexually available. He is also embittered by her apparent indifference to the attention women are giving him. But, since he is trying to prove how much he can do without her love, he stifles his concern and intensifies his flirtations. Thus, he sends Marie the nonverbal message that she cannot depend on him to be faithful to her.

Of course, the Furillos avoid all discussion of their tantalizing "soap opera." Instead, they revel in their seductiveness, and both regard their success in attracting admirers as proof that they could easily get along without one another. Meanwhile, each becomes more distrustful of the other, and their mutual suspicion leads them to become very jealous of each other's "conquests."

Although the Furillos do not enter into extramarital affairs, they keep one another in an agony of insecurity. In similar cases, however, when each spouse is thoroughly maddened by not knowing how far the other has gone, both of them may secretly begin actual affairs.

Suspecting, but not discussing, these affairs adds enormously to the distrust between spouses. Their jealousy becomes a tormenting obsession, indicating the depth of their concern about losing each other. Yet they feel even more threatened by the prospect of increasing their interdependence, and they persist in the defensive assertion of their "independence." They go on behaving in a detached manner, as if neither one could care less about what the other is doing on the side, and they do not talk about their growing suspicions of mutual infidelity. Consequently, each becomes less secure about depending on the other *and* more reluctant to be dependable for the other.

COMPLICITIES AND THE THREAT OF TRANSCENDING DIFFERENCES IN GENDER

Ideologically, Jack and Claire Reuben subscribe to the belief that men and women are equal as human beings. However, throughout the 6 years of their marriage, the opportunity to fulfill the promise of transcending their inherent and socially learned differences in gender has been very threatening to them, chronically stirring up their fear of loving. Defending themselves against that fear, they transform it into envy and spite and agree to act out those feelings by *emphasizing* their differences in gender while maintaining their sexual chauvinism and social inequality.

The most commonplace aspect of the complicity between the Reubens is their pattern of sexual self-segregation. Maintaining separate sets of friends, each of them has different evenings out. Claire has a regular class in aerobic dance with her female friends on one night and attends a child study group with them on another. Jack just as routinely gets together with his male friends to do political organizing and to play squash.

In these same-sex gatherings, they frequently join in with their friends to "let their hair down" in discussing the opposite—and absent—sex. The men in Jack's circle complain enviously about how the women have it made by changing or quitting jobs whenever they feel like it, knowing that their husbands feel obliged to go on working. On the other hand, they gleefully report how they spited their wives by refusing to give up a night at the gym, "even though she pleaded for me to go to the ballet with her."

Claire and the "gals" also swap stories of spiting their husbands. She once described with great relish how she absolutely refused to give up her dance class, although "Jack begged me to go to a party with him for one of the candidates he was backing." Often, the women confide in one another about how simplistic their husbands are in their basic outlook on life, "like big kids who know from nothing except their jobs and their power trips."

When they are together, the Reubens avoid communicating about issues they regard as the "specialty" of their own gender. Jack never asks Claire for advice on matters pertaining to his job, although he does share his occupational concerns with his buddies. Nor does he tell her any of the misgivings he may have about his physical condition, mental state, or sexual adequacy.

Claire is just as close-mouthed about whatever she finds troubling on her turf. She discloses none of her worries about her work outside the home and inside of it, which often includes all the cooking and housekeeping. She even refrains from consulting Jack about the rearing of their 3-year-old child, who, in terms of their complicity, is consigned to her exclusively. Finally, while conversing freely with female friends about her gynecological condition, she carefully keeps him in the dark about those details of her biological functioning.

The Reubens also express their sexism in a conventional approach to lovemaking. To move toward genuine equality in that realm of behavior would mean altering patterns of behavior that both of them have learned to associate with whatever success they have had in sexual intercourse. True, their success may be relatively meager in comparison with what they could achieve if they were to interact as fully equal sexual beings: equally active, equally passive, equally turned on, equally interested and involved. However, since Jack and Claire feel exceptionally threatened by the possibility of becoming more equal in those ways, they are willing to settle for whatever pleasure they do experience rather than face, grapple with, and subdue the fear of loving aroused by that threat.

Typically, the Reubens make love only at Jack's request. Taking on the "macho" role, he initiates their sexual interactions and determines the specific techniques they employ. Thus, he tries to convince Claire, and himself, that he is a paragon of dominance and virility, a much stronger and more self-assured male than he actually feels himself to be.

Meanwhile, he secretly longs for her to "come on" to him. He would like to know beyond any doubt that she really *does* regard him as a very desirable man whose body and genitals she finds attractive and exciting. True, she never turns down his advances. But is she *spontaneously* drawn to him? Does she have the same urgent need to get him into bed as he often feels and shows toward her? For a long time he has yearned to be more passive during lovemaking, wishing Claire would be more open in expressing her desires and more active in touching, kissing, and embracing him. In fact, he has had powerful and recurrent fantasies of surrendering to her impassioned advances, indicating how much he wants to be relieved of the pressure to assume all the responsibility for the programming of their sexual encounters. In one of his favorite fantasies, she begins to fondle his genitals after he has fallen asleep, on a night when he didn't press her into sexual intercourse. Then, after he gets an erection, she gets on top of him.

However, Jack never reveals this or any similar fantasy to Claire, nor does he try to enlist her help in changing their formula for making love. He worries that she might reject him as unmanly, if she knew what was going on in his mind. He is also concerned about losing his sexual potency if he deviated from adherence to his stereotyped notions of masculinity.

Sustaining her role in their complicity, Claire plays the part of the docile female who obediently acquiesces to Jack's sexual demands. By always waiting for him to come on to her, she gets proof of her attractiveness, and she can perceive herself as sexually desirable, no matter how many private doubts she may have about her femininity and physical allure. At the same time, she does not have to take the risk of revealing the intensity of *her* erotic appetite, which, she fears, might lead Jack either to rebuff her or to consider her wanton and aggressive. During their foreplay, she never requests any special stimulation from him, although she may be itching to have him stimulate her genitals orally, which he has never done. She also restrains her impulses to make advances toward him and she remains his "lady in waiting."

Like Jack, Claire has recurring daydreams about changing their approach to lovemaking. She is obsessed with thoughts of approaching *him* before bedtime—of unbuttoning his shirt or of unzipping his pants. Actually, her docility has been troubling her with questions that cannot be answered while she maintains it. How much would Jack still love her if she became as forward as she imagines being with him? How ready is he to accept her as an equal in sexuality—as the real woman she inwardly craves to be and not as the caricature she has been playing? Yet she does not test out these questions with him, worried that he would regard her as unfeminine and unappealing; threatened, too, that she might not be able to function sexually at all, although her current level of gratification is far from what she knows it could be.

In their lovemaking the Reubens suffer the consequences of their defensive scenario. While Claire yields to Jack's desires, she greatly inhibits her erotic responsivity. Indeed, she feels the penetration of his penis into her vagina as a defeat for herself. Because she is envious of the social power and sexual freedom his organ symbolizes, she is loathe to admit that she has any need of his penis for her own pleasure. Besides, she believes, if she were to have a really fulfilling orgasm, it would not belong to her. Instead, it would be *his* since she needed his penis to attain it. So, even as he thrusts himself inside of her, she restrains her own impulses to let go and to show all of her affection for him.

Enacting the same spitefulness, Jack tries to get their sexual intercourse over with as quickly as possible, with a minimal expression of tenderness and consideration. He rushes through foreplay, touching Claire just enough to get her barely lubricated. Envious of her for being able to "just lay back and spread her legs" instead of having to get and maintain an erection, he feels hostile about having to "perform" for her. So, suppressing the passion and affection that is really welling within him, he enters her vagina and "gets his rocks off" quickly. Immediately after his ejaculation he rolls off her body and, without a word, falls asleep.

Obviously, by such spiteful behavior the Reubens frustrate and deprive themselves, and they prevent themselves from learning how to appreciate and accept each other's inherent differences in gender. Thus, they lose the opportunity marriage offers for developing the ability to *utilize* those differences for their mutual gratification. Ironically, by failing to help one another to transcend their biological differences, they increasingly feel more envious of one another's sexual anatomy, more inadequate as sexual partners, and more locked into their gender-role stereotypes—all of which contribute to greater insecurity about their indentities as a male and a female.

COMPLICITIES AND THE THREAT OF IMMERSION
IN THE PLEASURE OF LOVEMAKING

In these complicities mates transform their fear of loving into a kind of antifeeling—a sensual numbness by which they turn themselves off from the possibility of erotic interaction. In keeping with this emotional transformation, they agree to shun possibilities for sexual intercourse *and* to avoid situations that might turn them on. Yet they do not communicate honestly about their chronic lack of desire, and they never discuss their mutual avoidance of lovemaking or of sensually exciting situations.

As newlyweds, Larry and Rona Stuart were quite passionate, making love several times weekly. But this degree of pleasure proved too menacing for them to bear. So, they devised a complicity for their mutual defense, elaborating it considerably over the next 14 years. Now, generally lacking erotic aliveness, they make love rarely and without the enjoyment that would motivate them to do it more often. For long periods they are completely celibate. Yet they rationalize their abstinence by saying to themselves, and even to others, that "sex isn't everything." This rationalization merely evades the bitter truth that, in *their* relationship, the sexual component of loving has become virtually nothing.

As they go through their daily activities, the Stuarts act as if the idea of making love never occurs to either of them, that lovemaking has no place among the multitude of domestic projects they have covertly agreed as necessary for them to go on doing—day and night. Accordingly, when they are home in the evening and throughout the weekends, they busy themselves with chores that they *must* catch up on.

In keeping with this agreement, they pursue different hobbies, entirely on their own. This arrangement further reduces their chances to come into physical contact. Each also extolls the virtues of the other's recreation, thus reinforcing its role in the continuation of their complicity. When they finally do turn in for the night, Larry and Rona withdraw into twin beds, using them as a barrier, but falsely convincing one another that separate beds are better for their personal comfort and health than a double bed would be. They then hammer one more nail into their sexual coffins by switching on a late-night television show. Captivated by whatever is shown, they sink into a trancelike state, becoming "dead to the world"—and to each other.

Over the years the Stuarts have also minimized the possibility of being together without someone else around. Instead, they do everything they can to remain in the company of others. Of course, the mere presence of these people is sufficient to foil even the slightest inclination they may feel, however unexpectedly, to make love.

Maintaining a constantly "open house," Rona and Larry give their friends, neighbors, and relatives a hearty welcome for dropping in to visit at any time—and without advance notice. They are quick to invite guests for the weekends and holidays. Regardless of their mood, they accept all the invitations they get to visit others, and they keep themselves "booked up" with reservations to a variety of cultural and sporting events. They never take vacations without their children or friends, and if nobody is available to travel with them, they join a group tour.

Coordinating a trip with other people obviously limits any couple's chances for making love as freely as they could if they traveled alone. Instead of being able to go off to their room any time they may be in the mood for love, these mates have to fit in with the preplanned schedules they have made with their traveling companions.

Still, the Stuarts sometimes go on an unaccompanied trip. However, on those occasions they make sure they have neither the time nor the energy to make love by arranging "vacations" that are even more debilitating and hectic than the schedules they ordinarily follow while they are working and at home. They set off on a whirl of tourism, hastening to all the historical sites, museums, theaters, concerts, races, restaurants, and nightclubs recommended as musts in their guidebooks. Between bouts of sightseeing they throw themselves into swimming, golf, and tennis.

On rainy days they trudge from shop to shop to buy mementos and bargains. Returning to the privacy of their room, they spend a great deal of time discussing how they will exhibit their trinkets when they get home. Then they may ruminate

for hours about whether they got stung or made a clever purchase. Extinguishing any flicker of erotic and affectionate feeling that could pass between them, they argue about who is to
blame for buying something they suddenly feel is a worthless
piece of junk. Finally, exhausted and disgruntled, they fall
asleep without having kissed or even smiled at one another.

Despite themselves, Rona and Larry do weaken on rare
occasions and engage in sexual intercourse. But even then
their motivation is not to celebrate their loving relationship by
creating an experience of supreme bliss. Rather, each feels obligated to do the other a favor in relieving the accumulated tension of their habitual abstinence. Or, after long periods of ab-
stention, both may feel they *must* have intercourse to
convince themselves of the ongoing reality of their marriage.

COMPLICITIES AND COLLUSIONS

Complicities are the most private of "deals" spouses
make. These "underground operations" are so heavily guarded
by husband and wife that they do not acknowledge what is
going on between them—much as secret agents who know one
another are pledged to avoid any signs of personal recognition
in public places where they may happen to meet.

Unlike spies, mates do not routinely conceal their marital
connection in public. They go forth as a couple among others,
often making a special point of letting people know they are
married, especially when they are feeling very good about
their relationship. However, mates are exceedingly wary about
having the "cover" of their complicities torn away. Yet this is
the very risk they incur every time they interact in public as a
couple. What if people notice the workings of their secret
pacts, the negative emotions they are trying to keep hidden
from each other or the fighting and fleeing behavior of their
scenarios? And what if, having detected those signs, others
confront them with questions they shudder to ask themselves?

Actually, spouses believe that any witness to their falsehoods might expose the truths about their silent agreements to
lie to each other. So in public they team up to *collude* in lying
to people in order to make it appear as if they do not have the
marital conflicts they are, in fact, privately enacting in their

complicities. When they are colluding, they temporarily paper over their marital discords, striving to convey the impression of having everything together and to dissuade people from searching too closely for problems in their relationship.

As could be expected, a couple ties the cloak of collusion most tightly around themselves whenever other people inadvertently stimulate threats over which they have formed complicities. For example, Roger and Madeline Taub, a newly married couple, devised a complicity similar to that of Marsha and Richard Crane to defend themselves against the threat of expanding the boundaries of their individuality. But the Taubs focus their scenario on a dispute about *where* to get an apartment when they leave the University of Minnesota to take jobs in the City University of New York—Madeline in sociology and Roger in mathematics. Since both of them are getting promotions, they are equally excited about their impending move, and they give each other immense help in figuring out how to conduct negotiations with the chairpersons of their prospective departments. But they have been unwilling to compromise in choosing a location for what they expect to be their permanent residence.

Early in April the Taubs fly into New York to find a place before starting their new jobs in September. Rushing from their hotel every morning, they look at a number of desirable rentals in Manhattan, Brooklyn, Queens, New Jersey, and Long Island. But these options only underscore the differences they had been arguing about for weeks. Madeline wants the relative quiet and open space of the suburbs, but Roger insists on being close to their jobs and the city's cultural institutions.

At a party held for them by their future colleagues, the Taubs collude to shield their divisiveness. Although they almost slip into revealing their differences, they catch themselves and act as if they were in unanimity about their housing plans. Thus, when someone asks where they intend to live, Madeline starts to disclose her preference. However, she picks up subtle but imperative visual cues from Roger, who is communicating his desire for her to remain silent. Then he interrupts her, in a very pleasant manner, injecting a joke about the high cost of urban gentrification, to show their friends that they would prefer living in Manhattan. Before Madeline has the slightest chance to disagree, a quickly passing chill in Roger's eyes that only she can interpret signals her to change the course of the conversation. So, she comments dreamily on how much they would *both* really *love* the Upper West Side. Soon, they join in an animated discussion with people who live in that neighborhood about the best streets there, exchanging information on real estate agents who are reputed to be helpful. Consequently, the Taubs impress everyone with their compatibility.

However, as soon as they leave the party, they begin a heated argument. Madeline accuses Roger of knowing *very well* that they don't have the money for a roomy apartment in Manhattan. Besides, she screams hatefully, hasn't she told him often enough that she would like to be in Long Island, close to some greenery and the beaches? Shouting back, he castigates her for being too cowardly to deviate from the same insipid lifestyle they had in Minneapolis. He also bemoans the time and expense involved in having to commute. Then, he tries to badger her into agreeing on how much better it would be for their careers if they lived near their offices. After this opening round, Madeline and Roger keep on battling without any respite. By the time they reach their hotel and get into bed, the tension between them is so abrasive they don't even kiss goodnight.

While staging such collusions, couples mystify themselves as well as the people they are trying to impress. If they spend a lot of time in the company of others, they can get carried away with their theatrical performances of perfect harmony. Indeed, if they consistently fool others about the existence of their mutual defenses, they may almost convince themselves that their marriage is completely free of conflict. To that extent, their public collusions have the effect of reinforcing their private complicities.

NOTES

1. Arieti, S., Arieti, J. *Love can be found.* New York: Harcourt Brace Jovanovich, 1977. pp. 14–15.
2. For a comprehensive account of these Freudian mechanisms, see

Sarnoff, I. *Personality dynamics and development.* New York: Wiley, 1962, Chapters 8, 9, and 10.

3. Peterson, D. P. Conflict. In Kelley et al., *Close relationships*, p. 382.

4. Laing, R. D. *The politics of the family.* New York: Pantheon, 1971, p. 13.

5. Indeed, married couples "read" each other's nonverbal messages better than do judges who are observing them. See Sabatelli, R. M., Buck, R., & Dryer, A. Nonverbal communication accuracy in married couples: Relationship with marital complaints. *Journal of Personality and Social Psychology,* 1982, *43,* pp. 1088–1097.

6. Peterson, op. cit., p. 390.

6

BREAKING THE COMPLICITIES

By preserving complicities and collusions, spouses obscure their insight into the particular aspects of loving they find most threatening. As a result, they cannot decrease the negative impact of those threats on their relationship, and they cannot learn how to react nondefensively to their fear. In the long run, therefore, a couple's interpersonal defenses *reinforce* the very anguish from which they originally sought to escape.

The most easily understood feature of their distress is chronic guilt. After all, when they married, they committed themselves to *true* love, to being honest in their communication. So, in being mutually dishonest, mates violate their own desired—and desirable—standards of marital morality, and this violation is bound to make them feel guilty.

Naturally, the more complicities they leave unbroken, the heavier will be their load of guilt and the worse they will feel about themselves. Ironically, however, by repeating the same lies over a long period of time, spouses produce a condition in which it appears to be out of the question to go from lying to being truthful. They exacerbate a vicious cycle: lying, feeling guilty, lying again, feeling even more guilty, and continuing to compound guilt with lies to the point that the very thought of telling the truth fills them with as much dread as the prospect of facing a firing squad. Indeed, they are inclined to endure all the discomforts of their deception and all the torments of their cumulative guilt rather than be truthful with each other.

Still, guilt can be reduced only by making amends for what was done to incur it. For mates in a complicity, a joint confession of their patterns of deceit would be the most beneficial method of securing expiation. Although they cannot undo the damage they have already done by lying to each other, they can reduce their level of discomfort and prevent the spread of their suffering. Otherwise, they are inwardly eaten by the acid of their guilt, and they may seek inappropriate ways of atoning for it by inflicting punishments on themselves—for example, by incurring injuries "accidentally on purpose."

An extremely varied array of other difficulties also can be understood as by-products of unbroken complicities. Because of the energy tied up in their defense pacts, couples often feel miserably bored. Boredom always arises when spouses are afraid to communicate what they really have in mind to say, when they are terrified to go beyond an impasse in their exchange of truths about what is happening between them. This common resistance can lead them to conclude, incorrectly, that they no longer have anything to say to each other—as they did in the past. Having closed off communication about the very things that most vitally concern them, they wrongly regard the resulting deadness of their interactions as a malady peculiar to their pairing.

These spouses imprison one another within the intricate fortifications of their falsehoods. They may choose to stay together for a lifetime, although they have more or less squeezed the life out of their relationship. However, they ultimately show the stigmata of their accumulated complicities. Many couples are ridden with psychosomatic ailments that express in bodily language the holistic character of their relational defensiveness.[1] Others inflict physical violence on each other, or they may displace their mutually throttled hatred onto their children, subjecting them to physical and psychological abuse.

As spouses react to these afflictions, they frequently begin to think about getting divorced. Many of them do break up their marriages instead of breaking their complicities. While they are single again, they may feel mightily relieved of their previous tensions since they are no longer participating in an intricate web of mutual invalidation. However, when they remarry, no matter to whom, they inevitably create complicities with their new mates. In time, the painful and destructive consequences of these interpersonal defenses can trouble them as much as the ones they contrived with their old mates.

Therefore, spouses can appropriately view their desire for divorce as a *remediable symptom* of their complicities rather than as a *viable solution* to their unhappiness. They can also adopt the same orientation toward their mutual feelings of boredom and guilt, as well as their tendencies to be abusive with each other or with their children.

INVALIDATION AND COMPLICITIES

As Bateson and his colleagues noted in describing destructive patterns of communication, invalidation occurs between people whenever their words and behavior do not match their thoughts, feelings, and intentions.[2] It is also mutually invalidating when either one pretends not to understand what the other is actually saying or when he or she does not listen earnestly to what the other is trying to get across.

By definition, every complicity rests on a fixed pattern of mutual invalidation. Having covertly pledged to sustain a commonly created lie, both mates *deliberately strive* to speak and to act as if they do not know *why* they made their agreement, *what* they agreed to do, and *how* they are doing it.

To uphold these paradoxical rules for relating to one another, mates simultaneously engage in *self-invalidation*. Both lie to themselves about the truths of their personal participation in their complicities. Specifically, they disavow their inner experience of the fear of loving and its emotional transformations. They also avoid acknowledging, to themselves, the roles they are playing individually in their defensive scenarios. Thus, spouses cut themselves off from large segments of their true thoughts and feelings, and this disavowal impedes their individual ability to make the most constructive use of their fears and defensive reactions.

Seen in the context of complicities, self-invalidation is a withholding of love from oneself—just as mutual invalidation blocks the sharing of love between mates. By inwardly resisting acknowledgment of being an accomplice in a collective falsehood, neither spouse can help the other to become more loving. So, their personal resistance to facing the truth about themselves is as damaging to their relationship as it is to each of them individually.

Predictably, in terms of our conceptual framework, the flight and fight reactions of interpersonal defensiveness show up in empirical investigations of couples as passive avoidance and cross-complaining, "in which the other's complaint is not listened to but met with a counterattack. . . . Dissatisfied spouses are observed repeatedly to engage in this form of interaction, setting off lengthy chains of reciprocal negativity. . . ."[3]

VALIDATION AND BREAKING COMPLICITIES

To break any complicity, both mates must switch from invalidation to validation. Actually, every person, single or married, has an unending need to validate his or her thoughts and feelings. With their capacity for self-awareness, all individuals feel intrinsically obligated to decide for themselves what to accept as the truths of their existence—no matter how honest or false they may be with others. By calling themselves to account in solitary reflection and introspection, people express a loving attitude toward themselves, a genuine desire to treat their own lives with the utmost consideration.

However, in unspoken rumination emotions and ideas often float through consciousness in a vague and fleeting manner, making it difficult for a person to bring them into clear and steady focus. People are also tempted to evade personal ownership for what they do not communicate, inclined to suspend themselves on an endless string of "maybes" and "yes, buts." Consequently, all people can gain in self-validation by disclosing themselves to others.

Actually, a number of studies have found that self-disclosure is significantly related to both satisfaction and intimacy between mates.[4] By making public what was once guardedly private, a person takes a firmer hold on the contents of his or her subjective experience. An empathic listener can also stimulate the speaker's memory and mental associations with unexpected questions and cogent replies. So, self-disclosure stimulates both mates to discover meaningful connections between their inner concerns and their patterns of behavior.

In addition, everyone has just as basic a need to *give* validation—to be accepted by others as competent to help them confirm what *they* privately think and feel. When giving validation, a husband and wife implicitly call on themselves to discern truth from falsehood as each listens to the other, and they are equally truthful in expressing their reactions to what the other is confiding.

Providing validation for a mate is not only a gift of love to him or her, it is also—and as much—a gift of love to oneself. When mates communicate honestly *about themselves*, they are telling the same truth *to themselves*, for they *confront* themselves as they *reveal* themselves.

The spouse who is speaking shows a desire to give of himself or herself to the other. Reciprocally, the listener, attending to what is said and letting it register fully, is bestowing an equally precious gift. Indeed, it is impossible for mates to profit emotionally from mutual revelation unless they *receive* what is revealed with the same sincerity as it is given.

It is wonderful to be reassured of your partner's love after you have revealed thoughts, feelings, and actions that you had feared might render you vulnerable to rejection. This acceptance gives you an incentive to go on disclosing things you think might make you unlovable to your mate. It is just as marvelous to reassure your mate, who has opened up about something he or she believed could provoke rejection from you. Knowing you are loving enough to accept your chosen partner, for better *and* for worse, increases your own ability to be compassionate and forgiving. Finally, by admitting they are troubled by the same worries, spouses fortify their feelings of commonality.

When a couple communicates with this affectionate candor, they are engaging in mutual validation, which researchers have verified as a characteristic of marital harmony. "Gottman and his colleagues have observed that highly satisfied spouses tend to listen to each other's expressions of 'problems' and to respond with some form of validation—that is, a non-judgmental expression of understanding."[5]

By practicing this kind of listening and responding, mates can buttress the strength of their relationship. Indeed, they repeatedly prove that they are sufficient unto themselves in this most vital area of human functioning, that they require no third party to mediate and monitor their lifelong quest to reap the rewards of their pairing, and that they can help one another to grow as loving persons.

STEPS TOWARD BREAKING COMPLICITIES

The Initial Confrontation

Fortunately, no couple's complicities are predetermined by any factors pertaining to the *individual* similarities or differences between partners. Rather, all mates create their complicities *collectively* while relating to each other. So, it is unprofitable for them to try sorting out which aspects of their separate backgrounds and personalities may have "determined" their *joint participation* in a particular complicity. Instead, they can concentrate on giving one another mutual validation by resolving to understand *what* they have agreed to do, *as a couple*, in forming a complicity; *how* they are doing it; *why* they go on maintaining it; and *how* they can break it.

Thus, it is absolutely essential for both mates to participate equally in the entire process of breaking a complicity. Of course, either of them can take the initiative to focus on their mutual defensiveness. Or they may confront one another at the same moment, each bursting with exasperation.

Their opening confrontation may erupt in the late hours of the night, even though they have to be at work the next morning. Perhaps, at other times, they may lose their tempers and start an argument while in the living room with their children. Or, after a lengthy exchange of pseudocommunication in a quiet restaurant, they may flare up in unison, each impatient to tear the wrapping off a package of lies they have been pretending, for years, did not exist.

Naturally, it is embarrassing for a couple to make a scene in public, and it is exhausting for them to stay awake most of the night in a tormenting discussion. However, mates can be kind and reasonable to themselves, and to anyone else in the vicinity, by agreeing to continue their confrontation later, under conditions more conducive to the fullness of mutual disclosure. They can honestly explain their outbursts to their children as unavoidable—and necessary—for improving their marriage, *and* they can add that this improvement will help them to become better parents.

After having sustained a complicity for months or years, mates cannot expect to undo it instantly. Rather, it will take them a lot of time just to vent their suppressed feelings, even before they clarify the origins and workings of their mutual deceit. So, as novices at communicating about these relational complexities, a couple may require marathon sessions that run over the course of a day or two, plus follow-up conversations to crystallize their psychological breakthroughs.

Obviously, mates need utter and uninterrupted privacy for the depth of revelation involved in unmasking their interpersonal machinations. If they are unable to sequester themselves at home, they can find some other place where there is no risk of intrusion or distraction.

The Catharsis and Containment of Fear

Just as they build their romance by choosing to communicate their loving thoughts, feelings, and hopes, spouses break through their complicities by daring to "rock the boat" and validate the reality of how they have been lying to each other. However, they have to brave extraordinary agony and turmoil while replacing the falsehood of a complicity with the truthfulness about everything they have agreed to cover up. Both must be ready to unleash and weather the full blast of the fear they had been defending themselves against.

In fact, mates must be willing to let themselves be shaken to the roots of their being. Once they open the "can of worms" in which they had stored their covert agreements to lie, they are in for an acute siege of jittery agitation. When they let their pent-up fear of loving emerge in its original intensity, it will rage within and between them, and they have to tolerate the presence of a psychological danger they had always considered to be lethal—unless they immediately defended themselves against it by fighting and fleeing. So, while getting their "basic training" as complicity breakers, it is perfectly normal for mates to tremble, moan, weep, or scream as they disarm themselves. Indeed, as their fear comes into the forefront of their consciousness, they may be stricken with depressing uncertainties about the worth of their relationship and their adequacy as individuals.

But spouses can change their attitude toward fear, regarding it as a warning signal to be heeded for their mutual benefit, and not as an enemy to be avoided at all costs. They will *not* fall apart, die, or disappear from the face of the earth when the fear of loving strikes them with its terrible force. Rather, the upsets they allow themselves to experience can help them to learn that it *is* possible to stand their ground and watch their fear as it hits and passes through them. Eventually, this emotional tempest will be followed by the couple's immense relief in seeing that they are still alive, and they will feel immeasurably better for having held still to face what they had assumed to be the end of their days.

Still, throughout their marriage, the involuntary imperatives of their fear will send mates scurrying into the trenches of their complicities. After they are dug in, they have to master their own wariness to dig themselves out, and this conscious struggle to make their love prevail must be repeated again and again. But by doing so, a couple develops the ability to impose voluntary control over the ways in which they respond to fear. With this control, they can prevent their love from being wiped out by their defensiveness.

Sorting Out the Threat behind the Fear

Of course, every couple is *always* maintaining complicities that originate from all four threats of love. However, they cannot break more than one complicity at a time since the process requires complete and undivided attention. But mates do not have to ponder the question of when to work on breaking which complicity. They can make this decision by paying attention to the *emotional* and *behavioral* signals that are bothering them most inescapably at a particular time. These signals point to the complicity that is most prominent in their thoughts and interactions. They can start the collective process of comprehending and eliminating it by scrutinizing either the *content of their inner experience* or the *patterning of their interpersonal behavior.*

If they begin by looking inward, they can detect the most disturbing negative emotions they are harboring toward each other. As soon as both air their commonly held rivalry, distrust, envy, or sensual numbness, they are actually beginning to uncover the deceitful agreement that is currently most troublesome to them. The particular feelings they identify reflect the threat that has been stimulating their fear of loving. Thus, they can see exactly what emotions they have been using as transformations of their fear. Then, they can connect their feelings to the behavioral scenario they are enacting to express those emotions.

Spouses can be most effective in draining off the incapacitating effects of their fear by disclosing their emotional transformations of it *as quickly as they can.* The more they shorten the gap between the time they first experience a negative emotion and the time they discuss it, the more relaxed they will feel and the more they will prevent the build-up of marital tension.

Alternatively, a couple can start by looking at the behavioral scenario they have repeated with nearly mechanical rigidity. The specifics of their script can inform them of the negative emotions they have been dramatizing. This information, in turn, permits them to identify the threat of love reflected in their emotions and actions.

Finally, couples can begin to understand a complicity by paying attention to what they are most careful to hide from others about the problematic aspects of their relationship. The very fact that spouses feel a common need to collude in hiding such information shows they suspect what is troubling them. Thus, they can get an accurate clue to the threat that currently has them "on the ropes" by examining the collusion they are most concerned to maintain in public. The substance of the dissension they are trying to obscure in front of people indicates what has been arousing their mutual defensiveness, and surely, if they can cooperate so spontaneously, and so effectively, to deceive others, they have the ability to cooperate in order to *stop* deceiving themselves.

Naturally, mates can juxtapose all of these strategies in working through a specific complicity, flexibly shifting their attention as they discuss the emotional transformations of their fear, their behavioral scenarios, and their collusions. During these discussions, each mate can inwardly search out the ways he and she has been participating in their defense pact. Then, as they exchange their thoughts and feelings, they may encounter disagreements between them about the meaning of their complicity. So, each has the personal responsibility of querying the other—and re-examining his and her views of their collective problem—until they can reconcile their differences.

Whenever one spouse tries to "play dumb" or deny some feature of a mutual defense, the other can press for greater honesty and raise questions calculated to ferret out what he or she is trying to hide. In this regard, the familiarity husbands and wives have with each other's modes of communication, including their nonverbal techniques of evasion, permits them to help each other when one temporarily shows more resistance to self-disclosure.

When they have gained an understanding that makes equal sense to each of them, mates attain self-validation *and* mutual validation. They will feel stronger as individuals for having affirmed their innermost selves—and better as a couple for having arrived at a common basis for making a desirable change in their relationship.

Translating Awareness into Action

Since a couple's hard-won insight dissipates the cloud of their past confusion, it can feel liberating in itself. Temporarily satisfied by their awareness, mates may believe they need do nothing more than accept it to end their complicity. However, if they do not *act promptly and appropriately* on the truth they have shared, their insight becomes an additional problem for them. Sooner or later, they may even begin to doubt the validity of their own awareness; they may slip back into their old pattern of behavior; and they will feel, quite correctly, that they have let each other down.

Consequently, it is important for mates to map out a course of action for permanently scrapping their complicity—as quickly as they can—after gaining an understanding of it. They can *explicitly* agree on what specific changes in behavior to make and on how to implement the action they decide to take. When they *participate together* in making the *actual changes* necessary to break their complicity, they prove that they do have the determination to make their relationship more loving. Then, to prevent themselves from resuming the same complicity, they can frequently assess and take note of their progress. In due course, with this complicity broken forever, they can proceed to break the next one that presses into the forefront of their consciousness.

When the concept of complicity dawned on us, it immediately illuminated the darkness of our marital misery. To paraphrase Aldous Huxley,[6] it cleansed the doors of our common perception and opened up previously unseen vistas for reducing our miseries and enriching the satisfactions of our marriage.

We began to apply the idea with growing effectiveness in freeing ourselves from complicities we had accumulated but had never understood as such. Our success, in turn, encouraged us to probe more deeply into the recesses of our marital closet and to exorcise many of the troublesome ghosts that had been rattling away inside it for so long.

Of course, we contrive new complicities and collusions as we go forward in fulfilling the promises of love. We never expect to be completely free of such defenses, any more than we expect to be free of the fear of loving. Now, however, we do not have to waste a lot of time and energy blaming one another for the tensions we have created jointly. Instead, we are highly motivated to detect the emotional transformations of our fear of loving, the scenarios we are using to enact those feelings, and the ways in which we collude in public to hide our defenses.

Still, every time we become embroiled in the heat of dismantling a complicity, we have to endure a great deal of emotional pain. But we have learned to approach the process without too much hesitation and with an underlying confidence in the benefits awaiting us. Sometimes, we find it hard to believe just how much we have benefited. In a relatively few years, we have markedly increased the liveliness and productivity of our relationship. Both of us have felt enormously empowered, as individuals, to handle whatever challenges we face in the world on our own, and in taking complete responsibility for improving our relationship, we have steadily strengthened our ability to validate ourselves and each other.

Our most delicious pay-off, however, is the enjoyment we now get in each other's company. Nothing we read or heard in psychology prepared us for the "charge" we feel just by "hanging out" together. Much of this specialness of feeling can be traced to our romance, which we take ample care to nurture. But just as much of it is the cumulative result of having become comfortable about airing our petty, mean, and nasty emotions along with the deviously defensive antics we employ.

On the other hand, we believe the undoing of a complicity is the most trying of all efforts spouses can make to reach each other. After what we have experienced in going through the process, we have an abiding compassion for couples who remain imprisoned by their defensiveness. Having created these fetters, however, they *can* provide for their own liberation.

Happily, human beings are the most inventive of all species, and spouses can succeed in using this inventiveness to awaken the loving harmony that is dormant in their relationship. But it is foolhardy for them to deny their intrinsic self-centeredness or to discount the fact that humans are also the most deadly creatures on earth, well on the way to obliterating *all* forms of life, including their own. They therefore have a better chance of subduing their own capacity for destruction by recognizing it. Then they can realistically join in the daily effort to actualize their love and to refrain from yielding excessively to their fear and defensiveness.

Thankfully, humans are also uniquely gifted with a sense of humor. The ultimate test—and reward—of a sense of humor is the ability to laugh at one's own folly. All laughter is beneficial, according to Norman Cousins.[7] But we believe its most healing effect comes from draining off tensions people accumulate in using deceit to be socially impressive. So, *laughing at oneself in front of others* is especially therapeutic since it also involves a liberation from the stress of *convincing oneself* that one is, indeed, fooling others.

In this regard, the increased honesty and validation mates derive from breaking their complicities can free them to "goof" on themselves, and they can enjoy laughing at the convoluted capers of their complicities. By joining in laughter at their own falseness, they attain relief from their vain efforts to impress themselves and each other. Since each is both actor and audience for the other, mates always have the chance to lighten their inevitable sufferings by taking turns as comedians, both recalling their hilarious maneuvers in past complicities. They can give themselves regular comic relief from the heaviness of their disaffections and disputes, and they can have fun together, even while going through the hardest of times.

Now, we will apply these guidelines to illustrate how the couples, described in the last chapter, can go about breaking the complicities they formed in reacting to each of the four threats of love.

OVERCOMING THE THREAT OF EXPANDING
THE BOUNDARIES OF INDIVIDUALITY

Richard and Marsha Crane, the couple involved in a scenario to avoid purchasing a house, can begin to break their complicity by recognizing the persistence and futility of their indecisive *pattern of behavior.* Of course, buying a house is a very important decision, and it is prudent for mates to take their time and give serious consideration to it. However, when they go on and on vacillating, passing up one viable alternative after another over a long and extensive search, they can help each other to draw the proper conclusion: namely, they are resisting a decision and *canceling out each other's desires* with irrational consistency.

Either Richard or Marsha can point to this irrationality as a symptom of *their* problem. Then, to establish the common origins of this symptom in *their relationship,* they can look at their individual behavior to see how absolutely each has vetoed the other's inclination to favor a particular house. They can also examine their personal fantasies about every place they turned down. This scrutiny will show how greedily they have adhered to their separate egoistic stipulations and how rivalrous they have been by giving no real thought to the preferences each has voiced to the other.

Facing the content of their negative emotions, Richard and Marsha can see that both of them have been reacting with the same kind of defensiveness to the threat of becoming more united as a couple. They might also realize how absurd it is to persist in competing with each other and depriving themselves of an improvement in their living quarters. After all, they would not have wanted to look for a new home in the first place if they were satisfied with their present residence. So, isn't it ridiculous for them to keep on rejecting *all* alternatives, any one of which would be an improvement over the place they have been willing to remain in?

Convinced of the relational meaning of their mutual invalidation, the Cranes can decide to end their competitive contest. Then, they can make more realistic compromises and take the appropriate action to enlarge their collective identity by actually purchasing a house that is sufficiently pleasing to *both* of them. After taking this cooperative step, they can accommodate their personal tastes and talents in the creative activities of decorating and furnishing their new abode. Richard can give Marsha the necessary "room" to express her individual yens in arranging the living room so they can entertain in the way she enjoys so much; she can let him make the structural changes and add whatever insulation he thinks is necessary to keep the place energy efficient. As a result, both will have a common space in which to get together more intimately and comfortably than ever before. Thus, they can turn their excruciating stalemate, which had them nailed to the fixety of selecting nothing, into the realization of their common desire for a better home and into a deeper fulfillment of the promise of expanding the boundaries of their individuality.

The Taubs, who are depriving themselves of the love inherent in further fulfillment of the same promise, can begin to understand the nature of their complicity by considering how they are colluding to hide their dispute from others. First, they can easily detect the gross discrepancy between their public pretension of a consensus on where they want to live and their private warfare about it. Then, like the Cranes, they can see that the sharing of a common, and probably permanent, abode in *any* location is the nub of their upset. This insight can point them directly to the threat they feel about becoming a more unified couple. They then can appreciate how all their arguing about where to locate themselves is an expression of the competition they wrote into their defensive scenario. With this awareness they can reach a compromise, taking an action that involves each giving something to the other in terms of their originally separate positions on the issue. Roger can yield on his former adamance about settling in Manhattan, and Madeline can meet him half way by forgoing her insistence on Long Island. For example, they can agree on a pleasant location in some borough of the city that is fairly accessible to both of their offices, and, having reached that agreement, they can cooperate—privately and publicly—to secure an apartment that suits their combined tastes.

OVERCOMING THE THREAT OF INCREASING INTERDEPENDENCE

The Furillos, who have been tormenting each other with jealousy, can break their complicity with a different opening move. Rather than continue to deny their feelings, Tony *or* Marie can venture to "lose face" by owning up to his or her jealousy. For they are only perpetuating the falsehood of their mutual defense by maintaining their false pride about showing the jealousy they actually feel.

To have a fruitful dialogue, the Furillos will also have to drop whatever erroneous ideas they might have picked up about the meaning of jealousy itself. Often depicted as a "green-eyed monster," jealousy has been condemned by some authorities as "pathological"—as a sure sign of excessive dependency and possessiveness. Admittedly, one can find instances in which a person's obsessive suspicions of infidelity are totally unfounded in the behavior of his or her mate. However, among many spouses like Tony and Marie, jealousy arises from their *mutual* detachment and distrust. So, in the psychology of interpersonal defense, their jealousy indicates how fearful they are of becoming as interdependent as they actually crave to be, how deeply they really do care for each other, how much they want to hold on to their loving relationship, and how crazed they are at the thought of losing one another.

Of course, no matter which one begins to express jealous feelings, both Tony and Marie are likely to react with acute alarm, and they may scream and bark at each other for hours. Still, whoever provokes the confrontation makes an offer of honesty that the other can scarcely refuse. In fact, this opening confession is precisely what both of them have been waiting to hear. It is also what both of them have been wanting to admit: basically, that they are sick and tired of pretending *not* to be dependent on one another's loyalty when they actually *do* need and cherish each other as a monogamous mate who can be trusted and depended on *unconditionally,* and that they are just as weary of their "no-win" displays of aloofness and unwillingness to be trustworthy and dependable.

Following this decisive breakthrough, Tony and Marie can compare notes, not only on the mental representations of their jealousy but also on how they have been carrying out their flirtations and trying to upset one another. In this discussion they can specify all the manifestations of their negative emotions. They can reveal exactly how suspicious they have been of each other; the distrustful fantasies they have had about how each might be cheating on the other with various people; and how they have imagined attracting strangers to them to assert their "independence" from one another. Likewise, they can admit how they visualized "getting theirs back" for every incident when each observed the other in a flirtation; how they did, in fact, incorporate the enactment of these fantasies into their scenario; and how they pretended not to notice what each could *see* the other doing.

Although Tony and Marie did not have full-fledged affairs with others, spouses who actually did would also need to bare those derelictions. Naturally, these admissions will be even more difficult for them to make than those about their jealousy, their emotional transformations of fear, and their flirtatious scenarios. They may feel compelled to air their distress for days before arriving at a consensus about the meaning of their infidelity. Nevertheless, complicities cannot be broken with half-truths. To break a defense pact securely—and for the everlasting good of their relationship—both mates have to go all the way in the truthfulness of their disclosures.

Of course, in exchanging such shattering revelations, a couple risks the possibility of losing whatever shreds of mutual trust they still retain. But what sustenance can their relationship give mates if they go on with their secret affairs—and with the bottled poison of their gnawing suspicions? And how can they ever restore their solidarity unless they achieve the level of candor necessary to reaffirm their faith in each other?

If they are willing to be totally honest, a husband and a wife can prove the unquestionable sincerity of their desire to stay together. Acknowledging their interdependence by breaking their complicity once and for all, they gain a quantum increase in mutual dependability, which is, of course, the whole point of wanting to end their tantalizing torture.

OVERCOMING THE THREAT OF TRANSCENDING DIFFERENCES IN GENDER

A similar conclusion applies to the Reubens, who have been in complicity to guard against transcending their inherent and socially learned differences in gender. They can begin to uncover both facets of this threat by discussing how rigidly each one has been playing stereotyped roles. Why has Jack been spending so much of his free time in political activities and athletics with his male friends? Why does he exclude Claire? Why doesn't he participate more in doing the household chores? And why doesn't he show a greater interest in the way Claire is rearing their child? Reciprocally, what about Claire's heavy involvement with the women in her aerobic class and the child study group? Why doesn't she include him? Why is she so critical every time Jack does attempt to pitch in with the cooking and cleaning? And couldn't she be more helpful to him, too, by urging him to talk about his occupational problems?

By candidly exploring these questions, the Reubens will see how much they have shunned the possibility of *sharing* all marital roles and of *combining* their similar interests in politics and exercise. Maintaining mutually exclusive associations with people of the same gender, they have been ignoring the sexism reflected by their social segregation. As they talk about their defensive modes of fleeing, they can also become aware of how they have been spitefully emphasizing their gender differences and yielding to the threat of progressing in relational equality.

Demonstrating a sincere desire to break their complicity, Jack and Claire can translate their insights into action by agreeing to stop going out at night separately. Next, they can decide on how to implement their similar interests in the community and in sports—as a couple. They could team up as political activists or join a committee together at their child's nursery school, and they can exercise in the same gym, choosing a sport they find equally enjoyable.

Moving beyond the combination of their outside activities, the Reubens can get down to the "nitty-gritty" of the differential roles they have been playing inside their own home. Claire can gripe about Jack's withdrawal from childrearing and housekeeping, even though he knows what a demanding job she has. Likewise, Jack can voice his resentments about Claire's tendency to neglect him for her occupational and recreational pursuits and how she disregards him in the unilateral plans she makes for their child and home.

After this catharsis, the Reubens would be ready to dig for deeper insight into what is threatening them. Eventually, Jack can admit his worries about becoming a "patsy" of a man if he participates in childcare and housework. Similarly, Claire can acknowledge her anxiety about losing her femininity if she *lets* him share the domestic roles that she has been playing alone.

With these new understandings, both Jack and Claire can become less spiteful and less sexist. He can stop evading responsibility for their household and family, and she can stop resisting his help. Both can explicitly agree to communicate about the problems either of them encounter in their careers and in making the changes required to equalize roles. They can also give each other regular praise for displaying traits they had previously considered unacceptable for people of their own gender.

Finally, the Reubens can move on to the more delicate issue of mutual dissatisfaction with their stereotypical approach to making love. Either one could broach the subject. Claire can tell Jack how much she wants to drop her sexual inhibitions. But why has she been so unwilling to give herself over to their lovemaking? Why is she envious of his male anatomy and the "masculine" prerogatives he assumes in doing whatever *he* wants to do in bed? Is that why she holds out on him and keeps herself from having an orgasm? In the same egalitarian spirit, Jack can confide his envy of Claire's ability to be sexually passive, the pressure he feels to keep an erection, and his spiteful reluctance to prolong their foreplay for *her* pleasure.

Having gone this far in honesty, the Reubens can hazard an exchange of their secret fantasies. Knowing they have been similarly obsessed with complementary wishes to alter their erotic interactions, they could better appreciate the full extent of their human commonality. Just as they change in other areas of activity, they can begin to relate to each other more equally in making love. Claire can initiate more of their sexual relations and *show* Jack the kind of stimulation she wants. She could also *ask* how to stimulate him in ways he finds most enjoyable. Jack can *let her* take this initiative by *allowing himself* to lay back and slow down, no longer feeling so compelled to assert his masculinity. Thus, both can gratify the sexual desires they had been too fearful even to admit to one another.

OVERCOMING THE THREAT OF IMMERSION IN THE PLEASURE OF LOVEMAKING

The Stuarts could regard their erotic numbness and seeming disinterest in sexual contact as symptoms of their mutual defensiveness. However, they may find it easier to start breaking their complicity by reviewing the details of their *behavioral scenario* rather than the emotional transformations of their fear. Why are they having guests so frequently on weekends, the only days they can be together in private? Is it necessary for them to buy tickets to a concert series every season? And what about their vacations? What does their inflexible habit of taking the kids along or of going on group tours mean for their relationship?

Collectively answering such questions, Rona and Larry can help each other to recognize that they have been in a pact to waste the time, energy, and opportunities they could be using for lovemaking. With this awareness they are ready to agree on changes in their lifestyle that will result in more sexual contact between them.

First, they can institute the practice of refusing dinner invitations for any night during the working week, and they can refrain from having house guests on the weekends. They might even decide to give away some of their concert tickets. Then, they can remove the television set from their bedroom and replace their twin beds with a double bed. At the same time, they can go to bed with the common intention of deconditioning themselves from the threat of erotic pleasure, and if they react negatively to *anything* they do, they can stop—right then and there—to talk about it.

Gently, but purposefully, Larry and Rona can delve into the

reasons why the very pleasure of lovemaking threatens them. Are they afraid about losing control in front of each other? Does Larry worry that if he lets go too much, Rona will reject him as a wild beast? Does she anticipate rejection if she urinates or passes gas in abandoning herself to orgasmic release? Are they terrified about neglecting their work and their children if they get too immersed in erotic pleasure?

Confessing such apprehensions could greatly calm and reassure them; by making these most intimate revelations in the warmth of their physical closeness, Larry and Rona will finally realize that all they have to lose by making love is a lot of unhappiness. Feeling much safer in each other's arms, they can be more daring about giving each other erotic stimulation, and they can remain steeped in sexual pleasure for longer and longer intervals.

After learning to tolerate more enjoyment in their lovemaking, the Stuarts can move on to discard some of their other strategies for avoiding it. Perhaps, for their next vacation, they can leave the children with their parents and pick out a beautiful and secluded spot where they can make sensual contact with one another and nature. Even if they prefer going to a large resort, they can stop any activity, at any time, to go back to their room and make love. They can also create their own romantic ambience by ordering room service instead of going down to the dining room for every meal, only to have inane conversations with the people at their table. Sometimes, when other guests are in the nightclub watching the floorshow, they can decide to stroll around the grounds to revel in the beauty of the stars.

Lastly, Larry and Rona can dispose of shopping as a substitute for the sexual contact they had feared. While they may still want to buy mementos of their trip, they will have less *need* to get emotionally involved in their purchases, and their new enjoyment in making love can help them appreciate how much better it feels to lavish attention on each other rather than on the acquisition of material objects.

NOTES

1. For a perspective on the somatic effects of chronically stressful patterns of dialogue, see Lynch, J. J. *Language of the heart.* New York: Basic Books, 1985.
2. Bateson, *Steps to an ecology of mind,* pp. 201–227.
3. Levinger, Development and change. In Kelley et al., *Close relationships,* p. 340.
4. Brehm, S. S. *Intimate relationships.* New York: Random House, 1985, p. 214.
5. Levinger, op. cit.
6. Huxley, A. *The doors of perception.* New York: Harper & Row, 1954.
7. Cousins, N. *The anatomy of an illness.* New York: Norton, 1979.

Part II

LOVING FOR LIFE

Part II

7

DEVELOPING A LOVE-CENTERED MARRIAGE

In its most basic meaning, the concept of development refers to the unfolding of potentials over the course of time. Within scientific psychology, this definition generally has been applied to capacities that are assumed to exist within individual organisms. For example, psychologists have studied the development of a person's capacity for visual perception, verbal communication, and concept formation. Generally, too, the capacity being unfolded is assumed to be positively and unequivocally desirable, that is, being able to see more clearly, to understand words better, and to form more sophisticated—even moral—concepts.

For many years the domain of developmental psychology was restricted to children—as if all desirable development suddenly ceased with the end of adolescence. However, adults now are included in the lifelong reach of developmental theory and research. Actually, attention to personality development in adulthood was pioneered many years ago by Carl Jung and carried forward by such influential investigators as Erik Erikson, Bernice Neugarten, Roger Gould, and Daniel Levinson. Subsequently, Gail Sheehy popularized their work in her widely read *Passages*.[1] It is currently quite fashionable to speak of stages of adult development, with special emphasis on regular turning points, predictable crises, and increases in various traits associated with psychological maturity.

Of course, at the beginning of this century, Freud established psychosexual development as a legitimate topic of study.[2] Still, to this very day, *the capacity to love*, in a holistic sense, has not been the subject of developmental investigation in either children or adults. This neglect may reflect the cultural impact of the loveless societies in which psychologists, like their compatriots, are conditioned.

Nevertheless, the capacity to love is the most personally and socially constructive of all human potentials, its development bringing harmony within and between people. In fact, loving is so crucial to everyone's sense of well-being that men and women equate it with the central organ of their existence—the heart, which pumps the vital energies of the blood throughout their bodies. When they love and are loved in return, people say their hearts are overflowing with joy. But when they are having trouble with their love life, they dolefully describe their anguish as heartache and heartbreak.

DEVELOPING THE CAPACITY TO LOVE
BEFORE ADULTHOOD

Like other human capacities, the potential for loving does not unfold outside of an *interpersonal context* conducive to its flowering. Even the most elemental maturation of a child's capacity for physical growth is contingent upon both the voluntarily given care of its parents and the child's equally voluntary acceptance of what they have to offer.

Similarly, from the moment of birth, people begin to develop their innate capacity to love within the context of relating to their parents. Receiving affection, acceptance, and reliable care, infants respond in kind: cuddling, smiling, cooing, and cooperating. As their relationships evolve, children and parents are motivated to give of themselves not only in the form of hugs and kisses but also by sharing their thoughts and feelings.

People reared in such an atmosphere of warmth, communion, and trust naturally will acquire many of the attitudes essential for maintaining a loving relationship with a spouse.

Nevertheless, some of the fundamental conditions of childrearing, even when carried out by the most loving of parents, are bound to instill relational orientations that actually run counter to those needed by couples who want to conduct a love-centered marriage.

First of all, the parent-child relationship is *inherently unequal* in power. Parents are the ones who choose to have the children, and, for many years, they necessarily assume most of the responsibility for determining the course of their children's lives. Certainly, loving parents let their children take more and more responsibility for themselves as they become physically and mentally capable of doing so. However, during the long years of their rearing, children are inclined to become dependent on and subordinate to the wishes of their parents.

Secondly, children and parents cannot express the sexual component of their mutual love. A similar restriction exists between siblings. To be sure, these taboos against incest serve very vital functions for the welfare of all members of the family. But children have to grow up without being able to express their love holistically with the very people toward whom they feel the strongest affection.

In marked contrast, adults choose spouses of their own volition. A husband and wife also are free to integrate eroticism and affection in relating to the one person they have finally selected to love more than anyone else in the world, and spouses mature enormously by learning to relate as *social equals* who are *completely interdependent* and who *possess the same power* to meet each other's needs and to direct their relationship.

Of course, the majority of mothers and fathers have not deliberately focused their parenting on helping their children to develop the capacity to love. However, good parents are more or less mindful of the kinds of psychosocial transitions their offspring will have to make in becoming loving mates. Consequently, they gradually let go of their originally intense attachments to their children, and, as their offspring begin to approach young adulthood, these parents encourage them to find someone with whom they can fully express the sexual and affectionate wholeness of loving.

In late adolescence sons and daughters begin the process

of attenuating the close attachments they had maintained previously with their parents. Greatly increasing the physical and emotional distance between themselves and their mothers and fathers, young men and women pour their energies into the crucial task of preparing to face the future on their own. They become deeply concerned with sorting out their personal philosophy and style of living, while seeking the kind of education or vocational training that will enable them to utilize their particular talents and interests. At the same time, they experience an inescapable need to become economically self-reliant in the midst of a highly competitive society.

As they grapple with these pressing concerns, young adults get used to thinking about pleasing nobody but themselves. But they also are prey to painful feelings of frustration and isolation. Thus, while crystallizing a sense of autonomy and competence, they begin to yearn for the intimacy and pleasure of a loving relationship.

Not surprisingly, therefore, Carin Rubenstein and Philip Shaver have found that the loneliest of all Americans are single men and women between the ages of 18 and 26.[3] This very loneliness—this relentless feeling of deprivation—is probably what spurs them into an active search for union in love with someone of the opposite sex. Eventually, most of them turn to marriage as a way of transforming their yearnings into a living reality.

MARRIAGE AS THE OPTIMAL PATHWAY FOR DEVELOPING LOVE IN ADULTHOOD

Thus, getting married is the culmination of a quest for the partner every adult needs for actual fulfillment in loving. Still, having found this indispensable person in one another, mates do not automatically actualize all of their individual potentials for loving. Rather, having committed themselves to marriage, a husband and wife now are in the position to *begin* the lifelong process of jointly maximizing their common capacity to love.

Previously, these spouses had viewed their psychological maturation as contingent upon cutting loose from childlike attachments to their parents, and they saw *individuation* as their pathway to responsible adulthood. But uniting in married love means *reversing* that very process of separation and individuation. Marriage involves an *unconditional reattachment of oneself to another human being,* an interpersonal merger whose depth and scope has no precedence in past relationships with family members. In fact, as husband and wife, adults are socially encouraged and expected to fulfill both the sexual and affectionate components of love that they had to compartmentalize in relating to their parents and siblings. Moreover, the marital commitment of love-centered mates is based on a joint decision to devote the entirety of their adult lives primarily to loving one another. Consequently, from a holistic standpoint, their mutual involvement is bound to become much more *extensive* and *intensive* than any other attachments they had ever formed.

However, it is extremely difficult for mates to shift away from the individualistic thrust of their earlier development and to concentrate, instead, on their *relational* development. It is also difficult for them to alter their previous view of adult maturity, which emphasized the ability to distance themselves from their parents as a necessary condition for enhancing their personal growth. By contrast, a love-centered marriage challenges husbands and wives to accept the paradoxical fact that it is through the very process of strengthening their collective identity—not by differentiating from one another—that they attain optimal individual development. So, the more deeply mates are willing to merge in body and mind, the more effective they can be in maximizing both their relational and personal growth.

THE SYNERGY BETWEEN RELATIONAL AND INDIVIDUAL DEVELOPMENT IN LOVING

This perspective represents a departure from the widespread idea that psychological development necessarily refers to the emergence of some trait that is contained, in germinal form, exclusively inside an individual organism. As we have explicitly pointed out, a relationship is a superordinate concept, encompassing the two people who jointly and simultaneously create it. Thus, it resides in the *common consciousness* they derive from and express in their face-to-face contacts.

In this respect, a marital relationship is always *shared* between mates as *their* creation. Accordingly, the constructive development of their relationship hinges on what both of them agree to do in augmenting the loving elements they have already set into place. Naturally, as they increase the sharing of their love, they improve their relationship. In the process of making this interpersonal improvement, they bring out from within their separate beings the characteristics of patience, empathy, and compassion. As a result, each mate becomes a more loving individual, and as they pool such personal resources through their ongoing interactions, both of them contribute more completely to the enrichment of their relationship. Thus, relational and personal development in marriage are connected synergistically.

Consequently, each time mates decide to fulfill a promise of love and add a new increment to their romance, they change their relational development for the better, and they do the same whenever they choose to break one of their complicities. These interpersonal changes have a cumulative effect, steadily bringing more joy and pleasure to a husband and wife, while imbuing them with greater and greater confidence in their joint ability to make good things happen for one another. Meanwhile, by voluntarily taking the emotional risks necessary to effect these relational changes, they develop equally in their personal strength to tolerate the threats of love without fleeing from or fighting with each other.

On the other hand, no pair of mates is superhuman. Even the most stalwart husbands and wives have limits on how much fear of loving they can absorb at a particular time without choosing to reduce it through the use of interpersonal defenses. Of course, they succeed in extending those limits as they evolve their ability to confront and break complicities. Still, because of their human vulnerabilities, all mates continue to form new complicities even after breaking old ones. Then, as they devise and maintain those mutual defenses, they produce fresh miseries for themselves and impede their own growth as loving individuals.

Therefore, every marital relationship is also replete with possibilities of being developed for the worse. In many cases, the worsening that results from the accumulation of unbroken complicities becomes so bad within a period of several years as to take precedence over whatever mates have done to improve their relationship.

This kind of relational development hardly can be regarded as desirable by couples. Nevertheless, given the intransigence of everyone's inherent fear of loving, no marital relationship is ever developed in an unequivocally positive direction. Instead, all mates actively contribute to the negative development of their marriages, even if they are doing their very best to fulfill all the promises of love.

Clearly, it takes every bit of cooperation, persistence, and courage a couple can muster to break even one of their many complicities. Although intellectually prepared by a knowledge of relational dynamics, mates still need to apply all of their will and energy in order to grapple successfully with the defensive manifestations of their common fear of loving.

However, while involved in such interpersonal entanglements, couples do not cease to participate in society, and this participation tempts them continually to become enmeshed in the self-centered pursuit of the values of aggrandizement. So, while struggling to liberate more love from the tentacles of their complicities, they also face the struggle of protecting their relationship from the vortex of vicious competition that surrounds them. Indeed, the cooperative and courageous determination required for couples to succeed in contending with the societal opposition to loving is as great as that which they need to overcome the divisive fearfulness of their own human nature.

But what force has the power to sustain mates in this endless double struggle? The answer, of course, is love itself—but not as an acute need occasionally expressed, as a hazy memory of satisfactions past, or as a dreamy hope of some fulfillment in the future. Instead, to insure a mutually fulfilling prophecy of success in face of the inescapable adversity they inevitably encounter *from within themselves and from without,* mates can rely on an unshakable commitment to develop their loving relationship as the supreme goal of their lifetime together. With this explicit and mutual commitment, they create the wellspring of value—the social philosophy—they can permanently draw upon for sufficient inspiration to make effective use of our relational psychology. So, while accepting their common susceptibility to the destructive pressures of society and to their own fear and defensiveness, love-centered couples would prevail in their double struggle by guiding the development of their marriage progressively toward the better rather than toward the worse.

TIME AND MARITAL DEVELOPMENT

Hypothetically, a husband and wife could go on making this progress on a daily basis, never giving a thought to the future. In reality, however, they cannot help but think about how their functioning as human organisms and as a couple is affected by the inexorable passage of time. Of course, at any single moment mates may not notice the impact of time on what they are doing to develop their marriage. Sometimes, while cradled in each other's arms, they may feel suspended in a timeless space of indescribable beauty. There may be other times when they feel elated at having broken through several barriers in their relationship within a few days. By contrast, couples often become depressingly aware of having attained little mutual satisfaction and fulfillment over the course of several days, weeks, or months.

Consequently, it is very important for spouses to take the time of their lives into their own hands and to agree on a set of priorities for using it to their best advantage in developing their relationship. Given the many and demanding roles they play in today's complex society—just to earn a modest income and to care reliably for children—spouses are required constantly to take responsibility for making relational development an indispensable feature of their daily schedules. Indeed, apart from love, time is the most precious "commodity" they have to share. Yet mates can easily let it "slip away," heedlessly pursuing personal ambitions or excessively carrying out routine chores. They need to be very diligent in preventing other aspirations and activities from gnawing away at the time they could be devoting to loving each other more completely.

Existential Constraints

As they live their years together, mates encounter periods when their realization of the passage of time motivates them to decide conclusively on how to improve their relationship.

Thus, time exerts an implacable influence over a couple's decision about whether or not to conceive a child. Of course, from the moment they become sexually intimate, a man and woman face their biological capacity for reproduction. Long before their wedding day, many couples have taken their stand on the use of contraception. Once married, they must continue to confront the issue of birth control every time they make love until the wife reaches menopause.

On the other hand, all couples realize that, if they do want children, they must conceive while the wife is still capable of doing so. They also know that the physical risks of pregnancy for the mother and the child she bears rise markedly as women approach their late thirties and early forties. A couple's decisions about having children always occur within their awareness of the setting on the wife's "biological clock."

The most troubling constraint of time on all husbands and wives is their pervasive sense of human mortality. Mates cannot help but anticipate their own eventual decline unto death. Even robust newlyweds in their early twenties know that they will not live forever and that their seemingly inexhaustible vigor is destined to run dry in the stony grip of old age. Surely, these dire anticipations are bound to arise with greater frequency among elderly mates than among youthful ones. Obviously, when separated by death they cannot go on developing the loving quality of their relationship. But long before this unavoidable separation, lifelong spouses feel the icy fingers of death reaching toward them in the various signs of their aging. As they notice these psychophysical changes—the withering of their skin, their lapses of memory, their susceptibility to fatigue—they dread the thought of getting older. Besides, these dreads are heightened greatly by the extremely positive value our society places on youth—along with its equally strong denigration of old age.

Societal Constraints

Consciousness of these existential restrictions of time is sharpened further by various schedules imposed on couples by the contrivances of social reality, and they often feel compelled to conform to societal prescriptions that dictate how they are supposed to behave and what they are supposed to accomplish at different periods of time in the course of their marriage. Many spouses get caught up in weighing the biological advantages of bearing children before the wife becomes 35 against the economic incentives for her to remain constantly at work in order to advance her career and safeguard the couple's income.

In this respect, entry into many interesting careers and professions requires years of additional education and training *after* graduation from college. Meeting such requirements while maintaining a marriage may appear to be an overwhelming challenge to a lot of men and women. They may shun the possibility of getting married until they complete all their educational preparations and become established in their chosen fields. By that time, however, the woman may be beyond her optimal age for childbearing, and the couple, having expended so much energy in career building, may lack the zest for the highest quality of parenting.

Alternatively, having already married in their twenties, many spouses may defer the conception of children in favor of doing everything possible to become firmly entrenched in their careers. This kind of deferment has already become widespread, leading to the so-called "baby-panic" that has hit so many careerist wives in their middle and late thirties. In fact, the emotional and physical concerns related to such a long postponement of conception have spawned a whole new specialty of counseling for delayed pregnancy.

Timetables set down by the socioeconomic system also coincide ominously with other intervals of existential apprehension. Many spouses know that they have "had it"—in terms of future advancement in their organizations of work—if they do not receive a particular level of promotion before they reach 40. But couples of this age also are being shaken deeply by the awareness of having already lived half of their lives. Inwardly assailed with questions and doubts about the meaning of their existence, they fearfully exchange regrets over missed opportunities, failed expectations, and personal limitations. In the midst of these disturbing ruminations and conversations, the certain knowledge of having gone as far as they will be going in status and power is especially disheartening to spouses whose morale is heavily linked to endless success in the pursuit of self-aggrandizement.

Similarly, although they may be high-level executives, some husbands and wives are designated for early retirement at precisely the era in their lives when they begin to worry in earnest about the undeniable and rapidly spreading stigmata of their aging. The prospect of having to give up their jobs may exacerbate their terror of becoming totally disabled and withdrawn from the world. In this dispirited condition they may wrap each other in cloaks of gloom well before their official date of retirement.

By contrast, many spouses would prefer to retire quite early but are financially unable to do so. Consequently, they feel forced to remain at unwanted jobs until they can collect pensions that are tied either to a fixed number of years of employment or to the attainment of a specified age. Meanwhile, they may feel increasingly disgruntled and hopelessly trapped.

Perhaps the most ironic cases are those couples who could realize their romantic dreams of early retirement, given the "golden parachute" of severance pay offered by their employers. Yet these mates often balk at the opportunity when it is within their grasp. Suddenly, the reality of losing their occupational status and roles looms before them, arousing tremendous anxiety about no longer being useful and worthy of any admiration or respect. Cultural reverence for the work ethic naturally increases their worries that once they do retire, they will be relegated to society's "slag heap." Going against their intuitive feelings about how leaving work would allow them to make enlivening changes in their marriage, such couples cling desperately to their jobs. As a result, they block their relational development and undermine their morale.

A LIFEPLAN FOR MARITAL DEVELOPMENT

Therefore, couples need a lifeplan that permits them to cope with the *existential and societal constraints of time* in a manner consistent with the aim of maximally developing the loving quality of their marital relationship. Otherwise, they would have no clear path through their dark periods of inescapable contact with the forbidding shadow of mortality, and they might easily go astray by deferring unduly to the various temporal pressures that impinge upon them from their inevitable involvement with the existing socioeconomic system.

Of course, scholars and practitioners have been trying to find out how lifelong marriages change over time. But the results vary markedly from study to study, reflecting wide differences in the samples of couples, the methods of investigation, and the concepts used to define a notable shift. For example, the number of stages proposed ranges from as few as three to as many as seven, and the alterations put forth as significant in one description of the marital life cycle may not even be mentioned in another.

Despite this empirical and conceptual diversity, some authors continue to write as if every married couple were *fated* to undergo the same sequence of temporal changes and that spouses would do well to brace themselves in advance for the upsets produced by the purportedly inevitable onset of those changes. One book in this vein is entitled *The Marriage Map: Understanding and Surviving the Stages of Marriage.*[4] A similar offering presenting different stages is contained in *Supermarriage: Overcoming the Predictable Crises of Married Life.*[5] And in her recent bestseller, *Intimate Partners: Patterns of Love and Marriage,*[6] Maggie Scarf makes extensive reference to a particular five-stage account, implicitly treating it as definitive for all marriages.[7]

In constructing our own approach to developing a relationship, we have drawn selectively on the literature concerning marital stages or phases. However, we do not view the development of any marriage as being determined—somehow—by forces entirely beyond a couple's volition and direction. Instead, we assume that mates have the ability to *initiate* the stages in their relational development by making and carrying out decisions.

Surely, the vast majority of husbands and wives *do* initiate their spousal relationship by *deciding* to marry for love. Then, as newlyweds, they hope to enjoy the blessings of loving each other for the rest of their lives. But while they have this cherished desire, they do not necessarily know what kinds of decisions would continue to guarantee its fullest realization throughout all their years together.

Addressing the lifelong need for this knowledge, we give prime consideration to the issue of how a couple could best develop their loving relationship as their principal goal in living and how they could best implement that overarching aim at different periods in a marital lifetime. Consequently, we portray what a marriage could become—*not* what the course of marriage is usually found to be.

Unfortunately, with a few exceptions, researchers have concluded that the typical marriage develops more for the worse than for the better. Thus, deterioration and divorce have been posited as standard developmental stages of contemporary marriage.[8] But deterioration and divorce obviously are interpersonal disasters—relational development gone awry. It does couples little good merely to get detailed descriptions of a developmental pattern they would ardently wish to avoid.

Accordingly, we emphasize what is both desirable and attainable, and we explain how the dynamics and development of a marriage are always intertwined. With this perspective, which reflects a love-centered philosophy, couples could apply our relational psychology in a *genuinely* timely fashion—on a daily basis and with a view toward making decisions that extend over intervals as long as decades. Thus, their decisions would be doubly appropriate, taking into consideration what is best for them to do in developing their relationship at a particular interval *and* in preparing them for advancing this development through all the subsequent years of their lifelong marriage.

Desirable Objectives

Our model offers a comprehensive and systematic framework for *planning* and *implementing* a lifetime of relational development, showing the *key opportunities* mates have to maximize their capacities for love, to minimize their interpersonal defensiveness, and to affirm their humane values. We spell out how a couple could benefit by setting their sights on a series of *six relational objectives for different periods of time* in their lifelong marriage. Meeting each of these objectives would permit them to make quantum leaps in the degree of love they are able to share. Conversely, if they miss the chance to achieve any of these objectives, they would have to settle for less than the optimal amount of fulfillment that is potentially possible at a particular juncture in their relationship.

Because each of these objectives is the central focus of a span of time, we regard that interval as a *stage of relational development*. From our point of view, a couple inaugurates six stages in a lifelong relationship—one stage for each objective to be attained. These stages are linked in an invariant sequence over time. By dealing with the challenges involved in attaining the desirable objective for one stage—and by experiencing the gratifications of that achievement—mates pave the way to engage the next objective.

Developmental Dialectics

As a couple goes through each developmental stage, they fulfill the four promises of love in new ways that are unique to the changing tasks involved in meeting the objective for that period of time. Meanwhile, they also evoke new manifestations of the four threats of love, and the incapacitating fear aroused by those threats inevitably spurs them into forming new complicities. Although these complicities become additional sources of anguish, limiting the degree of enjoyment mates can share during a particular stage, they would be completely unable to achieve *any* desirable objective and progress from stage to stage without recourse to those interpersonal defenses.

By acknowledging this inescapable dialectic, mates would fully prepare themselves to attain all the objectives. Specifically, as they move toward an objective, they could help one another to face and tolerate the fear of loving, instead of yielding automatically to their defensive tendencies to fight and flee. In addition, they could give each other the support needed to become aware of the complicities they do establish to prevent that fear from swamping their ability to function at all. Otherwise, not realizing the dialectical nature of marital development, mates may get bogged down in blaming each other for conflicts and tensions that *no couple can avoid*—if they want to unfold their lifelong potentials for loving.

Since the process of attaining the desirable objective for

each stage imparts its *particular characteristics* to a couple's interactions, mates would enact and experience the dialectic between fulfillment and defensiveness in somewhat different ways from stage to stage. We convey the essence of these differences in the *twin names* we have given to each stage. The first name stands for the *joint action* mates take to meet the specific objective for that stage, and the second name represents *the quality of their mutual defensiveness.*

For example, newlyweds launch stage one, Coupling and Concealing, by taking on the first objective: to establish their romance as the most important ingredient in their relationship, while also becoming economically and socially viable as a married pair. They do this by *coupling,* deliberately arranging every feature of their workaday lives to support them in making the promises of their love come true. Still, mates become threatened as they progress in making good on all of these promises. So, even as they are merging more deeply, they covertly agree to reduce their fear of loving by *concealing* themselves behind complicities, hiding their innermost thoughts and feelings and withdrawing from each other.

AGING AND RELATIONAL DEVELOPMENT

As we will elaborate in the coming chapters, love-centered mates would want to dovetail the decisions they make for their relational development with the emotional and physical realities of their own aging. Obviously, the activities involved in coupling successfully consume enormous amounts of energy. Given the connection between youth and vitality, it is apparent that early adulthood would be the ideal time for men and women to marry. In that prime period of their lives, they have the greatest intrinsic desire to form a loving relationship—and the greatest amount of strength to put it on a solid footing.

The second objective calls upon mates to intensify their mutual love by deciding on and trying to conceive, and by participating as equally as possible in the processes of pregnancy and birth. After becoming parents, they can turn toward the third objective of maintaining the primacy and gratifications of their own relationship while lovingly nurturing their children.

Consequently, it would be sensible for a couple to have and to rear their offspring while still young enough to cope fully with the exacting demands of infants and toddlers. It would also be prudent for them to complete their family before the wife is exposed to the complications that may accompany conception, pregnancy, and childbirth for women in their late thirties and early forties.

But as mates decide to stop reproducing—a decision linked to the fourth developmental objective—they are bound to notice some signs of their own aging. Looking into the mirror each day, both of them see the creases beginning to furrow into their foreheads, the tiny crow's feet creeping into place at the corners of their eyes, their first wisps of gray hair, a very slight sagging of flesh around their necks and jowls. At the same time, they may be shocked profoundly either by the dramatic worsening of their parents' health or by the death of a parent.

Thus, husband and wife are struck involuntarily with more apprehension about their own survival than they ever felt before. This dread reinforces their inherent self-centeredness, and they become more resistant to opening themselves to the emotional vulnerabilities involved in furthering the positive development of their relationship. Indeed, from this time forward they are more easily upset by all the threats of love.

During the last three stages of their lifelong marriage, therefore, spouses will experience greater and greater difficulty in their struggle to withstand the fear of loving and to develop the closeness of their merger. In fact, the impulse to defend themselves with complicities will begin to take precedence over their commitment to act in favor of fulfilling the promises of love. As they live through these stages, they have to mobilize more willful effort to tip the balance of their relational development for the better—toward meeting the desirable objective for each stage and overcoming the defensiveness aroused in that process.

On the other hand, mates have the freedom to choose how to respond to the implacable changes and preoccupations associated with their aging. Surely, it is within their power to communicate about how they are reacting to their own and each other's indications of physical and mental decline. Likewise, they can collaborate in forging a common understanding of how their separate reactions are affecting the development of their relationship.

With this awareness a husband and wife could minimize the damage of their defensiveness in relating to each other *and* in rearing their maturing children. Then, after their offspring leave home and go off into the adult world, mates would be ready to reap the erotic and emotional pleasures of unmediated intimacy. Similarly, in those years a couple could decide on the best arrangements for leaving their jobs while both of them still have the health and energy to enjoy whatever new activities they agree to take up in their retirement.

Thus, love-centered mates would not arrive at old age only to be shocked by the discovery that one of them feels "outgrown" or hopelessly misunderstood by the other. Rather, on reaching the end of their lives together, they would share the satisfaction of having succeeded in bringing the original fruitfulness of their marital solidarity to its ultimate ripening.

NOTES

1. Sheehy, *Passages.*
2. Freud, Three contributions to the theory of sex. In The basic writings of Sigmund Freud.
3. Rubenstein, C., & Shaver, P. *In search of intimacy.* New York: Delacorte, 1982.
4. Rock, M. *The marriage map: Understanding and surviving the stages of marriage.* Atlanta: Peachtree, 1986.
5. Ruben, H. L. *Supermarriage: Overcoming the predictable crises of married life.* New York: Bantam, 1986.
6. Scarf, M. *Intimate partners: Patterns in love and marriage.* New York: Random House, 1987.
7. Nadelson, C. C., Polonsky, D.C., & Matthews, M. A. Marriage as a developmental process. In C. C. Nadelson & D. C. Polonsky (Eds.), *Marriage and divorce: A contemporary perspective.* New York: Guilford Press, 1984.
8. Levinger, Development and change. In Kelley et al., *Close relationships,* p. 340. See also Ahrons, C. R., & Rogers, R. H. *Divorced families.* New York: Norton, 1987.

8

COUPLING AND CONCEALING

The first objective of love-centered marriage is for newly-weds to establish their romance as a more influential ingredi-ent in their relationship than their complicities. By doing this they affirm the primacy of love over the fear of loving and become passionate companions within the daily context of their married life. Spouses attain this objective through *coupling,* which occurs as they fulfill all the promises of love and integrate its sexual and affectionate components.

Evidently, newlyweds intuitively sense the importance of coupling. Studies show that they generally spend more time together, communicate more openly about everything they do and feel, and participate in more joint activities than at any other period in their married life.[1] Still, new mates can concen-trate on coupling *so* enjoyably that they will *always* feel more inclined to be together than apart, that they will *never* be able to forget—even during the hectic years of childrearing—the joys they created at the start of their marriage. Thus, coupling can "imprint" them with a common standard of how happy they can be as husband and wife. Subsequently, during any impasse of alienation, they can mentally evoke that standard and rouse themselves to restore the gratifications of their past intimacy.

In this respect, the first stage of marriage is analogous to a "critical period" of behavioral development: a limited span of time when some innate potential of an organism *has* to be brought out by a particular kind of stimulation from its environment. Otherwise, that behavior may fail to emerge altogether, or it may develop only in a partial and flawed form. For example, some varieties of birds, raised in isolation from birth, may never properly learn the vocalization specific to their species since they were deprived of hearing those sounds at precisely the period when their own maturation required the input.[2]

Naturally, the unfolding of a marital relationship is very different from the development of a baby bird's capacity to chirp like others of its kind. But coupling is the indispensable stimulation newlyweds need to maximize their potentials for becoming uniquely bonded as a loving pair. If they withhold that vital stimulation from one another and do not learn, right from the start, how to build their romance, they may find it exceptionally difficult later in their marriage to sit snugly together in their nest and, like a pair of lovebirds, sing their own sweet song of contentment.

Consequently, newlyweds have a heavy stake in the outcome of their coupling. At this stage all the promises of love are dazzling in novelty, variety, and abundance: a cornucopia of plenty, inviting mates to dip into it without reserve. Now, committed to be wholeheartedly loving in so many ways, they are particularly vulnerable to the threats of love, and they feel obliged to defend themselves against the fear of loving aroused by those threats.

So, in direct contrast to their coupling, newlyweds form complicities that have the effect of *concealing* themselves from one another, and this concealment, in turn, limits their fulfillment in loving. Yet concealment is just as susceptible to "imprinting" as is coupling. However, if they shift the balance of their relationship from the building of their romance to the maintenance of their complicities, they are in grave danger of jeopardizing their future chances for marital happiness.

MERGING AND WORKING

As Kurt Vonnegut has wryly observed, you are expected, in America, "to paddle your own canoe."[3] But newlyweds have climbed into the same boat. So, paddling in unison, and in the same loving direction, obviously is the way for them to travel through life. Still, having been reared on the ideology of individualism, it is extremely difficult for new mates to overlap the boundaries of their individuality and merge solidly into a collective identity. Repeatedly, they may have to remind each other of their pledge to put individualism permanently behind them and to dedicate their separate lives to the welfare of the relationship they are creating together.

Viewed in a societal framework, coupling is as radical a political activity as any spouses can carry out. Of course, newlyweds are not acclaimed as revolutionaries because they married for a lifetime of loving. But even the most genuinely love-centered mates have to reconcile what they are living for as a couple with their participation in the socioeconomic system. Nowadays, many men and women take on the crucial objective of coupling at the same time they are preparing for or embarking on careers. They need to give very careful thought to the best ways of making their work subservient to their married life. Otherwise, they may become so involved in self-centered strivings as to mount an insidious counterrevolution against their own revolutionary commitment to live for love.

Obviously, mates need a minimal income simply to exist. But why shouldn't they also have enough comfort and amenities to enhance the beauty of their relationship? Why should they be constantly hounded by the spectre of poverty in a country as affluent as America? Yet to make any sort of income, they have to participate in an interpersonal milieu where everyone is motivated to play the game of living by a set of rules more appropriate to a snake pit than a love nest. Accordingly, to obtain and retain a rewarding place in any field of endeavor, they have to compete relentlessly with others.

Faced with this gruesome fact, newlyweds are thrust into a tormenting double bind. If they shun competition altogether, they put their relationship at risk by not having enough money to support themselves and their future offspring. They may also forfeit their chances of doing the kind and level of work that would actualize their particular talents, be beneficial to others, and give them social validation for their accomplishments. On the other hand, if love-centered mates become too zealous in striving for money, recognition, and self-actualization, they not only go against their values and expose themselves to excruciating stress but also seriously endanger their marital satisfaction and harmony.

Renouncing these unpalatable extremes, newlyweds can take a middle course. By moderating their ambitions and choosing their occupations wisely, they can continue to develop their relationship as their chief goal in life and earn enough money for a decent standard of living. In addition, they can extend their values into the world by relating with genuine care to people in their fields and places of work and by joining with others to press for institutional changes that would produce more economic justice and social equality for everyone.

Meanwhile, working mates can take the necessary steps to remain in intimate contact and to funnel more emotional intensity into their own relationship than they do into their jobs. If they share the same vocational interest, they probably have communicated about it from the time they started to fall in love. Now married, they can incorporate their joint interests into their common dream. They can regularly discuss how to deal with issues on which both of them are knowledgeable, and this communication becomes an integral part of their closeness as a couple. So, they quite naturally reinforce the growth of their collective identity.

Spouses with different careers usually need to make more deliberate efforts in educating each other about what they are doing and why. Actually, it can be very stimulating for newlyweds to learn the "ins and outs" of each other's occupation. They can further connect by reading in depth about each other's field, and each can actively contribute toward helping the other to do work of high quality within the aspirational limitations they have set.

As newlyweds cooperate on these vocational matters, they turn each other on and become more lively companions. Well before the end of a working day, such mates may enjoy the romantic fantasy of reporting what they have done when they get home—each getting "high" on the image of the other's warm and welcoming response.

Nevertheless, this sharing can become most menacing. When they were single, they never disclosed themselves so thoroughly to the same person every day. Nor did they invest so much of themselves into the construction of a common future with anyone else. As they merge their inner lives and fuse their separate fates, newlyweds may worry about dissolving into one another, and this threat of losing their personal identity can flip a switch of alarm that calls forth their defenses against the fear of loving.

By the time Marc and Lois Simon married, they had begun their careers. Marc was a social worker, running a program for drug addicts. Lois was a consultant in computer programming, serving agricultural and environmental groups. Despite their occupational differences, Marc and Lois adhered to the same set of values. As veterans of the counterculture, they still lived by the love-consciousness they had acquired, and they viewed their careers as opportunities to act on their beliefs. In addition, they volunteered—as a team—to set up a computer network for the social service agencies in their locality; pooling their separate skills into this project gave them a marvelous feeling of unity and productivity.

Above all, the Simons were determined to make their own relationship an example of loving cooperation. While single, they had gone through the terrible experience of living with potential mates, only to end those relationships in bitterness and regret. Besides, they had seen many of their married friends, even those with "heads" like their own, break up in despair. Marc and Lois were especially careful to be considerate and truthful to each other.

In their first months of marriage, the Simons felt as if they had finally gotten everything together in their lives. During the week, they made telephone contact daily, seeking and getting solace from each other about hassles with their clients. After work, they rushed home to continue their conversations while preparing and eating dinner. When the dishes were washed, they took some time out for silent meditation. They then talked well into the night, until feeling so close they gladly shut up and got into lovemaking. On Saturday mornings they did their volunteer work, conferring with representatives of the agencies they were linking. For the remainder of the weekend, they caught up on their domestic chores, relaxed around the house, and got together with friends.

However, Lois and Marc soon began to back fearfully away from the cooperative unity they had succeeded in creating. In their defense pact, they covertly agreed to compete by getting much more involved in their separate occupations and by drastically curtailing their joint activity as unpaid volunteers. Their complicity also included the stipulation not to talk about this relational change. Thus, they blocked their coupling with an opaque screen of concealment.

Both of them stayed longer at their offices and stopped calling each other. They also took on more clients and broadened the range of their vocational activities. Marc started to write several papers about his clinical innovations, which he planned to publish and present at conventions. Asserting the need to spend time in the library after work and on Saturdays, he was hardly ever available for work on the social service network.

Lois did not object to Marc's revised schedule since she also wanted time for her new project. She had been thinking a lot about producing software under her own name. Now she was beginning to write and test these programs. This extra activity required visits to large computer facilities and much correspondence with potential distributors for her products.

Inexorably, the Simons eliminated their practice of being together for dinner. Each of them would come home at different times, often several hours after the end of their official working day. Marc would stop off at a shopping center to pick up some "fast food" for himself. He would peck at it alone while watching television. When Lois arrived, she would heat up a tray of frozen food and plop down near him to eat and watch the show. Although not totally silent, they acted as if they were too tired for anything but superficial summaries of what they had been doing. Actually, both of them were quite "gone," lost in private ruminations about their separate ambitions. While appearing engrossed in the video dramas, both were spinning elaborate fantasies of the stellar performances they would give in their individual sagas of future success.

Lois portrayed herself as a programming superstar, admired by other experts for her remarkable ingenuity. Her programs would be hailed as exactly what people needed to solve informational problems that had stumped them for years. This praise would also be reflected in brisk sales, permitting her to buy a wardrobe appropriate to her elevated status. Donating money, instead of time, to "good causes," she would not be distracted from her own career.

Munching on taco chips beside her, Marc projected himself as a leader in his field. Whenever he spoke at professional meetings, social workers from across the country would crowd in to hear him and clamor for copies of his papers. His publications would be reprinted in anthologies, and, eventually, he would write the definitive book on the treatment of addiction. Before then, however, he would become the head of his agency and an adjunct professor at a nearby college.

In these solitary daydreams Lois and Marc provided no role for one another, not even a minor supporting part of help-mate in the shadows behind the Great Man and the Great Woman. Rather, in their imaginings, as in the reality they were playing out, each greedily became the exclusive focus of his and her limelight. Of course, given their humane values, they did not actively undermine each other's projects. However, for-saking the common dream that had fueled their romance, they put a halt to spontaneous expressions of interest and offers of help. By keeping secret about the content and extent of their egoistic fantasies, they underscored their rivalry.

Like the Simons, by conjuring up fantasies that magnify their individual prowess, all mates engage in what we refer to, in our first book, as "mental masturbation."[4] Although they may not stimulate themselves physically, a husband and wife can be quite unrestrained in the number of psychological "strokes" they give themselves in their extravagant dreams of glory. Indeed, masturbatory fantasies represent the innermost refuge of willfulness and wish fulfillment. Inside this magical preserve, people can boost their egos beyond any constraint of social reality and any intrinsic barrier of human fallibility. Yet just because mates do not touch their genitals while stroking themselves mentally, they generally do not regard such fanta-sizing as a form of masturbation.

A large percentage of newlyweds also secretly engage in complete masturbation, furtively bringing themselves to or-gasm while mentally enacting a fantasy of exceptional achieve-ment. These mates may find it extremely difficult to open up about their masturbatory activity, having learned, from earliest childhood, to condemn it as socially unacceptable. Of course, as we point out in *Masturbation and Adult Sexuality*, even the most happily married newlyweds may get an urge to masturbate when they feel hemmed in by their marital commitment, "when they want to be completely free to follow their own desires, without any consideration of their mates."[5] In fact, according to Morton Hunt's national survey of sexual behavior, 72% of the husbands in their late twenties and early thirties and 68% of the wives said they were masturbating.[6]

Although commonplace, these separate masturbatory excursions inevitably contradict the essence of a couple's relationship, which involves the fullest possible sharing of their lives, both sexually and emotionally. Whenever they resist such sharing, a husband and wife work against the goal of unity they have set for themselves, and they undermine their enjoyment in being together. Besides, they may feel they are "cheating" sexually on each other, and this guilt further inhibits the willingness to talk about their solitary masturbation. Nevertheless, even if only one mate is secretly active in sexual self-stimulation, he or she can be sure that the other is maintaining an equivalent degree of involvement in private self-centeredness. Indeed, spouses insert such *quid pro quo* clauses into their complicities. They then strictly refrain from peeking into each other's closet.

DEFINING COUPLEHOOD AND REDEFINING RELATIONSHIPS WITH OTHERS

Before they met, newlyweds had separate and close relationships with other people. Naturally, while falling in love, they began to put more of themselves into one another and less into family and friends. However, this attenuation of old relationships is often rife with conflict. Parents and siblings protest vociferously about being neglected or rejected, and friends bitterly resent the erosion of their favored places as confidants.

Prospective mates can try to placate these aggrieved parties by "squeezing out" some time for staying in touch with them. Still, after becoming husband and wife, they cannot develop a love-centered marriage unless they *explicitly* resolve to give *all* other relationships a lower priority than their own. This does not mean they have to cut themselves off from relatives and friends or shy away from new friendships. However, knowing where they stand in devotion to their couplehood, they can no longer presume to have, with others, anything like the degree of intimacy and interdependence that exists between themselves.

This shift in attitude is crucial for newlyweds to make since the desirable objective of coupling hinges upon it. Clearly, to build their romance both of them have to affirm the supremacy of their marriage over any relationships they have with others. To put this affirmation into practice, mates have no choice but to dilute the attachments they might have maintained for a much longer time than they have known each other.

Changing previous ways of interacting with parents is especially difficult for newlyweds. One study of young couples found that the majority did not delineate themselves clearly from their families of origin. These spouses, classified as "traditional," remained so embedded within those familial configurations as to blur the lines of involvement between themselves, as a couple, and their roles as children. However, the same study uncovered a minority of newlyweds who had consciously set up very definite social and emotional markers around their relationship and similarly definite limits on relations with their parents.[7] In keeping with our viewpoint, these mates gave everyone "notice" of the specialness of their couplehood and how much they cherished it.

Of course, the marital gratifications enjoyed by such newlyweds permit them to withstand the troubles of convincing their relatives that they still do love them. But as they relegate familial relationships to positions of lesser importance, these mates emphasize the risk they are taking in depositing the bulk of their emotional eggs into their own relational basket. Thus, they often worry about not being able to fall back on their "Mommies and Daddies" as they encounter difficulties in their marriage, and they may vacillate about how much to hold on to their parents for whatever they might want to get from them.

Both sets of in-laws may similarly resist "giving up" their children. They frequently express this reluctance through various techniques of "seduction"—offering to buy the couple a house in their neighborhood, give them room and board in their own home, or provide detailed advice about exactly how the couple should manage their own affairs.

By jumping at these enticing offers, newlyweds can cripple the growth of their own interdependence. They have to guard against the possibility of weakening their mutual reliability by accepting unnecessary financial subsidies from their parents. Naturally, given the high cost of living, a couple may be sorely tempted to take such aid, and this temptation may be especially strong if each mate is earning only a minimal income at the outset of their marriage. Besides, one or both of them may still be getting educational credentials for a career. So, they could literally not survive, much less set up a domicile, without some outside help.

In such cases mates can apply for loans from lending institutions after having worked out feasible plans for repayment. As an alternative, they might want to get equivalent assistance from parents who can readily afford it. However, in such an arrangement newlyweds need to make sure they are keeping their relational interdependence intact. Thus, they may borrow money from their families and agree to pay it back as soon as possible, or within a fixed period, with or without interest. They may even safely accept an outright gift, *if* they *know* that there are "no strings attached" from their parents' point of view, that they can maintain their mutual respect and integrity without feeling "bought off," and that they will amply repay the generosity of their fathers and mothers by taking excellent care of their marital relationship as they earn more money on their own.

Still, in many cases, newlyweds become so threatened by fulfilling the promise of interdependence that they devise complicities to depend on their parents inappropriately. For example, they begin to take "pocket money" from their parents on the sly, neither telling—nor questioning—one another about what they have taken and what they have done with it. Obviously, these complicities damage the sense of mutual reliance newlyweds had previously built up. Moreover, such mates conceal how much it is costing them, in relational security, to depend so sneakily on their parents; how much energy they are wasting in concerns about pleasing their parental "benefactors" and in obsessive suspicions about what they are doing behind each other's back.

Of course, newlyweds often shoulder the full weight of their economic needs. Without any parental gifts or loans, they work for their joint income and carefully live within their means. They are also scrupulous about discussing the details of their financial plans, each depending on the other to be prudent about ways of managing and budgeting their money. Ironically, however, such a couple can become threatened by the very effectiveness of their mutual reliability.

Even before getting married, Charlotte and Larry Lanier were exemplary in "taking care of business." They never relied on either of their families for help. Proudly, they paid for their wedding out of their combined savings. Only 6 months later, they made a down payment on their own house. It needed a lot of work, but the "price was right." Both of them were very handy, and they had no difficulty meeting the mortgage payments.

Extremely goal oriented, the Laniers had arranged their schedules to have time for fixing up their home. Charlotte, who taught children with learning disabilities, returned from school promptly every afternoon, donned overalls, and, until Larry came home for dinner, scraped, sanded, and painted. Every Saturday at noon, Larry closed his store, which sold hi-fi equipment, and came home to work beside her.

The Laniers were thrilled to see how well everything was turning out, and their success increased their confidence in each other. When Larry was doing a particularly "tricky" job, like cutting an expensive piece of molding to fit against uneven walls, Charlotte knew he would do it perfectly. When she suggested a major revision in their original plans, he trusted her excellent judgment and went along with it.

Still, after their first anniversary, the Laniers were assailed with suffocating feelings of entrapment by having to be so dependable. Impulsively deciding that they "just couldn't put things off" any longer, they went on a shopping spree for household goods, although they had agreed originally to put off furnishing their house until they had paid all the bills for the building materials and had saved more money. Deceitfully, they told themselves what a "good deal" it was to take advantage of the yearly sales going on at all the stores. But they did not acknowledge the financial burden that went along with buying their expensive acquisitions on credit.

Gradually, they started to purchase things unilaterally. On her way home from work, Charlotte would turn off at a mall to browse in the decorating shops. Often, she would "pick up" a lamp or some unusual antique that caught her eye but that they didn't really need. "Oh, well," she mused, "it will only mean a few more dollars on our monthly bill."

Larry became equally irresponsible. On his lunch hours he frequented the stores that neighbored his own. Rubbing the "magical plastic lamp" in his pocket, he'd pull out his credit card and buy a microwave oven even though they already had a costly electric range. Or he would indulge himself with the latest model of a video camera and recorder.

More and more, each of the Laniers acted emotionally detached when the other suggested how great it would be to acquire another new item. "Sure, go ahead," Charlotte mumbled distractedly when Larry brought up the idea of trading in their old car for a station wagon. "Why not?" he blandly concurred when she proposed attaching a screened porch to the kitchen. Nevertheless, as they increased their economic unreliability, they seethed with mutual suspicion and distrust.

Soon, their extravagances put them into a deep financial hole. Charlotte's take-home pay and Larry's profits could no longer cover their escalating bills, and they had to figure out ways to make more money. Charlotte lined up appointments with students to do private tutoring, requiring her to stay out long after regular school hours. Larry kept his store open several nights a week and all day Saturday. Strained by her extra work, Charlotte developed a chronic bladder infection, but she refused to follow the doctor's orders to slow down. Larry could barely manage his additional employees and his expanded clientele. Buckling under this stress, he began to suffer from pains in his lower back. Unable to give each other emotional support, they began instead to give each other grief. Arguing incessantly about who was to blame for their predicament, each futilely berated the other, and both of them felt chained to a joyless treadmill.

Although the Laniers were unaware of our concept of complicity, their mounting unhappiness culminated in a liberating crisis. Distraught to the point of collapse, they finally had to admit that their harassment was entirely of their own doing. Realizing they were headed for disaster, they agreed to help each other "kick" their spending "habit." With their relational reliability again intact, they looked forward to easing up on their work and enjoying their beautiful home.

GIVING PRIORITY TO LOVEMAKING

In more prudish eras the honeymoon was regarded as a couple's first chance to experience the ecstasies of making love. But even today, when intercourse is commonplace—often expected—among couples who are in the process of falling in love, the honeymoon retains its historical emphasis on sexual activity. This focus reflects a lot of intuitive wisdom. Men and women still carry into married life whatever compartments they had imposed between the sexual and affectionate components of love. By openly encouraging complete immersion in the pleasure of lovemaking, the honeymoon permits the bride and groom to make a rapid start toward integrating those components *as a married pair.* Then, after the honeymoon is over, the intense satisfaction they have experienced helps them to sustain their marital romance in the "real world."

However, it is expected culturally that newlyweds are in for a jarring shock upon their return from "cloud nine," that when "the honeymoon is over" they will be unable to maintain whatever level of intimacy, sensuality, and passion they had enjoyed while they had nothing else to do—and nothing else they were supposed to do—except please each other, day after balmy day and night after sultry night.

Of course, the life of newly married couples in the workaday world *is* replete with unending domestic chores and economic obligations. These essential activities *do* sap their time and energy and *do* preoccupy them with many concerns other than making love and nourishing their romance. But of what use is their innate capacity to love if a couple can activate their romantic feelings only rarely and in very special circumstances?

Happily, just as newlyweds can voluntarily preserve the supremacy of their relationship while earning a livelihood and managing their household, they can keep lovemaking foremost among all their relational activities. Now, having sealed their commitment to each other, they have the opportunity to establish a gratifying rhythm of sexual relations and to improve the *quality* of their lovemaking.

Mates who have jobs with flexible working hours can arrange to be at home on the days they want to go to bed. The same applies to those who are self-employed or who work part time. These fortunate couples can set aside time for lovemaking in the morning or afternoon when they are most energetic and least downtrodden by the strains of their occupational activities.

However, most couples work on a conventional "9 to 5" schedule throughout the week. They must reserve lovemaking for evenings, weekends, and holidays. Occasionally, even at those times they may have to forgo the enjoyment of making love to handle unexpected emergencies, such as being asked to rush off to the aid of a stricken relative or an injured friend. Or they may feel it imperative to "show their faces" at a company party, knowing that refusal to attend would be *unquestionably* detrimental to their economic security.

Nevertheless, if newlyweds "imprint" themselves with a pleasurable rhythm for making love, they are constantly motivated to get back into it as soon as possible and to help each other avoid *unnecessary* engagements and distractions. Of course, they may want to partake in all kinds of recreation in their free time. But they cannot simultaneously make love and play tennis. Obviously, they will *always* have to give up some other activity to keep their sexual relations from deteriorating.

Before they do make love, however, it is best for mates to purge themselves of current grudges they may be holding against each other about *any* aspect of their lives. Since they make loving contact by extending their consciousness across any gap in their private thoughts, it is desirable for them to hear each other out. Then they can "tune in" unreservedly on each other.

This switch in mental focus may take some time, and mates may find it difficult to bring their minds and bodies into a common concentration on lovemaking. But, having finally cleared their heads enough to recall that this is "where it's at" for them as married lovers, they can reveal every nuance of their sexual yearnings. Communicating through intercourse, they heighten their erotic sensations in the physical display of their mutual affection, and as they revel in a common stream of sensual delight, they grow fonder of each other.

However, every time they make love newlyweds are confronted with their biological capacity for reproduction. Although they may often yearn to conceive a child, it is desirable for them to feel securely coupled *before* becoming parents. Thus, love-centered mates would want to postpone procreation until they are ready to integrate the challenges of parenthood with their ability to sustain the optimal development of their own relationship. Some couples reach this readiness within a year or two, whereas others may not attain it for many more years.

Nevertheless, even the most loving couples feel some ambivalence about the necessity of using birth control. No matter what form of contraception they employ, their spontaneity and pleasure will be inhibited in *some* way, either during the act of lovemaking or by their vigilance and preoccupation beforehand. Yet mates who spurn contraception are bound to worry about the risks they are taking, and the more they try to conceal their apprehension from each other, the more they withhold energy and reduce their pleasure.

In addition, some contraceptives may cause health problems. On taking birth control pills, for example, some women have suffered from headaches, high blood pressure, blood clotting, or increased susceptibility to vaginal infections.[8] On the other hand, some husbands break out with genital irritations as allergic reactions to the diaphragm or spermicidal cream used by their wives.[9]

Consequently, newlyweds ensure the long-term pleasures of their sexual intercourse by viewing contraception as their common problem—not as either "his" or "hers." Fully sharing this responsibility from the outset of their marriage, they benefit by *jointly* consulting the wife's gynecologist and thoroughly discussing the pros and cons of all contraceptives. As a result, their decision on birth control is based on what device will be safest and most effective for protecting *both* of them from any damage to their health—as well as from an unwanted pregnancy. Then they can utilize their chosen method with maximum enjoyment and reliability. As an added bonus, talking more openly about the nitty-gritty details of contraception may help a couple to communicate more honestly about other aspects of their relationship.

For newlyweds, however, the possibility of indulging in regular, intense, *and* frequent lovemaking is very threatening. Involuntarily drawn to the paradise of sexual consummation, both mates may long to quit their daily struggle with the realities of married life. Wouldn't it be better to stay in bed than to cope with all their responsibilities and all the challenges they see looming ahead? But these yearnings menace their very existence, not only as a couple but as individuals. It is commonplace for newlyweds, who have previously had an "absolutely marvelous sex life," to react with a great fear of loving and to defend themselves with complicities aimed at limiting their sexual enjoyment.

Some couples refrain from going beyond whatever degree of sexual pleasure and experimentation they have found tolerable already. Others may become unreliable about using contraception, making themselves insecure and greatly reducing their pleasure. Many couples turn themselves off so completely that they rarely experience a spontaneous urge to make love. Yielding to their deadened feelings, such mates avoid intercourse altogether; concealing what is really going on between them, they attribute their loss of desire to pressures from their jobs and household activities. Yet they falsely "forget" how well they had previously absorbed the same demands without feeling any diminution in their sexual appetites.

MAKING LOVE WITHOUT PLAYING ROLES

Actually, through their lovemaking newlyweds have an exquisite chance to make progress in transcending their differences in gender roles. Toward this end, both mates have been helped by the women's liberation movement, which stresses the idea that wives *deserve* as much erotic pleasure as their husbands. Thus, women no longer view their failure to have orgasms in sexual intercourse as an expectable source of marital misery that they should endure in silent resignation. Today, even the most "folksy" of women's magazines regularly contain articles on how wives can communicate and satisfy their orgasmic needs while making love; similar messages are presented in all the mass media.

These changes in women's attitudes have been getting across to men, who are becoming aware of what they could do to ensure their wives derive equal gratification in lovemaking. Meanwhile, the male liberation movement has been urging men to express their needs and desires to their wives, to take the lid off their own sensuality, and to be more passive and playful during sexual intercourse. Husbands may now relax from rigid adherence to the old "macho" image of the legendary American cowboy. The "slam-bam, thank you M'am" approach to making love is presently regarded as both selfish to a wife and self-denying to a husband. Men are being advised, instead, to savor the pleasures of foreplay as well as the "big bang" of the climax; to accept the tender and affectionate side of their own nature; and to enjoy erotic advances from their wives without feeling that unless they are taking the initiative at all times, they are losing their manhood.

By kissing and touching her husband *slowly,* and *all over his body,* a wife helps him to learn how to enjoy the sensuality of lovemaking without being so focused on his genital performance and so eager to prove how quickly he can reach the big "O" of intercourse. Simultaneously, *she* increases her own empathy with the nature of his sexual response while getting a fuller understanding of how she can better evoke it.

Reciprocally, a husband learns how to maximize his wife's arousal during foreplay by giving her the kind and amount of stimulation she requests. As he gently explores all parts of her body with his hands and his mouth, he gradually increases his awareness of how to contribute to the fullness of her sexual enjoyment, and he reassures her about the powerful allure of her femininity.

FAMILIARITY WITHOUT CONTEMPT

Mates may also wish to share oral-genital contact as a delightful end in itself. At certain times, when they feel too tired for genital interpenetration or desire a more passive form of lovemaking, they may prefer reaching an orgasm through this form of mutual stimulation rather than through sexual intercourse.

Kissing, licking, and sucking, each mate psychologically incorporates the particular sensations of the other's anatomy. Naturally, this kind of erotic activity can be uniquely pleasurable to them—if they have no inhibitions about it. But it does bring a husband and a wife "face-to-crotch," as it were, with their *intrinsic gender differences,* and it requires them to make oral contact with the fluids discharged in their differing modes of sexual response.

Thus, while progressing in this realm of transcendence, newlyweds may feel so threatened that they quake with the fear of loving. Forming complicities to reduce this fear, they frustrate each other by balking at further advances in accepting their intrinsic differences in gender.

One widespread scenario reflects the male chauvinism still prevalent in society. Establishing a rigid and repetitive pattern, the wife engages in fellatio with her husband without receiving equivalent stimulation from him. Although he fondles, pets, and probes his wife's vagina, he is careful to keep his face and lips away from it. Literally, he avoids facing her genital anatomy because it is the core of her womanhood. For him, as for other men, the structure of a woman's sexual organs symbolizes her ability to lay back and be passive, to get erotic pleasure without having to "perform" for it. Envying that in his wife, a husband is often inclined to quit performing as a man. But that inclination is horrifying to him since he associates it with emasculation. He reacts against it by avoiding oral contact with her genitals.

Playing her part in their complicity, the wife "goes down on him" because she knows how much he wants it. But she does it very reluctantly, resentful of his unwillingness to reciprocate. Besides, since the thought of having to taste or swallow his ejaculate disturbs her, she always takes his penis out of her mouth before his orgasm.

The wife's reluctance and vigilance makes her husband guilty about what she is doing "for him." It also tends to make him feel she is rejecting the very essence of his manhood, and

he winds up with an inner tension that cancels out his pleasure.[10] But how can he complain when he isn't even breathing
on her vulva, much less licking it?

The wife feels just as rejected because her husband never
gives her oral stimulation. Sometimes, she has fantasies of how
wonderful it might feel, and she envies the fact that he expects
her to do anything he wants sexually—just because he is a
man. On the other hand, a woman may believe her vagina is
dirty or has an unpleasant odor.[11] Even today, despite all efforts to dispel their feelings of inadequacy, many women have
this negative attitude about their *own* genitals. So, like these
women, the wife in this complicity feels she has no right to ask
her husband to engage in cunnilingus.

Mates may go on thwarting each other in these ways and
never speak about it. Thus, they conceal not only the threat of
accepting their intrinsic differences but also how they are spiting each other to defend themselves against becoming more
sexually equal.

Obviously, a couple's ability to enjoy oral-genital contact
rests on their willingness to break such a complicity by discussing and resolving whatever specific blocks either of them may
have about accepting one another's sex organs and secretions.
So, newlyweds can overcome conformity to mutually frustrating stereotypes by communicating openly about their sexual
attitudes, habits, and inhibitions.

By changing in these ways, newlyweds give each other
more sexual pleasure. As a result, both of them experience a
greater sense of personal adequacy, and each one feels more
complete as a human being. This feeling of completion enables
them to be more accepting of their own and each other's gender anatomy and physiological functioning. Such personal and
mutual acceptance adds enormously to their marital happiness.

CONCLUDING THE COUPLING STAGE

To stay centered on the welfare of their loving relationship, it is crucially important for newlyweds to remember that
all couples form complicities. Indeed, every husband and wife
resort to these mutual defenses *just because* they fulfill the
promises of love so much that they acutely arouse their fear of

loving. Thus, they can rightly regard their complicities as oblique indications of relational success rather than as unequivocal omens of marital doom.

Still, having begun married life in an unprecedented uplift of happiness, it is a jarring "downer" for new mates to become afflicted with the tensions of their defensiveness. If they forget or never realize that these afflictions are inevitable, they may suddenly feel something is fatally flawed in their marriage. Then, as they maintain their complicities, they may conclude erroneously that they are trapped hopelessly in a morass of misery. They ignore the gratifications they had generated collectively, and they brood helplessly about having to suffer in unremitting emotional pain for the rest of their lives.

Under this dreary cloud, newlyweds may begin to think about divorce as the only way out of a presumably irremediable situation. Eventually, they may split up even though they still share much love and fresh memories of how blissful they felt at the outset of their marriage. In fact, the divorce rate is staggeringly high for mates in the coupling stage. More couples get divorced within the first 2 to 3 years of marriage than at any subsequent interval[12]; most of their undoing may stem from a failure to undo their complicities.

Newlyweds would do well to "hang in there" and cooperate to break as many complicities as possible. After all, if they divorce and marry other people, they are bound to form the same kinds of interpersonal defenses with their new mates. Since there is no way of *ever* escaping from complicities in loving relationships, why not be willing from the outset of marriage to confront what needs to be done in breaking them?

Naturally, couples cannot break all the complicities they contrive as newlyweds. Still, to meet the objective of this stage, it is necessary to keep their complicities from usurping the love they are committed to share. Mates would benefit by considering several key questions as a means for assessing the state of their coupling. Have they succeeded in establishing the supremacy of their romance? How much have they integrated the sexual and affectionate components of love? To what extent have they fulfilled *all* of its promises? Which threats have they been finding most difficult to handle? Which complicities have they broken most easily? Which ones have they been most resistant to giving up?

As these questions imply, a couple's passage through the first stage of marriage can never be perfect in its satisfactions or in its resolution of conflicts. But it is desirable for both mates to feel they have made real progress in relational growth and to experience a common sense of closure about having met the objective of coupling well enough to go forward to the next challenge of deepening their love by becoming parents.

NOTES

1. Orthner, D. K. Leisure activity patterns and marital satisfaction over the marital career. *Journal of Marriage and the Family,* 1975, *37,* pp. 91–102.
2. Thorpe, W. W. Vocal communication in birds. In R. A. Hinde (Ed.), *Non-verbal communication.* Cambridge, England: Cambridge University Press, 1972, pp. 153–176.
3. Vonnegut, K. *Slapstick.* New York: Delta, 1976.
4. Sarnoff, S., & Sarnoff, I. *Masturbation and adult sexuality.* New York: Evans, 1985, pp. 61–65.
5. Ibid., p. 201.
6. Hunt, M. *Sexual behavior in the 1970s.* Chicago: Playboy Press, 1974, p. 86.
7. Goodrich, W., Ryder, R. G., & Rausch, H. L. Patterns of newly-wed marriage. *Journal of Marriage and the Family,* 1968, *30,* pp. 383–391.
8. Nass, G. D., Libby, R. W., & Fisher, M. P. *Sexual choices.* Monterey, Calif.: Wadsworth, 1981, p. 586.
9. Allgeier, E. R., & Allgeier, A. R. *Sexual interactions.* Lexington, Mass.: Heath, 1984, p. 349.
10. Nass, Libby, & Fisher, op. cit., p. 171.
11. Barbach, L. G. *For yourself.* New York: New American Library, 1975, pp. 148–149.
12. Aldous, J. *Family careers.* New York: Wiley, 1978, p. 150.

9

REPRODUCING AND RETREATING

By coupling successfully mates demonstrated the power of their joint creativity. Together, they made their symbolic creation—their loving relationship—gratifying and robust. Now they yearn to transform this intangible offspring of their love into an actual child whose entire existence would personify, enlarge, and celebrate the fruitfulness of their union.

Thus, the second objective of love-centered marriage invites a husband and wife to decide to reproduce, to implement their decision, and to heighten the intensity of their love throughout the entire process of going from the "gleam in their eyes" to the arrival of their baby. Just *wishing* to attain this objective is a great boost to a couple's relational development. Never have they presumed to be so daring and responsible, to put so much faith in their ability to face the unknown. Indeed, they may have to overcome many difficulties in conceiving, in going through pregnancy and birth, or in the unfolding of genetic defects, all of which exceed their power to predict, control, or remedy.

By reproducing, therefore, spouses can improve their ability to coordinate the involuntary and voluntary aspects of loving. In reaching a decision to conceive, they must cease their procrastination and opt in favor of their inner promptings. While attempting to conceive, they must accept their inability to exert voluntary control over the outcome of their intercourse. Obviously, they cannot guarantee that conception will take place precisely when they want it to occur. They are obliged to wait until the wife becomes pregnant and, subsequently, until the baby arrives. Likewise, they cannot willfully determine the gender of the fetus, its intrauterine development, or the exact time and course of its birth.

However, mates *do* have the power to *choose how they will relate to each other* during those involuntary intervals of waiting. In keeping with the desirable objective of this stage, they can decide to intensify their romance by fulfilling all the promises of love in ways that pertain specifically to the periods of decision making, conception, pregnancy, and birth. Knowing they are courageous enough to accept the benefits and burdens of reproducing, spouses become stronger as individuals. They also increase their mutual respect, setting into motion a self-fulfilling prophecy about how loving they will be as parents.

Although they can fulfill the promises of love in special ways at each juncture in the reproductive process, mates are prey to the accompanying threats. Consequently, they defend themselves against their fear of loving by devising complicities in which they temporarily *retreat* from reproducing *and* from a concomitant increase in their intimacy. They may shy away from the decision to procreate. Even after making a decision, they may avoid putting it into effect. Then, once having conceived, they may withdraw excessively from one another.

DECIDING TO CONCEIVE

By meeting their past commitments, spouses validated their mutual trust and cemented their collective identity. They now are considering an irrevocable pledge of love and devotion not only to each other but also to any child they produce. Of course, they can revel in constructing new romantic images for their common dream by exchanging fantasies of how they will literally merge their separate beings by combining their genes, the biological core of each one's uniqueness, and they can anticipate how well their individual characteristics will be fused within their child. Regarding their imagined offspring as an embodiment of the archetypical wish to ensure their personal and relational continuity, they can also look forward to satisfying their existential longings for immortality as individuals and as a couple.

Still, the commitment to become parents is more sobering than any they have made since agreeing to marry. Now, they are contemplating an offer of unfailing dependability to a human being who will have to rely on the success of their unity and interdependence for many years after his or her birth.

The solemnity surrounding this decision encourages spouses to be fully accountable for telling the truth. They have the greatest possible incentive to say what they mean and to mean what they say. To guarantee the future of their marital well-being, each needs unequivocal reassurance of the other's motivation and aptitude for parenting. Both want to know that their desires for a child are equally intense and authentic, that one partner is not merely accommodating the other's stronger wish for a baby. Each needs to believe in the other's ability to be a source of emotional support *no matter what happens* after they decide to conceive. Certainly, neither mate can feel secure about opting for parenthood if he or she thinks the other will fold up under the pressure of any complications that might occur. Similarly, both need to feel they can count on each other, *without any reservations,* to cooperate in providing the patience, wisdom, and firmness for guiding their child's physical and emotional development.

Envisioning another person to feed, clothe, and shelter, a couple's financial arrangements for the future become linked with sheer survival. Despite their intention to share all their marital roles equally, pregnancy may interfere with a wife's earning power. It is thus highly appropriate for couples to ask themselves how reproducing could affect their family income. How long will the wife remain on her job during pregnancy? How soon do they want her to return to work after their baby is born? What maternity benefits does she have? Does the husband have equivalent paternity benefits? Can they afford to have a child if she is required, for reasons of health, to stop working altogether? What about medical provisions? Do they have insurance to cover prenatal care, hospitalization, and other expenses they may incur after the baby is born? Or do they have enough money saved up for those purposes?

While spouses may answer these practical questions to their mutual reassurance, they remain vulnerable to the psychological threats connected with irrevocable increases in their interpersonal merger and interdependence. Therefore, although they have no rational reasons to delay reproduction, they may yield to those apprehensions by shrinking away from a definite decision to conceive.

Some mates feel particularly threatened by the thought of how thoroughly conception will overlap the boundaries of their individuality. Anticipating an irreversible loss of their personal identities, they worry about "losing out" to each other by having a child. So, they formulate complicities in which they forestall a decision to reproduce and retreat, instead, into intense occupational rivalry. Thus, they defensively strive to emphasize their separateness.

The Clarks designed just such a scenario. Married for 3 years, they had talked about having a child. Yet they were adamant about postponing parenthood indefinitely in favor of pursuing their careers. Ruth, a corporate executive, wanted to put it off for "at least" a few more years when, she claimed, she would be securely established in her position. She also believed but did not tell George, her husband, that motherhood would put her at a comparative disadvantage, allowing him to "go upward and onward" in his dental career, while forcing her out of the vocational arena.

George was well aware of Ruth's competitiveness. But since he secretly felt just as rivalrous toward her, he could not accuse her of wanting to "get one up" on him without exposing himself to the same accusation. He also expressed a desire for more time to consolidate his practice, and, like Ruth, he advocated a delay in conception until his professional progress could not be blocked by the demands of childrearing.

Sometimes, however, the Clarks showed signs of "weakening." After one very successful week, George felt moved to start a discussion about when they should try to conceive. But Ruth immediately clamped a lid on his opening, insisting that she was still not completely secure about her job. George acquiesced without protest since her insistence inflamed his own ambitions, which were simmering quietly under his stated craving to be a father.

On a subsequent occasion, after a wretched day at her office, Ruth began to wonder about the blessings of her own vocational success. In an unguarded moment of doubt, she asked when they really ought to have a child. This time *George* became indignant. How could they possibly go ahead while he had some empty hours in his weekly schedule? Besides, he was just offered an appointment to teach at his old dental school where he could do research that would make a name for him in the field. No, they *had* to wait. Spurred by his reaction into vivid fantasies of her own advancement, Ruth quietly dropped the subject.

The Clarks stuck to these rationalizations as they continued to compete in their pursuit of personal achievement. Then, the night before Ruth's thirty-fourth birthday, she had a full-blown panic over the fact that she was "running out of time." Like so many of her female contemporaries, she *suddenly felt* with implacable force what she *actually knew* all along: it is medically advisable for a woman to have her first baby before she is 35—especially if she intends to have more than one child. She berated herself for worrying more about her career than her health—and the health of any baby she could have. Curling up in George's arms, she was seized by a convulsion of sobs between which she pleaded for both of them to stop procrastinating.

Shattered by her outburst, George could not deny the truth of her concern. Given his training, he too had been worrying about the same realistic dangers. How could he justify any further delay? Of course, they would have to make some changes in their lives. His research might not progress as rapidly as he had hoped, and Ruth might not get a promotion. But who are we kidding? How can we possibly compare any of those accomplishments to how wonderful it would feel to have our own child? If we're ever going to be parents, we have to start *now!*

In deciding, finally, to reproduce, the Clarks had to lessen their rivalry and discard their rationalizations. Otherwise, the possibility of enlarging their collective identity would have remained an unrequited promise of love, dividing rather than uniting them.

For many other couples, the threat of increased interdependence motivates their vacillation. In one widespread complicity mates act as if the choice to have a child really is not theirs to make. These couples tacitly agree to take chances about conceiving. Forming a pact to avoid any discussion of what they are doing, both of them pretend they are not taking the risk of having an "accident."

The wife becomes erratic about inserting her diaphragm when they have intercourse. Sometimes she does and sometimes she doesn't. In her own mind she makes all kinds of excuses for her behavior: it's too cold to get out of bed, she's already too aroused and doesn't want to spoil her enjoyment, or she's fed up with having to be vigilant about contraception.

When her husband sees that she isn't getting up to go to the bathroom—as she has always done before becoming involved in foreplay—he *knows* she has not inserted her diaphragm. However, as a full accomplice in this contraception charade, he pretends not to notice. Meanwhile, he lies to himself, "If we're meant to become parents, she'll get pregnant. If it's not meant to be, she won't. So, why worry about it?"

The more mates persist in these mutual deceits, the less dependable each one feels and the more distrustful both of them become. Sometimes, however, a husband and a wife are fortunate to get so anxious about what they are doing that they catch themselves before their dangerous complicity catches them. Thus, they grow increasingly nervous whenever they have intercourse, especially on those occasions when they are "forgetting" to use contraception. Eventually, they spew out their tension in a big blowup. The husband may erupt first, ventilating his tormenting mistrust by attacking his wife for being unreliable. "What the hell are we doing to each other? Wouldn't it be better to *make a definite agreement and plan* the whole thing? Besides, if we can't trust each other now, how can we expect to count on one another if we do have a baby?"

Alternatively, the wife may expose their complicity, letting loose her boiling resentment about being the only one saddled with the mechanics of contraception. "Why didn't *you* bring the issue up sooner? You *never* mentioned it. What if *you* had to use a goddam diaphragm? Would you be as dependable as I've been up until now? How can I expect you to be a good parent if you can't even share the responsibility for birth control?"

By airing such recriminations and anxieties, mates realize the value of becoming more mutually reliable, and this insight could be just the impetus they need to end their indecisiveness. They then can honestly agree either to go forward with conception or to keep on using contraception diligently.

However, couples often fail to end their contraception charade soon enough to make a clear-cut decision about conceiving a child. In toying deceitfully with one another, many spouses "get caught." When the wife *does* get pregnant, they are *forced* to decide what they want to do next. They can "let nature run its course" and accept the pregnancy, or if they feel too unprepared to become parents, they can opt for an abortion.

Such a conflict gravely weakens a couple's sense of interdependence. Ironically, they got into this unpleasant situation because they *would not* depend on each other to make a responsible decision. Now they must come to an even more difficult agreement about whether or not to terminate the life they started from the falseness of their complicity. Consequently, they may begin a round of withering disputes, regretting their previous unreliability and verbally lacerating each other for it.

Spouses who choose abortion are prone to feelings of ambivalence and distrust, even after the procedure is over and the wife emerges from it with her physical health unimpaired. Similarly, couples who "decide by default" to have the baby they "accidentally" conceived often feel resentful, martyred, and joyless throughout pregnancy and may remain unforgiving and hostile after their child is born. Such parents are likely to displace their mutual recriminations onto their child, whom they scapegoat as the cause of their own failure in interdependence. They may also increase the emotional distance between themselves, their detachment indicating how threatened they still feel about being either dependable for or dependent on each other.

In many cases, however, an "accidental" conception may shock a couple into a new level of honesty. Burnt by reacting defensively to the threat of interdependence, spouses often wake up to the fact that they can readily turn it into a promise of love fulfilled; and, by pledging to be more reliable, they are able to deal with the conception as a unified team.

If they choose to have the baby, a couple is motivated to overcome the remnants of their ambivalence before its arrival. Taking full responsibility for *this* decision enables them to implement it by doing all the planning necessary to welcome their child into an emotionally warm and economically secure environment.

On the other hand, if they decide on an abortion, mates may approach it with a new mutuality of emotional support. Being considerate, kind, and tender, they minimize the inevitable suffering involved in this painful choice. And, when the abortion is over, they maintain the momentum of their deepening interdependence by using contraception faithfully until they reach a deliberate, well-considered, and unequivocal decision to have a child.

Exhilarated by talking about the possibility of conception, we too felt very threatened. True, we *thought* we were emotionally ready for this challenge. We were also doing everything possible to anticipate the economic demands of pregnancy and parenthood. Irv was earning a good salary as a psychotherapist at the University of Michigan Student Health Service and supplementing his income by teaching an undergraduate course. Sue was making just as much money as a psychiatric social worker at the State Mental Hospital. We planned on her working for at least a year so we could save most of her salary. In addition, we knew her Blue Cross policy required that she be insured for at least 6 months before becoming pregnant to qualify for hospitalization benefits during delivery. So we were very careful about accommodating those stipulations in our plans.

Still, could we *really* depend on each other to raise a child? What if we were still too immature? What if our relationship proved too fragile to withstand the constant presence and demands of a baby?

Of course, we regarded ourselves as much too dependable to play Russian Roulette with our decision to conceive. Instead, like some contemporary couples, we used the fearful state of world affairs to mask and rationalize our fear about taking on such a heavy responsibility. At that time a, "cold war" was raging on the symbolic "front" with the Soviet Union, and a shooting war in Korea seemed likely to erupt. Inflation was rampant without any end in sight. Food, housing, baby clothes, and diapers were soaring in price, and many of our friends who had recently become parents complained about their struggle to make ends meet.

Rather than admit the *inner* threat of becoming more interdependent, we attributed it entirely to the menace outside of us. Falsely, we wove those *external* dangers into the scenario of our complicity, pointing to those conditions as the source of our vacillation. Engaging in dismal discussions on the uncertainty of everyone's future, we lamented over how little we could depend upon the world to give us the reassurance we wanted before having a child. What if Irv was called back into service and shipped overseas? Could Sue cope with an infant on her own? Would Irv be strong enough to bear such a separation, knowing he was leaving Sue and our baby to risk his life in a war we believed was unnecessary?

After procrastinating in this way for several months, we realized that the more we tried to retreat from making a definite decision, the less we felt we could count on each other *or* society to give us the crucial push to "go over the line." Ultimately, our desire to become parents outweighed our concerns about international tensions and the national economy. Trusting ourselves to do the best we could to take care of business on our own "home front," we finally decided to have a child. By that time, Sue was sure of receiving the maternity benefits from her insurance. Allowing 9 months for gestation, we looked forward to a spring birth when the weather would be ideal for taking a newborn baby out-of-doors. Finally, in June of 1950 we threw away our crippling caution and began to make love more passionately than ever before.

MAKING LOVE TO MAKE A BABY

Once spouses decide to conceive, their sexual intercourse gives them a fresh appreciation for one another. They infuse their physical contact with increased tenderness and affection, and the specialness of this emotional exchange feeds into their erotic sensibilities. As a result, they discard many old compart-

ments between their psychological affinity and their bodily reactions. By blending the affectionate and erotic components of
their love more fully, they add tremendous energy to their romance.

Every time we went to bed, we were charged with ela-
tion. This could be *it!* This could be *the* moment when we
would ring the great gong of conception! Of course, we never
could be sure we had succeeded. But this uncertainty did not
cause us any apprehension. Instead, it added to the excitement
of our gamble with the uncontrollable forces of impregnation
that would meld one of Irv's sperm with one of Sue's eggs into
the evolving miracle of *our* child.

Repeatedly, we were awed by the fact that a new life
could result from the same sexual coupling we had done so
often in the past. There we were, doing nothing different at
all, and yet now it could be *for real!* This marvelous drama
affected us more powerfully than any aphrodisiac we could
have taken. Feeling so turned on, we could hardly wait for the
next chance to make love.

Mates also benefit, as we did, from freeing themselves of
all the unpleasurable constrictions of contraception. For the
first time in their marriage, neither one has to think about any
form of birth control. Without any device or chemicals to trouble their minds or reduce their physical sensations, they can be
completely spontaneous, making love in the most natural and
holistic way. They don't have to mar the delights of foreplay by
stopping to insert a diaphragm or don a condom, and they
don't have to worry about the health hazards of the pill or an
I.U.D. Rather, they amplify their excitement largely because
they are *planfully* trying to achieve the very outcome they had
just as carefully sought to prevent. Besides, since they joyfully
hope they will conceive whenever they have intercourse, they
are inclined to make love more frequently than ever before.

Both partners now have the greatest incentive to maximize the depth of their sexual interpenetration. The more
deeply they "get into" each other emotionally, the more complete will be their erotic pleasure. But it is also highly functional for the husband to thrust his penis as far as possible into
his wife's vagina as he approaches orgasm. This thrusting en-
sures the furthest reach of his ejaculate, which must deliver

his sperm cells up through his wife's cervix, into her uterus, and then make contact with the egg cell that has been released into her fallopian tubes—where conception usually occurs.[1]

Reciprocally, it is best for the wife to be as relaxed and lubricated as possible during intercourse. By yielding happily to her husband's thrusts and climactic ejaculation, she can receive his sperm with the greatest accessibility to her ovum. And when she enjoys sexual intercourse to orgasm, many of the physical reactions that accompany her climax may serve to facilitate conception.

Of course, it is not necessary for a woman to have an orgasm in order to become pregnant. However, Masters and Johnson have found that strong contractions in the "orgasmic platform"—the outer third of a woman's vagina—that occur during climax can help to force out all the semen from her husband's penis. Right after orgasm her uterus rapidly descends, dipping the mouth of the cervix into the seminal pool and making it easier for the sperm to move up into her uterus and fallopian tubes. Without orgasm this lowering of the uterus occurs more slowly.[2]

Recent research has also found that uterine suction immediately follows orgasm, helping to draw up the sperm more effectively for fertilization. This suction may be due to the hormone oxytocin, released during orgasm, which stimulates muscular waves in the woman's vagina, uterus, and fallopian tubes from an *outer to an inner* direction.[3]

Now, mates long to give up all self-control and stay forever in a mindless ocean of sensual pleasure. In fact, most authorities advise couples to engage in sexual intercourse every 2 to 3 days in order to maximize their chances for conception.[4] Yet a husband and a wife can become very threatened by this prescription for immersion in erotic fulfillment, especially since they feel more tempted than ever before to forgo all their worldly responsibilities and do nothing else but make love. Of course, they know that abstinence is not conducive to reproducing. So, they do not renounce sexual relations. However, to quell the fear stimulated by their erotic desires, they contrive complicities for *minimizing their feelings of pleasure,* as exemplified by the case of Alice and Martin Benedict.

The first time Alice stopped using a diaphragm, she and

Martin were ecstatic. For about 3 weeks they made love every day, more frequently than ever before. But the spontaneity and pleasure of their sexual contacts soon began to overwhelm them. Feeling happily spent by the morning, they longed to luxuriate in bed, and they hated to get up and go to work. On a few occasions Alice came in late for the important editorial meetings at the publishing house where she worked. Similarly, arriving at his law office much later than usual, Martin could barely keep his mind on the complicated briefs he had to prepare.

Failing to conceive for 2 months, the Benedicts began to question their fertility, long before they had a realistic basis for suspecting any difficulty. Creating a scenario to enact their unwarranted concern, they agreed to have Alice take her temperature every day to detect exactly when she ovulated, and they avoided intercourse except when the temperature chart suggested she was ovulating. They also strictly avoided orgasms, by any means, until the time of the month when *they* thought Martin's ejaculation could be put to its best physiological use. This procedure, which they initiated without any medical consultation, cast a pall over their sexual spontaneity. But the Benedicts rationalized their behavior by saying it was best for Martin to "save up" his sperm for Alice's most fertile days. Soon, their bedroom took on the ambience of an examining room in a gynecologist's office, and their perfectly timed copulations became as emotionally bland as artificial insemination.

Like the Benedicts, a couple may persist in denying their actual reasons for performing the mechanics of intercourse. But their rigid and medical approach makes their lovemaking more frustrating and tense than pleasurable and relaxing. Even if they do not have any bodily barriers to pregnancy, such mates could seriously diminish their chances of conceiving by maintaining this high level of emotional stress. Actually, among couples complaining of infertility, an estimated 20% have *no* detectable organic problems.[5] It is known that stress can prevent ovulation or cause an abnormal chemical balance in a woman's cervical secretions, either killing or immobilizing her husband's sperm. Stress can also weaken the production and motility of a man's sperm, and it can cause muscle spasms in his sperm ducts, interfering with the normal transmission of those cells.[6]

For a minority of couples, it may take only a month of trying for the wife to become pregnant. But most spouses go through a much longer period before conception takes place. Only one fourth of all couples conceive in the first month; on average, it takes 4 to 6 months. Some couples have to keep on trying for a whole year, even when they are in perfect health. Consequently, most doctors suggest waiting for that length of time before consulting them.[7]

Sometimes, however, when a couple does not conceive for a year, both mates may begin to doubt their reproductive powers. Threatened by the need to increase their interdependence by confronting this problem, they defend themselves from facing the possibility that one or both of them might have some physical obstacle to conception. They devise a complicity in which they *pretend not to recognize* that they could be infertile, and they resist taking the responsibility of going *together* for a medical consultation. Instead, *each suspects the other* of having a secret malady, yet they do not voice what is on their minds.

The wife may wonder if her husband knew he was sterile before they got married. Maybe he had a bad case of the mumps, ruining his capacity to produce sperm. Or maybe he had something much more shameful—a sexually transmitted disease! *That* could certainly have wiped out his ability to reproduce. But even if he didn't have an illness, couldn't he be lowering his sperm count by exposing himself so often to the heat in the steam room at his gym?

Similarly, the husband privately condemns his wife. Could she possibly have had gonorrhea before he met her? Perhaps some scar tissue was left in her fallopian tubes that was preventing fertilization. Or maybe she had an abortion that was badly botched. Could her uterus be so messed up that it can't ever be fixed?

Stewing in the rancid juices of their suspicions, these mates get caught up in a vicious cycle of mutual misgivings. Each becomes more and more unreliable in the eyes of the other, and they actually begin to act less and less dependably. Yet they behave as if no problem exists; while they continue trying to conceive, their defensiveness widens the gulf of detachment between them. Through this mutual and unexpressed paranoia, a couple can sink quickly into a slough of relational stress and disharmony; by preventing themselves from taking any action to remedy what might be a *physical* problem, they reinforce their complicity.

By contrast, mates can relieve their tensions by talking about what they have been thinking. This communication permits them to let go of groundless suspicions about one another. Then they can consult a doctor to find out what malfunction is at the root of their infertility. Given this information, they can reaffirm their relational reliability by doing whatever is necessary to improve their reproductive ability.

INFERTILITY

Unfortunately, in 15% of all couples, one or both mates have a physical condition leading to infertility.[8] Although it was typically viewed as a "female problem" in the past, infertility among mates is equally attributable to both sexes. In 40% of infertile couples, the problem is with the husband and, in another 40%, with the wife. For the remaining 20%, both spouses are problematic or the cause of their infertility is unknown.[9] However, gender stereotypes die hard. Even today, many men associate fertility with manhood. Husbands often resist going for a medical examination, reluctant to risk the deflation of their "masculinity" by being found with a defect in fertility. Nevertheless, testing the man first is much easier than doing a diagnostic work-up for a woman.[10] It is a relatively simple procedure to obtain and evaluate a sample of semen. A woman, on the other hand, may require not only examination of her internal organs but also testing of her hormone levels, ovulatory cycle, and vaginal secretions. In some cases exploratory surgery may also be necessary.[11] Like a husband, a wife may dread the loss of her "femininity" if some weakness in her reproductive system is detected. Female "barrenness" has even been considered a legitimate basis for divorce. Thus, infertile mates need to muster an exceptional degree of compassion for themselves and an equal amount of empathy for one another.

Frequently, these husbands and wives must take a medical orientation to their lovemaking—*out of necessity*—doing it only in the exact manner and at the precise time suggested by their physician. Naturally, these couples can continue to express their mutual affection whenever they make love. But intercourse on a medical regimen can produce severe stress that is exacerbated by uncertainty about the outcome. It would be good for infertile couples to know it is estimated that 60% of them can overcome their difficulties and that the medical techniques for reversing infertility are continually improving.[12]

Still, some mates become so distraught they want psychological assistance. To meet this need, psychotherapists have been going beyond the usual methods of marital counseling, organizing groups in which couples can share their feelings and aid each other in coping with their common problems. Similarly, on their own initiative couples have organized groups for mutual help.[13]

PREGNANCY

Whenever they do conceive, mates can exult in their good fortune, feeling blessed by their ability to fuse into one. Knowing it is possible for them to create a child, they are apt to feel deeply validated about their suitability for each other.

The expansion of the wife's abdomen is joyful evidence of their success in expanding the boundaries of their individuality. Later, when "quickening" begins, the couple can share the exhilaration of seeing *and* feeling movements made by the active fetus, and they can rightly regard the process of gestation as *their* pregnancy—not merely as the wife's.

Pregnancy provides spouses with an additional and external source for building their romance. Previously, they could anchor their loving interactions only in *mental* representations. But now they can regard the fetus as a tangible locus of their collective identity, and they can see themselves as united in love within the physical reality of a being who is actually growing as a fruition of their common dream.

Spouses magnify their romance by melding their individual talents and efforts in preparations for their infant's arrival. Some couples remodel an extra room they had been using for their individual hobbies into a nursery, gladly relinquishing their "personal space" for the cooperative project of raising their baby under optimal conditions. Others get involved happily in the challenge of finding and moving to a larger home where the literal expansion of their living quarters reflects the physical and psychological expansion they have already achieved through conception.

Nevertheless, pregnancy is also threatening proof of how completely the wife and husband have merged their individual beings, and both may become panicky at the thought of permanently losing their personal identity. No longer able to retreat from conception, spouses often defend themselves by *retreating from each other.* Impeding their closeness and cooperation, couples may establish a complicity based on controversies over whose preference will prevail in naming their baby. They argue vehemently about who should select the name or whose relatives the child should be named after. This scenario can be especially ghoulish if the parents or grandparents of both mates are already deceased. In such cases a couple may become embroiled in a tenacious struggle, each one greedily vying to co-opt *their* child as a means for carrying on the identity of *his or her own family.*

Because this form of rivalry is so direct *and* so utterly absurd, spouses may be struck by their own folly before they do appreciable damage to their relationship. Then, after a hearty laugh at themselves, they can reduce their competitiveness sufficiently to agree on a name that gives neither of them a "one-up" advantage over the other.

In other cases, however, spouses "go underground" and compete indirectly through masturbatory daydreams that they do not disclose. The wife has extravagant fantasies about how she is going to outdo her husband in being the "best parent" in their child's eyes. Meanwhile, the husband inflates balloons inside his head about how much better a parent he will be, especially as the mightiest of all breadwinners.

In addition, many mates secretly resort to physical masturbation, accompanied by whatever mental stimulation they need to glorify themselves.[14] Both spouses may privately justify this practice as a "substitute" for sexual intercourse that could become more awkward and less enjoyable as pregnancy progresses. However, the secrecy of their behavior indicates its true meaning as an individualistic escape from honest interaction with one another.

These spouses may keep on avoiding a return to honesty about their masturbatory secrets. With birth and parenting looming before them, they may feel too insecure for mutual self-disclosure. However, they eventually will have to react to their child's display of sexual self-stimulation. So, if they can bring themselves to communicate with each other—*now*—about their own masturbation, they will be equipped emotionally to educate their child about it in a candid and accepting manner.

Mutual Accountability

Almost as if by "divine design," the shift in attitude required for conception—from the pursuit of personal aspirations to the attainment of an interpersonal goal—prepares mates for the degree of interdependence desirable for prospective parents. Relying upon one another, they can meet the vicissitudes of pregnancy; maintain their physical, mental, and economic well-being; and make all the preparations to welcome their child into an emotionally secure environment.

The more mates depend on each other, the more they reinforce their mutual trust and their romantic image of themselves as a trustworthy pair, building their confidence to be loving parents. Still, because of her physical vulnerability, a pregnant wife cannot deny that she might have to call on her husband to play the role of compassionate nurse in coping with unforeseen problems. Sometimes, when there is a possibility of miscarriage, a woman may have to stay in bed for weeks, and she might have to give up her job prior to giving birth. In such a situation, she would want to count on her husband to take care of her, to run their household, and to relate lovingly to her.

The husband also has to face these possibilities and be ready to sustain an income for both of them. However, he is just as dependent on his wife's willingness to be reliable in preserving her health and morale. If complications in pregnancy force her to leave her job, she is the one who is carrying *their* child. Thus, while he provides help for her, he is also dependent on her to do everything possible to remedy her condition and protect the fetus.

Because couples are required to increase their interdependence in these crucial ways, the actual reality of their pregnancy can be very threatening. With their baby soon to appear, husbands and wives often reexperience the old threat of being "stuck" with one another forever. Under these circumstances, they may want to retreat from the responsibilities they have assumed in conceiving, and they may form complicities by which they *reduce* their relational reliability.

In one widespread scenario, spouses turn away from each other in detachment and distrust, and they covertly agree to rely instead on their parents. Whenever the wife has any question regarding pregnancy, she telephones her mother for detailed instructions about what she should do. She may even ask her mother to accompany her on visits to the doctor. Other women routinely take their mothers along when shopping for the baby, relying totally on their mother's taste, and they put more credence in their father's opinions than in their husband's about how to remodel a room for their child.

Sometimes, the wife resumes a childlike dependency on her father. As a little girl, she often relied on "Daddy's" judgment on many important matters. Now feeling distrustful of her own husband, she consults "Dear Old Dad" for advice on managing her finances or on how to continue her career after she gives birth.

Resuming exactly the same kind of clinging with his own parents, the husband does not protest against the wife's behavior—just as she raises no objection to his. "After all," the husband reasons as he retreats in distrust from his wife, "didn't my mom understand my problems better than anyone else? And she *never* failed me." So *he* starts to call *his* mother whenever he is anxious about the pregnancy, questioning her on topics ranging from how to treat his wife's morning sickness to what kinds of furnishings are best for the baby. He might also arrange frequent visits to his parents' home, where he can be fed by his mother who happily slaves all day to prepare his favorite dishes.

At the same time, the husband begins to act like a naive boy in relating to his father. He airs his vocational dilemmas with him, instead of with his wife, and he gets "The Old Man" into lengthy conversations about how to invest savings for his family's future.

Other mates contrive complicities of unreliability in matters of health during pregnancy. In their scenario, the Brenners endangered themselves *and* their future offspring. Kathy, a legal secretary, was well aware of the detrimental effects of smoking on fetal development. Still, she smoked her usual pack or two every day, viewing her behavior as essential for "getting some relief" from the pressures of working during pregnancy. She also told herself that smoking helped her to stay on the diet her doctor had recommended.

Her husband, Carl, did not *insist* that she break her unhealthy habit. Sometimes, he would mumble a "dig" about her puffing like a chimney. But he usually ignored her smoking, knowing that in return for his permissiveness, she would tolerate his growing alcoholism. Struggling to "make it" as a commercial artist in a high-powered advertising agency, Carl felt "entitled" to stop off at a bar on his way home from work every day—just to relax with a quick drink.

Over a period of months, he began coming home later and later—and drunker and drunker. Eventually, he could barely pull himself out of bed to go to work in the morning. Although Kathy did bark at him occasionally for jeopardizing his job, she never put Carl "up against the wall" about his drinking. How could she demand that he stop, once and for all, without inviting him to make exactly the same demand about her smoking?

By avoiding a decisive confrontation, the Brenners have increased their individual unreliability *and* their mutual distrust. As a result, they are depriving each other of love throughout pregnancy while suffering, and permitting their unborn child to suffer, the negative consequences of their destructive pact. Ironically, because of this defensive retreat from interdependence, Kathy and Carl could be saddled with much heavier responsibilities, once their baby is born, than any they tried to shed during pregnancy. Kathy's smoking may cause physical and mental impairments in their child.[15] Or even if they are extraordinarily lucky and the baby is not handicapped, they will not be able to give it proper care if Carl is fired from his job for excessive drinking.

Equality within Diversity

Having proven the normalcy of their reproductive organs, spouses may feel they have finally attained "real" manhood and womanhood.[16] Seeing each other as unquestionably equal in their contributions to conception, they reach a new plateau in their ability to appreciate and accept their intrinsic gender differences. Now they can marvel at nature's way of saying, "Vive la difference!" in the creation of human life.

However, mates can be very threatened by the opportunity that pregnancy offers for continuing to transcend their differences in gender. Both may balk at acknowledging the biological limitations of each one's gender in the process of gestation and birth. For example, a husband may feel very envious of his wife's capacity to carry their child within her for 9 months, to give birth to it, and to feed it from her own breasts. This is a formidable combination of powers that nature reserves exclusively for the female sex and that induces feelings of inadequacy and deprivation in men. Indeed, according to Karen Horney, even young boys have expressed "wishes to possess breasts or to have a child,"[17] and Benjamin Spock has also remarked on how much boys envy girls for their ability to bear children.[18]

A wife can just as intensely covet the freedom her husband enjoys from the danger and pain of bearing and giving birth to children. Contemplating her exclusive assumption of these physical burdens, she may fret about "what we women have to go through." She may also regard the prospect of breast-feeding as a physically draining and emotionally coercive chore that will ruin the shape of her bosom, restrict her participation in other activities, and keep her tied to a stereotyped gender role.

Consequently, a husband may want to spite his wife because she *is* pregnant, while she wants to spite him because he is *not!* Together, they contrive complicities in which they express their spiteful feelings and "get back" at each other. Sometimes they can be downright vengeful, ostentatiously spurning each other's company to spend time in gender-typed pursuits, either alone or with members of their own sex. Naturally, mates are also spiting themselves in these sexist defense

pacts that impede their ability to accept their gender differences and to progress in relational equality.

Appropriating the fetus as hers—and hers alone—the wife
may blot out the husband's part in its creation. Like a queen
bee, she considers him a mere drone. Quitting her job, she in-
dulges her "feminine" whims by becoming excessively focused
on her appearance. Constantly looking at herself in the mirror
and checking her weight, she spends lavishly on chic maternity
clothes without consulting her husband. Whenever she has any
worries about her pregnancy, rather than discuss her concerns
with him, she telephones a "girlfriend" for advice. Afraid of
losing her sex appeal by exposing her husband to the nitty-
gritty details of her physiological changes, she never suggests
that he go with her to the obstetrician for her regular examina-
tions. When shopping for the layette, she relies totally on the
judgment of the saleswomen. At home she refuses to let her
husband get into *her* act, rejecting his suggestions about what
they should buy for the baby.

Meanwhile, the husband adopts a pose of "masculine"
perfection in an effort to become the "top man" in his field. Of
course, he may rationalize this preoccupation with his work on
the grounds of preparing to meet the economic demands of
parenthood. But he goes far beyond the "call of duty" and
spends inordinate amounts of time with his male colleagues,
staying late at the office and going out with them after work to
bowl or play cards.

Further exaggerating his stereotyped gender role, the husband projects his "masculine" prowess into the future, visualizing himself in a brilliant career while "keeping" his "little
woman" and a child in an ever improving style of comfort. At
the same time he spitefully avoids discussing the physical aspects of his wife's pregnancy, and he never offers to accompany her to the doctor or become better informed about the
birthing process.

Of course, the developing fetus literally is part of the
wife's body, and her husband can only empathize vicariously
with her unique experience. Still, cognizant of the desirability
of promoting their relational equality, mates can share as many
aspects of pregnancy and birth as possible.[19]

Visiting *their* obstetrician together, a couple can become

equally aware of any special precautions the wife may be advised to take in preventing physical complications, and the husband can help her to follow whatever regimen the doctor prescribes. Similarly, they can agree on a particular type of birthing procedure. Mates can also participate, *as a couple*, in classes on prenatal care and preparations for birth. Sitting side by side in these classes, they acquire a commonality of roles as expectant parents. Like the wife, the husband can learn about the physiology of her changes. With this knowledge he can help her to stay in good condition and, later, to deliver the baby. By assisting her and sharing her experience, he can express the soft, tender side of his nature that he may have suppressed previously.

The wife can foster the couple's relational equality by enthusiastically welcoming her husband's involvement in every aspect of her prenatal care and delivery. If he is resistant to such participation, she can prod him into it, and her prodding may evoke productive discussions of the gender-role stereotypes they are still reluctant to relinquish. If she has a job she can continue working, unless the doctor advises her to stop, and she can remain at work until she is almost ready to give birth. Thus, she can avoid becoming overly self-absorbed, develop her occupational skills and interests, and responsibly contribute to the family income.

BIRTH

When the wife goes into labor, the couple can apply everything they were taught for the climactic episode of birth. Comforting and encouraging his wife, the husband can help her with the breathing and pushing exercises they had practiced. Even if unexpected complications, such as a weak fetal heartbeat or a breech position, require the wife to undergo a caesarean section, these egalitarian mates are optimally prepared to tolerate the attendant shock and to deal with their common disappointment at being unable to go through with the natural delivery they had planned.

With the husband present when the baby is born, *both* parents can usher it into life, and the infant can immediately form the same kind of loving bond with its father as it does with its mother. Spouses also add new strength to the loving bond between them. In fact, Lorna and Philip Sarrel regard the physiology of labor and delivery as a very sexual event. After all, birth ". . . is the culmination of an act of intercourse, the product of male-female union, and unless there is heavy sedation or a caesarean delivery, it is a moment of surrender to natural body rhythms and processes."[20] Women actually have described the birth of a baby as similar to an orgasmic response, both physically and psychologically. Thus, when delivery is shared by a husband and a wife, it can be one of their most intimate experiences.[21] Indeed, they can attain lasting emotional benefits for themselves and the baby—advantages that show up in many aspects of their postnatal contacts with their child and each other.

Richard, a former student of ours, told us how much it helped his marriage for him to assist in the birth of his first child. Since he and his wife, Sharon, were living in a remote section of Oregon, they had no access to courses on preparation for childbirth. Still, they prepared themselves by reading everything they could find on various methods of natural birthing. When Sharon went into labor, Richard took off from work and remained at her bedside, where they could implement everything they had learned.

Their doctor had agreed to let them do their own thing. But he remained "on call," coming in periodically to check on Sharon's progress while the couple got into their breathing exercises. Carefully, they timed the length of every contraction and the intervals between them. Every time Sharon felt a pain coming on, she grabbed Richard's hand and held it tight while he soothed her head and gently rubbed her belly, telling her how much he loved her. Soon, they were functioning like an obstetrical team.

Within a few hours, however, the rhythm and strength of the contractions declined. Eventually, they ceased completely, leaving Sharon and Richard emotionally deflated. Still, something *had* happened. But the doctor said there was nothing they—or anyone else—could do, either to predict when her labor would begin again or to spur it on.

Sharon remained in intermittent labor for over 24 hours. During this long span she had a number of very severe contrac-

tions, but her cervix was not dilating much, and she grew increasingly anxious and exhausted. But Richard's warm and
constant presence helped to relieve her torment and sustain
her morale. As their harrowing ordeal continued, they felt like
lovers grappling with a life-and-death danger in which everything they valued was on the line. With Richard's efforts syn-
chronized with Sharon's, they were united in the same lifesav-
ing mission, and they cherished each other more than ever
before.

Suddenly, *it* happened again! Yes, again and again! Much
stronger and more quickly. One stab of pain after another.
Harder and harder, lasting longer and longer. Sharon could
barely ride out one wave of cramping spasms before another
began. Curling her legs up against her huge belly for comfort,
she urged Richard to ring for the nurse.

Yes, the nurse announced, the baby was on its way.
Quickly, she called for the doctor. But there had been an unexpected rush of births and he was still busy with another patient. While they waited for him, the nurse summoned an or-
derly to take Sharon into the delivery room. Before they
started to move her, the baby decided to come into the world,
and Richard was right there beside the nurse to catch it! After
the cord was cut, he put the lovely little girl on Sharon's chest.
Drunk with the ecstasy of knowing their baby was alive and
well, they were awed by her angelic beauty: the halo of fuzz
around her luminous head, the symmetry of her full lips, the
velvet folds of her tiny neck, and the exquisite shape of her
little hands and feet. Yes, she was certainly worth waiting for.
She made everything they had just suffered—and everything
they had ever gone through in their marriage—meaningful and
worthwhile. Sharon and Richard experienced a sense of communion that went beyond their fondest imaginings of spiritual
transcendence, and the human commonality they felt could
not be diminished by any of their differences in gender, either
intrinsic or learned. Later, they discovered that they had permanently improved not only their ability to communicate as
husband and wife but also their ability to make passionate
love.

NOTES

1. Hyde, J. S. *Understanding human sexuality.* New York: McGraw-Hill, 1986, pp. 119–120.
2. Masters and Johnson, *Human sexual response,* pp. 68–126.
3. Gadpaille, W. J. *The cycles of sex.* New York: Scribner's, 1975, p. 387.
4. Rosen, R., & Rosen, L. R. *Human sexuality.* New York: Knopf, 1981, p. 345.
5. Coleman, *Intimate relationships, marriage, and family,* p. 422.
6. Adams, V. The odds on psychosomatic childlessness. *Psychology Today,* May 1980, pp. 33–34.
7. Rosen and Rosen, op. cit., p. 344.
8. Ibid.
9. Coleman, op. cit., p. 422.
10. Cox, F. D. *Human intimacy: Marriage, the family, and its meaning.* St. Paul: West, 1987, p. 386.
11. Coleman, op. cit., p. 423.
12. Ibid.
13. Mazor, M. D. Barren couples. *Psychology Today,* May 1979, p. 101.
14. Sarnoff and Sarnoff, *Masturbation and adult sexuality,* pp. 214–215.
15. Katchadourian, H. A. *Fundamentals of human sexuality.* New York: Holt, Rinehart & Winston, 1985, p. 131.
16. Gadpaille, op. cit., p. 387.
17. Horney, K. *Feminine psychology.* New York: Norton, 1973, p. 151.
18. Spock, B. *A teenager's guide to life and love.* New York: Simon and Schuster, 1970, p. 14.
19. Gadpaille, op. cit., p. 387.
20. Sarrel, L., & Sarrel, P. Sexual passages. Part II: Pregnancy and becoming parents. *Redbook,* July 1979, p. 70.
21. Ibid.

10

NURTURING AND NEGATING

Inspired by the arrival of a newborn infant, mates uncork all the reserves of love they had been storing up for it. In every glance and touch, they communicate their adoration. Feeling their love, which is as essential as food to its well-being, the baby reciprocates in its own infantile way. Snuggling and sleeping in their embrace, an infant's utter contentment satisfies the need its mother and father have to be loved by their own offspring. Reveling in the validation of the infant's response to them, they intensify their love for one another and feel mutually grateful for having produced this miracle of their joint creativity.

Building on this wonderful reciprocity of feeling, mates can meet the triple objective for this stage: developing their own relationship for the better while raising a loving child and making a living sufficient for the increased size of their family. However, this complex challenge can throw them into a chaos of disorientation and a whirl of cross-purposes. Now, with another life entirely in their hands, a husband and wife must make extremely rapid adjustments in behavior and mental set, altering their previous routines of eating, sleeping, working, making love, and relating to other people. In fact, following the birth of their first child, spouses may feel *really married* for the first time. Looking back, we recall our childless years as very lighthearted and carefree, indeed, as if we had only been "shacking up," as cohabitation was referred to in those days. But once we had a baby to raise into adulthood, we *knew* how "heavy" the very fruitfulness of marriage could be.

The demands made on the physical and emotional resources of young parents often coincide with mounting pressures in their occupations. Typically, husbands and wives have their children while vigorously striving to advance their careers; many studies reveal that couples usually underestimate the difficulties of coping with parenting and working. Frequently, spouses become resentful about the decrease in their leisure time. In addition, they may have more conflicts about money, and they tend to put greater emphasis on financial security.[1]

Fortunately, love-centered mates can keep their heads and hearts in harmony by appropriately fitting children and work into their humane scale of values. While coupling and reproducing, they had already kept the cultivation of their marriage above their occupational pursuits. Now, they will want to preserve the primacy of their couplehood and install their children firmly in *second place*. They need to relegate their careers to a position well below the loving relationship they want to nurture with each other and with their offspring.

Clear about these priorities, spouses can cater amply to each other without worrying about neglecting their children. Simultaneously, they can be optimally responsible parents, having decided to nurture their children much more than their careers. Thus, they can remain true to the existential significance of their marriage, which antedates the birth of their babies. After all, didn't they want children to celebrate and personify the emotional abundance of their relationship? Aren't they working for an economic base to support the sharing of their love as well as their offspring? And, after retiring, with their children as self-sufficient adults, won't they be left on their own again? Yes, wise are the mates who never forget that they will end up as a couple, just as they began—that between the beginning and ending of their lives together, the vitality of their relationship is the essential factor ensuring their happiness with each other, their children, *and* their work.

Of course, love-centered mates cannot expect to become

the most affluent, famous, or powerful members of their vocational fields and still give one another and their children an adequate amount of care. Predictably, excessive involvement in work on the part of both husband and wife often leads to marital dissatisfaction because they neglect their home, their children, *and* their relationship. So, aiming to "have it all ways" is a cultural fantasy of insatiability—not a sound principle for good parenting or for the attainment of marital happiness.

Nevertheless, many couples have taken up, as a self-evident article of faith, the mission of earning enough money to give their children the latest and the best of everything. Pursuing this goal with quasi-religious fervor, spouses become martyrs, crucifying themselves on the cross of economic striving. These mates take on more hours of employment than they did before becoming parents, placing undue strain on their bodies and minds. Consequently, they subvert not only their own marriages but also their relationships with the very children they had intended to benefit.

Obviously, if parents push themselves to the point of illness and incapacity to work, they *prevent* their children from depending on their earning power. Couples forestall such an ironic catastrophe only by accepting the limitations of a modest income. Indeed, by retaining their zest as loving mates and parents, they teach their children most effectively how to approach both the making and the spending of money.

Surely, love-centered mates would take a humane stand on all sorts of local, state, and national issues. Having ushered their offspring into a dangerous world, they cannot *avoid* such involvement in the community. Specifically, they can throw their weight in support of social, political, and economic changes that would result in more loving, peaceful, and healthy conditions, not only for their own family but also for other people.

Accordingly, parents would protect the health of their family from the environmental hazards of modern technology. As far as it is financially possible, they would avoid living in an area with dangerously polluted land, air, or water. But, no matter what their income, they can exercise the vigilance to limit their family's intake of foods known to have been tainted with herbicides or chemical additives. Some of these treated foods are carcinogenic to people of all ages; others produce allergies, hyperactivity, and learning disabilities in children.

Similarly, parents face the challenge of coping with the noxious effects of "cultural pollution," especially as emitted by television. Commercial television exploits the appeals of self-aggrandizement to promote the sale of merchandise that is either inessential or of dubious value to children. The manipulative, hostile, and deceitful content of many programs also spreads fear and paranoia while suggesting that violence is an appropriate means of settling conflict between individuals and groups—not communication, cooperation, and negotiation. In fact, "By the age of 18, the average child will have witnessed more than 18,000 murders and been subjected to more than 650,000 commercials."[2] Finally, rather than portraying sexual activity within the context of interpersonal care and consideration, television dramas often link it with domination and aggression. This negative association induces a tendency to split the sexual and affectionate wholeness of love, making it harder for children to integrate those two components when they are ready to form loving relationships of their own. With these considerations in mind, parents would want their children to view only programs of clear educational or aesthetic value. Certainly, they would not use television as a babysitting device or to substitute for personal interaction with them.

By departing in these ways from conventional norms, mothers and fathers put their offspring in a position to be questioned or criticized by others. They frequently have to explain why it is best for their children to resist the physically or emotionally destructive practices they may see routinely on the mass media or in their schools and neighborhoods. As humane mentors, however, parents would not teach in the authoritarian manner often followed in formal schooling. Rather, by providing an intellectually honest and stimulating atmosphere at home, they permit their children to ask provocative questions, discuss controversial issues, and seek guidance in dealing with the problems encountered in being nonconformist. Thus, by affirming their values in the crucible of daily life, love-centered mates not only demonstrate their courage but also serve as excellent role models, offering their children a genuine incentive to emulate them. Simultaneously, they bestow the imperishable gifts of real love and truly wholesome living.

NURTURING AS A MIRROR OF MARITAL DEVELOPMENT

In the process of helping their children to grow as loving persons, spouses fulfill all the promises of their marital love in new ways. For example, in showing children how to be considerate and honest, parents increase their own ability to cooperate, make compromises, and communicate honestly, thereby expanding the boundaries of their individuality and the strength of their unity. By being economically and emotionally reliable in parenting, mates intensify their own interdependence and motivate their children to become trusting and trustworthy. By sharing the diverse tasks of rearing in a nonsexist manner, husband and wife progress in transcending their own differences in gender and foster similarly egalitarian behavior in their children. Finally, while teaching children to integrate the erotic and affectionate components of their needs for love, mates can advance in the same integration and become more fully immersed in the pleasure of lovemaking.

Yet couples cannot attain the fulfillments of childrearing without succumbing, in varying degrees, to the inherent threats of love. As in every stage of marriage, they form complicities that contain pockets of alienation between them. Now, however, they can include the children in their pacts, often weaving disagreements about parenting into their scenarios. They may also use their children—rather than their *own* inner feelings of threat—as an excuse for their defensiveness. Thus, they expose a son or daughter to their own fear of loving, to the negative emotions into which they have transformed that fear, and to their methods of fighting and fleeing.

As a defense against the threat of expanding the boundaries of their individuality, mates may covertly agree to compete for a child's allegiance. By this dramatization of their own rivalry, they encourage the child to employ the same egocentric and divisive tactics in relating to them and others. Similarly, when feeling threatened by the increase in interdependance required for parenting, spouses enact their distrust and detachment, becoming mutually unreliable in meeting their responsibilities; as they let themselves "off the hook," they disregard a child's inclination to be undependable. Defending against the threat of transcending their gender differences, mates may stop accepting each other's intrinsic characteristics and feel dissatisfied with a child's particular gender. Locking themselves into stereotypical roles, they revert back to a sexist type of parenting, which limits the child's acceptance of its own gender and makes it more difficult for him or her to reject gender-role stereotypes. Lastly, in reacting against the threat of immersion in the pleasure of lovemaking, mates reduce their own erotic enjoyment and become more repressive toward a child's sexual feelings and behavior, thereby inhibiting his or her ability to integrate the sexual and affectionate components of love.

Thus, all couples frequently stand before their children as examples of how to be unloving, of how thoroughly mates can upset one another, and of how miserable they can feel about their relationship. Indeed, from the perspective of evolving the ability to love, spouses cannot fail to induce their offspring to develop for the *worse*, even as they motivate them to develop for the *better*. In this respect the impact mates exert on every child's personal development mirrors the dialectic of their own relational development: while parenting they are nurturing *and* negating not only their own potentials for loving but also their children's.

The simultaneity of this nurturance and negation produces both joy and anguish for spouses. This mixture of feelings may account for the contradictory findings that have been reported on the relationship between parenting and marital satisfaction. In some retrospective studies, a majority of spouses viewed their years of childrearing as the unhappiest in their marriage.[3] By contrast, in other research most of the mates said they were satisfied with their children and their roles as parents.[4] Likewise, a large national survey conducted by Yankelovich and his associates found that 90% of the couples would have children again.[5]

Reacting to these discrepant results, Frank Cox, author of a leading text on marriage, concludes that emotional ambivalence is intrinsic to parenting: ". . . the 'lows' and 'highs' are so extreme that you want to cry at one moment and laugh at the next."[6] Of course, even love-centered mates swing between these polarities in reacting to uncontrollable strokes of misfortune and good luck in a child's development. However, they can keep the balance of their "homemade" ambivalence consistently on the "high" side by promptly breaking the complicities in which they have implicated their children. By this parental diligence, mates further the constructive development of their relationship and free their children to go on actualizing their own capacity for love.

THE COUPLE IN THE FAMILY

Seeing themselves as partners in parenting as well as in marriage, spouses permanently enlarge their collective identity. They also transform a major element of their common dream into a living reality; this transformation gives them a tremendous uplift in personal and relational potency.

From this time forward they can enrich their romance by sending each other waves of loving appreciation whenever they make enjoyable contact with *their* child and whenever they fondly review his or her endearing qualities. Similarly, when away from one another, spouses can energize themselves by invoking mental representations of those interactions and conversations.

But a child is not a toy or a doll who exists solely to fortify the couple's morale and romance. A child needs to live and grow for its own sake. Mates now have in their midst someone of their flesh and blood but with a separately functioning body and mind; someone who belongs to them, but whom they do not possess; someone they influence but who, with a will of his or her own, also influences them.

The First Child

A couple's first-born child immediately changes their interpersonal configuration from a dyad to a triad. As loving mates, a husband and wife continue to interact as equals. But as parents they become heads of a new social structure: the family. In guiding their marital development, they must consider how they relate, *as individuals and as a couple,* to the child. In addition, all three of them interrelate as members of the same familial group. Thus, while upholding the exclusiveness and preeminence of their relationship, a husband and wife are no longer alone in their own abode; they must adapt to a mediating force—"a little stranger" whose omnipresence both facilitates and inhibits their unity.

As Georg Simmel commented many decades ago, the triad is an inherently volatile social structure since any two of the participants may be tempted to form an alliance against the third.[7] Besides, these alliances can be altered at any time, with either partner in a clique abandoning the other to join forces with the previous "outsider."

Consequently, even as they merge more deeply through parenting, spouses often feel exceedingly rivalrous toward each other, and they begin to subvert the depth of their union. In their complicities they strive to establish separate coalitions with a child, each deliberately seeking to become the "best" parent. They may also play out seemingly irreconcilable disagreements over the specifics of rearing, both mates trying to enlist a child as an ally in their competitive contest.

Jane and Gregory Kaufman were intoxicated by the milky scent of their newborn daughter. Her flawless skin, so sweet with the freshness of life, was similar to Jane's smooth and rosy complexion. Waiting breathlessly for the baby's gentle gurgles and voiceless yawns, they even imagined she was speaking to them. Could she be smiling, too? After all, since she had so many of their features, she must be as intelligent!

Sizzling with enthusiasm, the Kaufmans took on their parental roles as if they had always known how to be Mom and Dad. They had decided that Jane, an elementary school teacher, would take a 2-year maternity leave to be at home and get the baby off to a good start. Although Greg remained on his job as Assistant Principal in a local high school, he rushed home every afternoon to share in the baby's care.

The Kaufmans basked in the infant's reflected glory when her grandparents arrived to examine and praise her. But the "old folks" were scarcely interested in Jane and Greg. Rather, they made the Kaufmans feel like breeding horses who, having done their duty to continue the stock, should be let out to pasture while they doted on the foal in the barn. By contrast, when friends came to visit, everyone marveled at how well Jane and Greg were managing. Soon they were regarded as proven experts in parenting, and all the expectant couples in their crowd turned to them for advice.

Jane and Greg gleefully tracked their daughter's remarkable progress in sleeping through the night; in switching from breast to bottle to cup; in eating solid foods and sprouting teeth; in sitting up, standing, crawling, and walking; in moving from babble to genuine speech. Given their common interests in education, they were entranced by her intellectual and social development, thrilled by the keen twinkle in her big eyes, by her ability to concentrate on a story or a record, by the quickness of her understanding and fascinated interest in her surroundings. Respecting her insatiable curiosity, they answered all of her questions candidly. They also encouraged her to be honest in communicating with them about whatever was on her mind, making her feel comfortable enough to talk about things that might be disturbing her.

Eventually, however, the Kaufmans' successful teamwork began to threaten them. Sometimes, they felt they had become a pair of indistinct blobs by fusing so totally as parents. Gradually, they became more and more rivalrous. Jane started to resent being the one who was stuck at home, unable to do stimulating work like Greg. Hadn't *she* been in line to become a supervisor of the new math curriculum? Maybe she should have gone back to work right away. Meanwhile, Greg was worried about his inability to spend as much time with their child as Jane did and to have as much influence over her. Drawing a wedge of competition between them, they soon engaged in a bitter struggle, each fighting tenaciously to prevail over the other in matters of childrearing and to secure their daughter's allegiance.

On the benign face of their complicity, Jane and Greg tried to impress the child with their special talents. Utilizing her skills, Jane demonstrated how she could cook, bake, and clean while functioning as the most understanding and devoted of mothers. She also tried to convince her daughter of what an exceptionally patient and charming companion she could be, cheerfully "on call" during the child's long hours of daily play in the park.

Pulling out his bag of tricks, Greg sought to captivate the child with verbal fireworks. Night after night, he mesmerized her with exciting tales of chivalrous knights and the beautiful princesses they saved. The more bug-eyed the girl became, the more he embellished the exploits of the fictitious heroes and heroines—all of whom were unbridled projections of his own individualistic aspirations.

But the Kaufmans did not restrict their competitiveness to these peaceful means of winning their daughter's favor. Frequently, they erupted into vicious arguments about how they should raise the child. Jane felt she needed more discipline. She should be taught to apologize when she misbehaved; she should go to bed on time, rather than insist on staying up to hear more stories; and she should not get *every* toy she craved. Invariably, Greg would side with the child, casting Jane in the role of a hateful shrew and presenting himself as an all-bountiful protector of the "poor dear." Jane would fight back, discrediting Greg as a father and pointing out how bad his unwarranted indulgence was for their daughter's psychological development. He would then counterpunch with the charge that she was expecting too much from the child and that her proposed discipline was unjust or overly severe.

Most of these battles took place behind the child's back. Occasionally, however, the Kaufmans staged their fights with her as a witness. Arguing the merits of their opposing stands, each hoped, like lawyers in an adversary proceeding, that she would rule against the other in rendering her judgment about who was in the right—and with whom it would be best to align herself. Invariably, their arguments ended in a stalemate—but not until they were fuming at each other and not before their daughter was abysmally confused and abashed, feeling she was the actual cause and object of their combat.

Such warring parents impose a cruel hoax on a child, leading him or her to believe it is possible to move from filial to parental status within the family. Indeed, they treat the child as a social peer by implicitly inviting him or her to adjudicate their publicly staged disputes over parenting. In these scenarios, spouses reveal a sharp rupture in their co-leadership of the family, and they offer a child the chance to exercise an authority that they ordinarily—and ideally—do not relinquish.

Thrust into the position of a pseudomate, the child is saddled with the crippling strain of playing a hopelessly unrealistic role. He or she is also stressed by feeling compelled to solve problems that originate in the spouses' own relationship. The child is therefore doubly victimized: first, as an object of the couple's competitiveness and, second, as the presumably decisive party in the outcome of their rivalry.

Is it surprising, therefore, to learn from Ivan Boszormenyi-Nagy and Geraldine Spark,[8] as well as from other family therapists, about the emotional casualties found among children who are subjected to such parentification? Or to hear, from the same sources, how bitterly spouses also suffer in attempting to shift their parental responsibilities onto their children?

Exposed to the parental ploy of "divide and conquer," a child may be motivated to become an active manipulator, secretly proposing separate "deals" with each parent, cagily withholding information about concessions extracted from one or the other, and egging both of them on to fiercer combat when they argue. Besides, such a child is likely to employ the same unsavory tactics of exploitation and deceit in relating to other people.

Beyond the First Child

In conceiving and rearing a second child, spouses can derive the same fulfillments as they did in going through those stages with the first one. Having already experienced the incomparable rewards of creating and caring for one child, mates are likely to want another. Besides, a couple often makes the decision to reproduce again while they are buoyed up by the proven success of their parenting; the transports of their ongoing experiences act as powerful incentives for them to enlarge their family.

With another baby in their home, spouses can feel more virile than ever before. Loving and being loved by this new child, they add a lasting source of energy to their romance, and they strengthen their relationship even as they give more of themselves in parenting.

The younger child also can be a great boon to the older one, who now has a permanent companion and playmate. In sharing parental care with this sibling, the older child learns to be more patient, cooperative, and considerate. The first born is also no longer a "loner" or the sole subject of parental authority. He or she now has a brother or sister with whom to find emotional support in coping with the world.

Still, each additional child multiplies the network of relationships within the family. As a childless couple, mates had communication only in two directions. However, as Cox observes, "Add one child and this becomes six-way communication; add two children, and there is now twelve-way communication."[9] Thus, the difficulty of maintaining good communication between mates and their offspring goes up in a geometric progression with every increase in family size.

Naturally, too, in having another child, mates stimulate the same threats of love as they did with their first one, and they can now incorporate *both* children into their complicities. For example, they can contrive scenarios that call for each mate to have a "special" relationship with one of their children. These alliances may require a lot of sneaky fighting between the husband's clique and the one led by the wife. Such parents subject their "troops"—the children—to the same stressful competition they are enacting with each other, and the hostile rivalry between "enemy camps" can continually foment familial tension. Ironically, these mates also set a precedent for their children to "gang up" against them at some later point in their lives. Thus, mimicking the couple's subversion of their own relationship, formerly rivalrous siblings may become allies, secretly hatching plans to exploit the disunity of their parents.

Surely, it is essential for every child to be loved equally by each parent; it is just as desirable for each parent to be equally loved, as an individual, by every child. Otherwise, someone in the family will feel gravely deprived and invalidated, and his or her resentment could depress the morale of the entire group.

To maintain their intimacy within this matrix of interpersonal complexity, it is crucially important for husband and wife to exchange the significant details of their personal interactions with the children. Cooperating as a parenting team, they can share their experiences and observations, continually making compromises on whatever differences arise between them. Perceiving the couple's solidarity—as mates *and* as parents—the children are motivated to drop whatever efforts they may have been making to divide them.

Thus, husbands and wives can retain a firm grip on the primacy of their own relationship and make sure it is not diluted. Indeed, each mate can speak for both of them whenever either has a separate contact with any child. Under these conditions, each child feels just as secure in relating to one parent as to the other; all the children know that their welfare is being adequately considered; and they can honestly express their thoughts and feelings about anything, without worrying about being entangled in parental rivalries. Consequently, even while remaining outside the perimeters of the couple's relationship, the children feel lovingly accepted as an integral part of the familial group, and everyone's well-being is enhanced by the growing closeness between husband and wife.

SEX AND THE LOVING FAMILY

While producing a child, the physiological changes of pregnancy and birth can contribute to a couple's sexual satisfaction. Mothers show an increase in the supply of blood flowing into the pelvic region, which can heighten their responsiveness to genital stimulation and penetration. After having a baby, some women have an orgasm for the first time.[10] In turn, the intensification of a wife's eroticism is likely to affect her husband in kind, arousing him more keenly than ever before.

By its very presence, a newborn also stimulates a fresh charge of erotic feeling among mates. In addition to being turned on by the baby's proof of their fruitfulness, loving parents get a "rush" from the very act of giving their children care, and they go "sky high" from a child's expressions of love for them—its cuddling, cooing, and smiling. The routine nurturance of a baby actually *requires* parents to make a lot of sensual contact with it. Nursing is more than a mere act of feeding. It also involves contact between highly erogenous zones: the mother's nipples and the sensitive tissues around the baby's mouth. Fathers can participate vicariously by watching the baby suck on the wife's breast; they can also get a much more direct experience of this process by giving the baby a bottle. Cradling the child in the haven of his arms, a husband can derive the pleasure of a literally warm communion between himself and the baby.

Through the medium of touch, both mates have many opportunities to impart their affection to the baby—changing its diapers, bathing and dressing it, calming its hurts and fears in a tender embrace. As Ashley Montagu has reported, many studies attest to the crucial effects of parental touching for a child's optimal growth.[11] This tactile contact is just as vital for the happiness of the parents and for the bonding they crave with their child. Besides, holding, stroking, and fondling a child leads mates to revive long-lost traces of their own sensuality and to break down inhibitions about touching each other.[12]

Steve and Lois Stampler created a ritual they jokingly called "The Heat Treatment" that linked them enjoyably to their child *and* to each other. After giving the baby his last breast-feeding for the night, Lois would pass him on to Steve, who was already reclining in bed. He placed the baby face down on his bare chest, hugging him and whispering endearments. Then, Steve would put the baby in the same position on Lois, who was now lying beside him. After Lois had her "turn" with "the treatment," she and Steve would snuggle together with the baby draped across both of them. Sometimes, the Stamplers felt so cozily enveloped in a glow of emotional and physical warmth that they wanted to keep their son with them all through the night.

Alternatively, such idyllic interludes may inspire a couple to put the baby back in its crib so that they can make love. However, most women need to wait for several weeks after delivery in order to resume sexual intercourse without physical discomfort.[13] This interval, combined with their abstinence during the last few weeks of pregnancy, interrupts the pattern of lovemaking that mates had established in the first two stages of their marriage. Then, both husband and wife must readjust to the use of contraception. After all the freedom and spontaneity they had enjoyed while trying to conceive and throughout pregnancy, mates often perceive the need to resume any form of birth control as onerous. But if they want the peace of mind essential for their erotic pleasure, they have to accept responsibility for avoiding another pregnancy until they truly desire it.

Still, a baby's omnipresent demands for prompt gratification of its needs can intrude implacably on a couple's freedom to make love. Of course, some babies learn quickly to sleep through the night. But other infants, and even older children, are restless sleepers, waking nightly and keeping parents on edge about when or whether to make love.

Couples may also suffer from a lack of space. Today, with the soaring costs of housing, millions of families must live in cramped quarters that are not conducive to romantic intercourse between parents. Many spouses have to keep an infant in their own room. Or their bedroom may be adjacent to a child's room and lack adequate soundproofing to muffle their voices and sexual movements.

One young mother complained to us despairingly about such an inhibiting situation. "What can I do? I'm going bananas! My kids just won't fall asleep until late. Even when they do, they're *very* light sleepers. Every time we start to make love, they're up and crying for something."

Another couple reported a humorous variation of this plight. Presumably asleep in an adjoining room, their 5-year-old son developed the habit of lying awake to hear them make love. One night, frustrated by their silence, he pounded on the wall and shouted indignantly, "What's the matter? Aren't you going to do it tonight?" After this episode the parents shifted the boy's location. Living in a large apartment, they could easily put him in a room more distant from their own.

Even if they succeed in conquering the problems of creating a romantic space, mates still have to provide themselves with ample time for using it. Generally, new parents do a lot of juggling before evolving a consistent schedule for pleasurable intercourse. Surely, they will encounter times when they must give a seriously ill child "top billing"; times when the ceaseless rigors of parenting jangle their nerves, weary their bodies, and deflate their spirits; times when crises and emergencies at work siphon off the energy they could be putting into making love. Nevertheless, even during those harrowing times, mates can remind each other of the top priority they have given to lovemaking in the cultivation of their relationship. Likewise,

they can share responsibility for restoring their erotic fulfillment as quickly as possible.

Some couples have the option of arranging their hours of
work to be at home to make love while their children are in
school. Under these ideal conditions, a husband and wife can
be as carefree as they were before becoming parents. However,
couples who must work from morning to evening can do a lot
of daytime lovemaking on weekends and holidays. They can
send their children off on outings with a reliable sitter or leave
the children and sitter at home, going off by themselves for a
day or two of uninterrupted privacy in a place of natural
beauty.

Nevertheless, after becoming parents, mates may become
particularly threatened by immersion in the pleasure of lovemaking. As a defense, they frequently design complicities in
which they agree to *desexualize* themselves. Such scenarios
often call for the wife to turn herself into a virtual Madonna
before her husband, children, and the rest of the world. She
trims her hair, purging its soft and tumbling sensuality. Wearing
only the plainest of clothes—tailored blouses and skirts in dull
colors that are vaguely reminiscent of habits prescribed for a
religious order—she may even strap herself into a girdle to blot
out any suggestion of her shapeliness. And setting her face into
a prim expression, she limits her conversations with her husband to the practical details of their parental and occupational
roles.

Subjecting himself to similar asceticism, the husband
avoids any hint of flamboyance in his attire. A dark, three-
button suit becomes his standard uniform, which he modifies
on weekends only by shedding his tie and replacing his jacket
with a sweater or windbreaker. Formerly jocular and quick to
smile, he now affects a chronically serious mien that befits the
Priest he presumes to be for his wife, children, and other people. No longer telling risque stories or giving vent to frivolous
flights of fancy, he soberly concentrates on issues that concern
his family and job.

Putting sexuality behind them, parenthood is now this
couple's principal reason for being married. And they *are* outstanding as parents, discussing all the details of rearing their
children as an affectionate and unified pair. Still, these mates

sacrifice their own erotic pleasure because they are so threatened by its allure. Indeed, because they feel that immersion in lovemaking might tempt them to throw over the responsibilities of parenting altogether, they shun that temptation by becoming so immersed in the tasks of childrearing that they scarcely think or talk about anything else when they are together.

In a few years such mates appear much older than they actually are. While in her mid-thirties, the mother may exude the wasted air of a "matron" in her late forties, flattened out and weighed down by slaving for her family. Her husband, about the same chronological age, has the tired and pale look of an elderly man who has spent too many decades carrying all the troubles of the universe on his stooping shoulders. Seeing this would-be Madonna and Priest presiding at a family dinner in the dining room, earnestly engrossed with their young children on the topic of table manners, one would be hard pressed to imagine how they could possibly have "sunk so low" as to engage in the intercourse necessary to have a family.

For some of these couples, however, the sexless and "straight" demeanor they show in public may reveal only one side of a complicity by which they separate the sexual and affectionate components of their love. Like polished actors, such mates do not bring out the erotic side until they go "on stage" inside their own bedroom after the children are asleep.

Gretchen and Edward Meyers maintain this kind of literally dramatic compartmentalization. When they are together during the day, Edward, a foreman in a construction crew, and Gretchen, a saleslady in a local dress shop, are considerate but reserved and formal in relating to each other. Colluding with great artistry in front of their children, Gretchen refers to Edward as "Father," and he calls her "Mother." What names could be more indicative of parental devotion, untainted by fleshy desire?

But once safely hidden behind the closed door of their own room, this "saintly" couple changes their script and drops their daytime collusion. Gretchen, the erstwhile Madonna, becomes a bewitching Whore; and Edward, the fatherly Priest, becomes a shameless Pimp. While he strips off his shirt, she rushes into the bathroom—emerging quickly in skimpy black

panties and bra, a lascivious leer on her parted lips. Half naked, he stalks toward her, his eyes flashing wildly. As he approaches, she backs up against the wall. Then, he reaches out
and pulls down her bra. Shuddering, she wraps her arms
around her breasts and starts to move away. But he blocks her
path, his body now pressed hungrily against hers.

Concluding this well-rehearsed skit, they stumble into bed
and, without a smile or a whispered endearment, "take each
other." Early in the morning they jump into the shower, wash
off all traces of their intercourse, and resume their daytime
roles before waking the children for breakfast.

Of course, in this type of complicity mates do give each
other some sexual release. But their compartmentalization of
sex from affection is so rigid that it has several negative effects. First, they turn their sexual intercourse into a porno-
graphic caricature that lacks the humanizing element of the
affectionate tenderness they really feel for one another. Second, they make their usual interactions unnecessarily passionless and dead. Finally, they give their children the false impression that eroticism is totally absent from their loving
relationship.

With this type of public pretense, such spouses strongly
reinforce their silent agreements to lie about the actual existence and content of their complicities. After years of skillful
collusion, they may mystify themselves and their children into
believing that their parental posture of having "no problems"
is the unquestionable truth of their marital relationship. Certainly, loving parents do not like to admit they have been systematically deceitful in presenting themselves to their offspring. It is hard for them to acknowledge their habitual
facades of collusion. But they will have to make precisely that
admission to each other *before* they can do the still more painful work of breaking the complicities they had been masking
publicly.

It is especially difficult, however, for mates to break the
complicities they form while parenting. When they were childless, they had nobody in their household to observe the existence of their marital problems. They could enact their defensive scenarios quite blatantly, making it easier to detect and
confront them. As parents, however, they have omnipresent

witnesses to their interpersonal behavior—children who may see through the web of deceit they are maintaining for their mutual defense. Under these altered conditions, they have the incentive to form and maintain collusions, just as they would in the presence of anyone else, pretending to be free of the very complicities they are striving to keep their offspring from perceiving.

Actually, mates can get clues to what is threatening them the most by paying attention to the kinds of interactions that make them feel particularly "uptight" and collusive in front of their children. This insight can stimulate them to examine more carefully the meaning of what they are trying to hide and to communicate more honestly about what is really troubling them. Once they are able to break a particular complicity, they no longer have to suffer from it and they do not have to worry about imposing its destructive effects on any of their children. Now having less to conceal, they can also lessen the extent and inflexibility of their collusions. As a result, they can be much more spontaneous and relaxed when they interact with their family.

By learning to tolerate their fear of sexual pleasure, mates can begin to view themselves as true Sensual Lovers. In bed or out of it, they can obtain the enjoyment of relating in ways that combine eroticism and affection, and they are not shackled by the compulsion to affect contradictory and hypocritical personas at different times of the day or night. Of course, even Sensual Lovers need a private setting for sexual intercourse. Otherwise, their freedom of expression can be so dampened as to extinguish their passion. But they do not confuse privacy with prudery, and they know how good it feels to hug and kiss whenever and wherever they are moved to exchange physical demonstrations of their mutual love.

This degree of spontaneity is equally good for a couple's children, who may be in the vicinity to observe them. Through these observations a son or a daughter can connect affection with physical demonstrativeness, a connection that enables them to appreciate the true holism of love. Witnessing the joy their parents take in an embrace, children are also validated in their own discoveries of the pleasure that goes along with sexual self-stimulation.[14]

Indeed, without any instruction children naturally explore their genitals and find out how much fun it can be to masturbate. Parents who accept and enjoy their own sexual relations are in the best position to confirm a child's personal experience. Thus, they can openly assist their child in developing accurate knowledge of his or her sexual functioning and a positive attitude toward the place of eroticism in the behavior of a loving person.

Surely, spouses will be called upon to clarify many puzzlements in teaching their children the "facts of love." They will probably encounter many negative attitudes and erroneous notions their children pick up from other sources. For, despite its supposed "liberation," our society continues to reek with sexual repression, the noxious effects of which crop up in pornography, secrecy, and other forms of separating the erotic and affectionate wholeness of love. In spelling out their alternative approach to loving, a couple may have to spend considerable time correcting these cultural "kinks."

Given an honest sex education by their parents, children can grow up without feeling bedeviled and secretive about their own erotic yearnings and activities. Such children know they can always consult either their mother or their father on anything that may be particularly troubling to them: their masturbation, their bodily changes, and their sexual reactions to other people.

The Oedipal Conflict and Its Resolution

All mates are destined to become part of a problem in childrearing that is both universal in scope and difficult to resolve. Ironically, this dilemma arises from the very feelings of love that pass between them and their children. Labeling it the Oedipal conflict, Freud described[15] how a child between the ages of 3 and 6 becomes erotically and emotionally drawn to its parent of the opposite sex. At the same time, the child develops rivalrous hostility toward the parent of the same sex, who reacts in kind. Consequently, both parents become anxious about the status of their own relationship.

However, Freud did not adhere to a holistic conception of love. He did not point out that in loving *both* parents, every child is bound to have affectionate *and* erotic feelings toward the father *and* the mother. Of course, it seems safe to assume that this blend may be instinctively more evoked between members of the opposite sex whose genital coupling is indispensible for the perpetuation of the species. Still, prior to their conditioning in sexual repression and homophobia, baby boys may be aroused sexually in expressing love to their fathers, just as baby girls may react in loving their mothers.

Freud also neglected to emphasize the fact that the sexual overtones of love naturally go from parent to child. Thus, fathers and mothers are turned on to both sons and daughters. Of course, given the taboo against incest, an erotic reaction to a child of the opposite sex may be very upsetting for most parents to admit. However, an erotic reaction to a child of the *same* sex can be doubly frightening since it also conflicts with society's disapproval of homosexuality. Indeed, some fathers are so homophobic that they suppress any impulse to kiss or hug their own sons. Likewise, as Lonnie Barbach found, mothers have been appalled at having fantasies of sexual contact with their daughters.[16]

Thus, even if they have children of only one gender, both parents can experience erotic attractions toward them, paving the way for Oedipal involvements that are homoerotic. Still, parents, like their children, are likely to be more strongly attracted to people of the opposite sex. So, as we first explained in *Masturbation and Adult Sexuality,* fathers and mothers go through what we have called the Reverse Oedipal,[17] developing a special affinity to their children of the opposite sex and regarding each other as rivals in those relationships.

Although mutual attractions between parents and children emerge involuntarily, it is exceedingly important for all concerned to use their volition to renounce these involvements in a manner that permits the parents to further their relational development and that frees the child to become a responsible adult who can integrate the sexual and affectionate components of love in a relationship with someone of his or her own choosing.

Unfortunately, this happy outcome is often precluded by complicities that spouses use to defend themselves against the threat of immersion in the pleasure of lovemaking. Such mates formulate scenarios in which they negate their own sexual re-

lations, instead becoming excessively involved in Reverse Oedipal patterns. In some cases parents allow this involvement to
extend into overt sexual abuse of their children. More frequently, however, while restricting their erotic feelings to fantasy, parents foster such close ties with their children of the
opposite sex as to put the erotic component of their marital
relationship into total eclipse.

Vincent and Sally Flanagan are classic examples of this
kind of negation. They met while seniors at college, majoring in
accounting. After a few months, they gave in to the temptation to make love for the first time, and they liked it *very*
much. By the time of their graduation, they were planning to
marry. Taking jobs in different firms, they worked until they
could save up for a comfortable home near Newport, Rhode
Island. With enough money on hand, they got married, buying
themselves a small sloop as a wedding present. They then settled into a routine of sailing as often as they could on weekends. Exploring cove after cove of Narragansett Bay, they
looked for the most romantic spots to drop anchor for a night
of lovemaking.

Approaching their fourth anniversary, the Flanagans had
their first child, Danny. They were so enthralled by his dimpled
smile and big brown eyes that they decided to make a major
occupational change. They would go into business on their
own, working in their house, so they could be closer to Danny
and spend more time with him during the day.

The Flanagans were surprised by the speed of their success. In 3 years they were making more money than they had
as employees; new clients were signing up with them every
week. Meanwhile, they added Eileen to their family. With her
red hair and shining blue eyes, she was a fitting complement to
Danny.

By now, however, the Flanagans were well entrenched in
a mutual defense against the threat of indulging in erotic pleasure. After Danny's birth they had drastically reduced the frequency of their intercourse. They also suspended their sailing
activities; when they did begin to sail again, they took Danny
with them. Actually, they could have made love in their bunk
with a fair amount of privacy by letting Danny fall asleep in his
cradle on the deck. But they told themselves it would be bad to

make any noise that might disturb him. Besides, they were hardly ever "in the mood." So why bother?

But while they became cooler as a couple, Sally grew passionate in declaring her feelings for Danny. "What a fantastic boy!" she would rave to friends and relatives. "I could just eat him up, he's *so* delicious!" She got so engrossed in pampering the boy that she often seemed unaware of Vincent's existence. Even when they were alone in their own room, she would go on and on about what Danny had done and would do—what he needed and what she wanted to get for him.

Occasionally, Sally's preoccupation with Danny got on Vincent's nerves, and he was more impatient and demanding than Sally in dealing with the boy. Usually, however, he let her take over on almost everything that concerned their son.

With Eileen, however, Vincent suddenly woke up as a vitally interested parent. Now, he was the one who trumpeted the child's virtues. "What a living doll! She's so gorgeous, and what an amazing disposition. So *sweet!*" He also participated much more directly in her feeding and changing than he had with Danny. When visiting friends, he bubbled over in describing her delightful antics, and he steeped himself in fantasies of how wonderful she would become with the passing years.

Sally felt twinges of alarm at Vincent's absorption with Eileen. But she was generally calm about it because she and Vincent had added a new element to their complicity after Eileen's birth. From then on they tacitly agreed that Sally would "have" Danny as "Momma's Main Man"; and Vincent would "have" Eileen as "Daddy's Little Girl." Thus, they became quite mutually exclusive as parents of their son and daughter, the better to exclude sexual relations from their marriage.

In these cases mates intensely eroticize their interactions with their children, foisting upon them mute desires for gratification that no child can possibly provide. As a result, the children become emotionally oppressed by the parental attention lavished on them. Yet, being so needful and dependent, a child is readily "hooked" by an ardently doting parent. Since this exceptionally "favored" position is very difficult to renounce, the child may grow up with a reluctance to break such close ties.

However, mates who never stop immersing themselves in the pleasure of lovemaking can most effectively help each other—and their offspring—to untie their Oedipal knots. Given the depth of their own sexual fulfillment, these parents have no burning need to transform their children into vicarious consorts. Of course, like Sally and Vincent, these mothers and fathers cannot help but feel the erotic nuances that go along with the affection they experience in loving their children. But the proven satisfactions of their own "love life" help them to renounce erotically tinged mental attachments to a child. Similarly, these spouses can best empathize with the sexual feelings that arouse and distress their children. United in a sympathetic understanding of the whole situation, they can encourage their offspring to talk openly about it to them. Thus, both parents and children can learn to accept their incestuous desires as normal *and* controllable.

Parents actually increase their children's self-respect by giving serious consideration to their Oedipal feelings. Of course, as Alice Balint, a child psychoanalyst, advises, a mother and father must frankly assert the impossibility of a child's hope to secure either of them as a lover. At the same time, however, they can realistically point out, in terms the child can understand, that as an adult the child can, like themselves, find fulfillment in love with his or her own mate. In this way parents can display their respect for the child's feelings and communicate the fact that they regard him or her as a very lovable person.[18]

Naturally, it may require any number of tense conversations before all members of the family become fully tuned into the same wavelength of intellectual comprehension and emotional closure. But the parents and the children are rewarded abundantly for their persistence and their pains. Having weathered this momentous test of their relational priorities, mates emerge with proof of their success in upholding the primacy of their relationship. Likewise, they strengthen their personal and collective ability to tolerate the most disquieting truths about feelings that parents are "not supposed" to experience. Simultaneously, their children enjoy the manifold blessings of consciously accepting the taboo against incest, which includes the ability to face inner and interpersonal conflict, to construct a moral code based on consideration for oneself *and* others, and to see that fulfillment can flow from renunciation as well as consummation.

Finally, having "buried the hatchet" with their parent of the same sex, these children can willingly identify with him or her. "Instead of trying in vain to displace his father, a boy begins to model himself after him, acquiring a personal sense of the strength and maturity he represents. Similarly, as a girl accepts the futility of competing with her mother for the love of her father, she identifies with the mother; and by modeling herself on the strengths she perceives in her, she strengthens her own self-image."[19] Meanwhile, the formerly rivalrous parent also makes his or her peace with the children of the same sex. Accordingly, the family atmosphere reflects a harmony that occurs only when all of its members are clear and secure about how they stand in relation to one another on the bedrock issue of love.

NOTES

1. Cowan, P., Cowan, C., Coie, L., & Coie, J. The impact of children upon their parents. In L. Newman & W. Miller (Eds.), *The first child and family formation*. Chapel Hill: University of North Carolina Press, 1978. In addition, see Aldous, *Family Careers*, pp. 164–167.
2. Coleman, *Intimate relationships, marriage, and family*, p. 441.
3. Bell, R. R. *Marriage and family interaction*. Homewood, Ill: Dorsey, 1975.
4. Chilman, C. S. Parent satisfactions, concerns, and goals for their children. *Family Relations*, 1980, *29*, pp. 339–436.
5. Yankelovich, Skelley, & White, Inc. *Raising children in a changing society: The General Mills American family report*. Minneapolis: General Mills, 1977.
6. Cox, *Human intimacy*, p. 442.
7. Simmel, G. The triad. In K. H. Wolff (Ed.), *The sociology of Georg Simmel*. New York: Free Press, 1950, pp. 145–169.
8. Boszormenyi-Nagy, I., & Spark, G. M. *Invisible loyalties*. New York: Harper & Row, 1973.
9. Cox, op. cit. p. 443.
10. Barbach, *For yourself*, p. 155.
11. Montagu, A. *Touching*. New York: Harper & Row, 1971.

12. Gadpaille, *The cycles of sex,* pp. 380–415.
13. Brecher, R., & Brecher, E. M. (Eds.). *An analysis of sexual response.* New York: New American Library, 1966, pp. 88–96.
14. Sarnoff and Sarnoff, *Masturbation and adult sexuality,* pp. 100–101.
15. Freud, Three contributions to the theory of sex. In *The basic writings of Sigmund Freud.*
16. Barbach, op. cit., pp. 166–167.
17. Sarnoff and Sarnoff, op. cit., p. 122.
18. Balint, A. *The psycho-analysis of the nursery.* London: Routledge and Kegan Paul, 1953, pp. 50–51.
19. Sarnoff and Sarnoff, op. cit., p. 124.

11

FOCUSING AND FRAGMENTING

Approaching this stage of marriage, a couple has already progressed through half their relational development. They now are about to embark on the last half, which coincides with inescapable signs of their aging. While their future is replete with opportunity, it is also fraught with existential dread.

Even in their mid-thirties, mates display the visible handiwork of Father Time in wrinkles and crinkles, in patches of graying or thinning hair. More importantly, they are less exuberant than they were a mere 10 years ago, and they cannot "bounce back" as quickly from an illness or a night of dissipation.

These liabilities accelerate from year to year. From now on a husband and a wife would be increasingly depleted by any child they added to their family, making them feel like mechanical drones at precisely the time when it would be desirable to inject a fresh charge of vitality into their interactions. Indeed, if they have been raising two children, a couple is in danger of losing the effectiveness of their juggling act, simultaneously handling the challenges of developing their relationship, parenting, and working.

To keep from dropping the crucial "ball"—their relational development—spouses need to impose *new* and *lasting limits* on the expenditure of their energies. Perhaps, during their own childhood, they believed that admitting to being finite was equivalent to a confession of abysmal failure. Besides, their cultural conditioning in the mystique of limitless aspiration did nothing to dispel this mistaken belief. But now, as mature adults, they know that Supermom and Superdad are as fictitious as Superman and Superwoman.

By acknowledging and accepting their human limitations, spouses are free to become even stronger as a couple, for they can take the appropriate action of giving greater attention to one another, which requires some major alterations in the distribution of their efforts. Consequently, the fourth objective of marital development calls upon mates to focus more time and energy toward intensifying the loving quality of their own relationship in two ways: by ending procreation *and* by eliminating parental practices that are no longer essential or beneficial to their growing children.

TEMPTATIONS TO CONTINUE REPRODUCTION

At an earlier stage in their marriage, many mates commit themselves to having a family of a specific size. Upon reaching that goal, they derive a common sense of completion. They then settle into the goal of cultivating their marital merger while continuing to rear their children with optimal care and consideration. However, the special joys and fulfillments of parenthood may tempt some couples to go beyond the quota they had set originally. They begin to waver and talk about "reopening their options." Other couples never pinned themselves down to a fixed number of children, and they continue to resist such a limit, despite the fact that they are barely coping with their various responsibilities.

Certainly, Americans are enjoined to equate success in living with the *quantity* of their tangible achievements rather than with the *quality* of their inner experiences. For many couples the idea of having more and more children is comparable to the continual acquisition of material possessions. These mates feel driven to have child after child even though, in the process, they undermine the quality of their marital experience *and* the quality of their parenting.

Similarly, the American emphasis on "having it all" incites

couples to be dissatisfied with children of only one sex. If they already have two boys or two girls, they may feel sorely deprived. So they may push themselves to have as many additional children as it takes to conceive a child of the opposite sex. Citing a longitudinal study in which the same couples were followed over a period of 16 years, Letha and John Scanzoni report that mates who did not have both a boy and a girl were likely to conceive more children than they originally agreed upon. Some couples had a third, a fourth, or even a fifth child in seeking at least one of each sex.[1]

Because of these rigidly held gender preferences, mates put themselves under tremendous pressure. With every pregnancy beyond their second child, they anxiously wait and wonder, "What will it be this time?" If they do not get a baby of the desired sex, they may be chronically disappointed in it and in themselves. Sometimes, they may even treat the child as if he or she actually personified the gender they had so intently wished to produce.

One of the couples we interviewed told us that, after having two daughters, they were implacably determined to conceive a son. While the wife was pregnant, she had recurrent fantasies of how strong and handsome her child would become as a young man. Meanwhile, the husband often imagined his son-to-be as a baseball or football star. When the wife went into labor, the husband paced the floor of the waiting room, regaling other expectant fathers with stories of how he would encourage his "boy" to become an outstanding athlete. Finally, a nurse came in to announce the arrival of the couple's third girl. But the husband, persisting in his mental set, immediately denied the reality of the child's gender and shouted, "How is *he?*"

In a similar case, a couple with two boys yearned desperately for a daughter. When the wife became pregnant again, they adamantly refused to consider the possibility of having another son. Although both mates were educated professionals, they gullibly accepted the superstitions of "old wives tales," taking the particular changes in the wife's facial features and abdominal shape as "evidence" that the fetus was female. From the moment the pregnancy was confirmed, they threw out all the baby clothes from their sons and bought a new layette—entirely in pink. When the baby turned out to be another boy, both of them went into a tailspin of disbelief and depression. Ultimately, they did succeed in cherishing him as a healthy and lovable member of their family. To satirize their own folly, however, they jokingly began to call the boy "Pink." This became his permanent nickname, but *he* never appreciated its humorous connotations since it always made him feel self-conscious and insecure about his parents' basic acceptance of him as a male.

Naturally, by rearing a son and a daughter, spouses learn about the emotional and physical functioning of members of their *own and the opposite sex*. This experience, in turn, helps a husband and wife to empathize with and accept their own intrinsic gender differences. However, a couple cannot be sure of having children of both sexes, no matter how many they go on conceiving, and they may end up with a large family of either boys or girls.

It would be good for mates to realize that the intimacy of *their own marital pairing* offers both of them the lifelong opportunity to go on increasing their ability to accept their intrinsic gender differences, to reject sex-role stereotypes, and to express all the traits and inclinations they share as human beings. Besides, by scuttling any unrealistic expectations they have about controlling the sex of their offspring, they are better equipped to give an equal amount of love and acceptance to the children they already have.

Still, researchers report that having *any* number of children is likely to be associated with *some* problems for the offspring *and* the parents.[2] A solitary child may suffer from the absence of the companionship and stimulation of a sibling. At the same time, the parents may be inclined to overprotect and overindulge an only child. By contrast, three or more siblings may establish bitter patterns of rivalry and make one another chronically insecure as they shift alliances among themselves. Meanwhile, the parents are buffeted by this complex competition and constantly pressed to sustain familial harmony.

To be sure, a family limited to two children is not immune to sibling rivalry. Likewise, as we pointed out in the last chapter, parents may exacerbate such competitiveness by involving both children in their own marital complicities. Nevertheless, considering the advantages and disadvantages of various family sizes, it appears that a two-child family may be most balanced on the positive side. From the standpoint of the children, it provides each with a companion, while requiring them to learn how to be cooperative and make compromises with a peer. Having two children also helps parents to set themselves clearly apart as leaders of the family, making it harder for them—than it would be with an only child—to lapse into parentification or the formation of "hot-house" trios.

Aside from these benefits, the two-child family permits a couple to end procreation and parenting of infants and toddlers before those extremely demanding activities seriously dilute the quality of their marital intimacy. Actually, the majority of couples now seem to have an awareness of these considerations, viewing two children as the ideal size for a family.[3] Most couples also consider 3 years as the best interval for spacing those children.[4] This span of time enables the older child not only to complete toilet training but also to form a stronger sense of self for meeting the challenge of sharing parental attention with another brother or sister.

RELATIONAL BENEFITS OF LIMITING FAMILY SIZE

In voluntarily renouncing further procreation, mates immediately benefit by admitting they are doing it for the explicit purpose of intensifying their relationship. This admission reaffirms the values on which they founded their love-centered marriage. The couple's commitment to the primacy of their relationship is refreshed, and they can advance their relational development without being impeded by the unresolved question of having more children.

True, on their way to resolving that question, mates may uncover sticky areas of ambivalence. Even if they have adorable children of both sexes, why stop enlarging the family? Since these offspring have turned out so well, why not go ahead and have one or two more? Or, since they have felt so good about being parents, wouldn't they feel even better with each additional child they brought into the world? Surely, if they have had only boys or girls, giving up the chance of conceiving a child of the opposite sex—*forever*—may be especially difficult to face.

A husband and a wife may need to air such doubts extensively. In fact, their vacillation may be just as troubling as it was before they decided to reproduce for the first time. But this indecisiveness, while painful to endure, cannot be banished unless and until both of them have thoroughly examined all of its facets. Thus, in making the decision to limit their family to its existing size, they benefit by probing themselves—and each other—with the utmost seriousness of purpose.

Of course, love-centered mates generally communicate with as much candor as they can muster. However, most of their joint decisions do not confront them with such absolute and momentous finality. After all, houses can be rented, bought, and sold. Jobs can be left or changed. But forsaking reproduction is a lifelong decision—reminiscent, in its awesome implications, of the irreversible act of conceiving a child. In exercising their freedom of choice on this issue, mates achieve new levels of honesty and solidarity.

At the same time, they liberate themselves from the wearing preoccupations they had been harboring while still retaining procreation as an option. For as long as they even *thought* of having more children, they could not help but wonder when to conceive and how to readjust their lives to accommodate another child. What would be the *right* time for themselves *and* for the entire family? How could they be sure of having enough time, energy, and money to satisfy *everyone's* essential needs for love and security?

Besides, mates could not avoid a lot of stressful fantasizing about those potential offspring. What if they had trouble conceiving another child? Even if they conceived promptly, what detrimental effects might another pregnancy and birth have on the wife's health? What if the baby were born with a mental or physical defect? Could they, as parents, cope with it emotionally and economically? How would such a misfortune affect their other children? And even if a new baby arrived in good health and was the gender they had hoped for, how would his or her siblings react? Would they be receptive or rejecting?

What a relief, therefore, to be done with all such misgivings once and for all! How much lighter and looser mates feel now that they no longer carry around *any* concerns about this vital aspect of their future! Indeed, it is only after shedding those concerns that both of them are likely to see how much energy they had tied up in imagining what they would or would not do about a child they might or might not have.

Now, mates can focus all of that energy on the immediate and direct enrichment of their relationship, bringing it into the vivid forefront of their consciousness. As a by-product of their increased level of liveliness and fulfillment, they improve their general well-being. As happier persons, they are able to relate with less irritability and greater generosity toward their children, and they have less need to seek substitute gratifications via excessive parenting. They are motivated to stop pampering and overprotecting their offspring and to let them become more self-reliant in every way that is appropriate to their actual level of physical, mental, and emotional maturation. In short, a husband and wife become better parents as they better fulfill the promises of their love for each other.

When their marital history became relevant for illustrating the complexities of this stage, the Slaters were already the parents of two children—Becky, 9, and Pam, 6—and owners of a small but charming house in Connecticut. Scott, a physical therapist, was employed in the rehabilitation department of an urban medical center, while Liz, a registered nurse, worked at a small community hospital.

After their first daughter was born, the Slaters agreed it would be best for Liz to continue working. She enjoyed the stimulation of her profession, and they needed a double income to meet the escalating costs of raising a family. Besides, each wanted to participate in all the responsibilities of childrearing and earning a living. Scott remained on an 8 AM to 4 PM schedule and Liz changed to a new "tailored-time" shift from 5 PM to 1 AM. So, Scott was on hand to be with Becky before Liz left for work.

For several years the Slaters were pleased with this arrangement. Scott had the unique experience of being close to their baby daughter every day, marveling at each change in her behavior. When Pam was born, he diapered, fed, and doted over her just as he had with Becky. Meanwhile, knowing the children were getting plenty of love during her absence, Liz could concentrate on her work without worrying about them.

Eventually, however, the disadvantages of the split schedule outweighed its advantages. Becky and Pam had become clinging and whiny, refusing to play by themselves and vying for attention whenever Scott and Liz were at home together. But the Slaters were even more upset by the damage to their own relationship. Gradually, they had fallen into the appalling habit of taking each other for granted, plodding through their separate routines like preprogrammed robots.

Their deadness was most painfully apparent in bed, which Liz did not enter until Scott was fast asleep. Usually, he didn't even wake up to greet her, much less to make love. Freighted with fatigue, she also lacked any desire for either mental or sexual intercourse. When they began working on different shifts, they had squeezed in a little lovemaking on a Saturday or Sunday night. But after so many years of abstinence during the week, they felt awkward about initiating sexual relations on their days off, and they sank into a profound lethargy about reaching out to each other with their former playfulness and "joie de vivre."

Eventually, they grew hungry for the pleasures of the romance they had known before becoming parents. They saw it was stupid to go on denying their estrangement as a couple. Besides, hadn't they been keeping Becky and Pam immature by hovering over them day and night? Wouldn't it be foolish to go on tantalizing themselves with the possibility of having another baby? True, they had always hoped for a boy—some day. But Liz was already 37, and they couldn't put off another pregnancy much longer. Yet with their kids and jobs, hadn't their relationship suffered enough? Finally, they had to agree, however reluctantly, that it would be best to give up the idea of ever having another child.

Following this difficult decision, the Slaters concentrated on finding ways to revitalize their marriage. After a few brainstorming sessions, they came up with a practical plan for spending more time with each other. Liz would go back to the day shift *and* try to get a job at Scott's facility. Soon, given the national nursing shortage, she made the change. As a result, they could drive back and forth to work in one car and have lunch together regularly. They started to use babysitters, giving themselves an evening out every week, and they even began going off for a few days at a time without the children.

Exhilarated by these changes, the Slaters reveled in the delicious experience of meeting for lunch at the hospital. These encounters felt as thrilling as the dates during their courtship. Gleefully, they savored the rare pleasure of being intimate under workaday conditions, like lovers keeping a tryst while everyone else remained stuck in their passionless ruts. Of course, in the cafeteria they kept some wraps over their romantic feelings. Still, they got intensely high from daring to display their closeness by sitting at a table for two and by the unmistakable ardor of their communication.

On their way home Scott and Liz exchanged solace for the frustration they experienced during the day and let off steam about anything else that bothered them. By the time they arrived at the house, they were ready to give their undivided attention to the girls, observing and responding to them as a coordinated team. Encouraged by this unity, Becky and Pam accepted their parents as role models of reliability, keeping their rooms and clothes in order and offering to help with other household chores. Sometimes, Becky started supper with Pam as her assistant, permitting Liz to take a shower and relax after returning from a busy day at the hospital. On weekends Becky also showed consideration, giving her parents a respite by taking Pam along on visits to friends. Once used to being left with sitters, both girls related well to other adults; without Daddy as their chief playmate after school, they formed much closer ties to Liz and their classmates.

Seeing how well their daughters were maturing, Scott and Liz felt they were on the right track. Their willingness to give themselves periodic breaks from the demands of parenting also paid off in terms of their own morale as a couple. These rewards were especially evident when they took brief vacations without the girls. But Liz and Scott did not save up their lovemaking for these occasional trips. Instead, they resumed a delightful pattern of sexual relations during the week, and on weekends they often had their own wonderful "matineé" after sending the children to the movies with a sitter.

Many other husbands and wives have divided their roles

with the same split schedules the Slaters followed—with the same ultimate results. When queried by a researcher, these mates uniformly complained of having no time to talk to each other, to do things together, or for sex. In fact, one couple saw each other for only 45 minutes a day. This wife, also a nurse, worked on the day shift, while her husband, a plant foreman, worked from 5 PM to 1 AM. She got home at 3:30 after picking up the kids from school, and he left less than an hour later to go to work. They, too, had to confine their lovemaking to weekends. Occasionally, they took a day of sick leave to get more time to be together during the week.[5]

Nevertheless, it is rapidly becoming an economic necessity for both spouses to work, as it is for the Slaters. A comprehensive study of America's families, conducted by the Joint Center for Urban Studies of M.I.T. and Harvard, predicted that in the 1990s the joint income of spouses will be essential for a middle-class style of life.[6]

THE DUAL-CAREER COUPLE AND THE CHALLENGE OF FOCUSING

Fortunately, couples may also derive some psychological and relational benefits from sharing the responsibilities of securing an income. Working enables both mates to satisfy their desires for intellectual stimulation and for making a social contribution through vocational accomplishment. Thus, several studies show that wives with careers—as compared to those who are housewives exclusively—are physically and emotionally healthier, have higher self-esteem, feel less socially isolated, and seem happier in general. In addition, these working wives regard childrearing more in terms of self-fulfillment than as self-sacrifice.[7] Reciprocally, when their wives work, husbands feel freer to change jobs, turn down promotions, and take time off for either advanced training or retraining for a different occupation. Besides, a dual-career marriage provides a man with a "buffer" of economic security against the unexpected loss of employment.[8]

There also is evidence that mates experience a more zestful life when both of them work. Each takes pride in what the other is doing, which adds to their *mutual esteem as a couple.*

By playing similar economic roles, they equalize decision making and power sharing in their relationship.[9] One study found that such spouses usually evolve a division of labor based on their personal interests and skills. When both of them balk at doing a particular kind of housework, they often rotate it. Typically, their allocation of tasks diverges from traditional gender-role stereotypes. Equally willing to cook, clean, shop for the children, get the car fixed, or arrange for home repairs, these mates readily interchange functions. This change of set often is required among dual-career couples due to illness or the demands of their jobs, which may include travel away from home. But these spouses can quickly trade "flexibility for predictability;"[10] and they ". . . accommodate shifting stances frequently."[11] Thus, they can count on *and* support each other whenever their personal, professional, or family needs require it.

Of course, as Karen Weingarten observes, these busy husbands and wives also need ". . . each other to unwind, to celebrate, to commiserate, to clarify and to sympathize."[12] Punctuating their basic sense of trust, both of them are inclined to be exceptionally thoughtful of each other. For example, when a wife has to go on a business trip, she telephones her husband in order to stay in emotional contact with him. During her absence, the husband reciprocates this consideration by taking good care of their children and giving them special attention. "He knows that his wife will feel better about being away if she is sure the children are happy."[13]

On the other hand, dual-career couples with children are extremely vulnerable to the stress of "role strain." Like Liz and Scott, they face a double day—one on the job and one at home—each of which tends to be very demanding. Mates are easily smitten by "burnout." Frequently, both of them are prey to chronic anxiety and fatigue, becoming easily irritated by their children, their colleagues, *and one another.* They may also find it difficult to think clearly, work efficiently, or concentrate on solving their common problems. Consequently, many spouses regularly take tranquilizers or alcohol to dull the pain of unremitting tensions and frustrations.[14]

The most devastating relational impact of burnout manifests itself on the sexual level. When husbands and wives feel swamped by their "overload," sexual contact becomes a duty rather than a pleasure, or it "flies out the window" completely. As Ellen Frank and Carol Anderson state: "Things seem to fall apart a bit in the middle years, when more husbands and wives report that they are distracted from their sexual relations."[15] Other investigators have discovered that some husbands maintain an interest in sex but begin to show signs of performance anxiety or impotence.[16] Many wives, especially those in high-level careers, experience inhibited sexual desire; if they don't lose all interest in sex, they may not relax enough to enjoy foreplay or to attain orgasmic release.[17]

Unfortunately, as Marcia and Thomas Laswell point out, couples often expend the bulk of their energies working and parenting. Each partner gets "what is left over . . . only a nervous and exhausted mate."[18] For those who want to spend more time focusing on loving one another, "the dilemma of how to carve out that time for themselves when most of it (or all of it) is already spoken for . . . becomes a central issue."[19] In this respect, Joseph Procaccini points toward a constructive way out. Beyond proposing that couples make a "time and energy audit," he recommends that they question their value system and adopt more realistic goals in regard to their children's needs and their *own limitations*.[20]

Questioning spouses about happiness and understanding between them, researchers have found that greater amounts of togetherness *do* produce more satisfying marriages. However, only certain kinds of shared activities produced this positive effect. The time couples spent together on child care, housework, watching television, or community activities had *no* significant effect on their marital relationship. However, "The more time together in activities such as eating, playing and conversing, the more satisfying the marriage." In short, having *fun* is the key factor. Accordingly, the authors of this study advise spouses to match their work schedules as closely as possible, as Liz and Scott decided to do. Otherwise, mates may "depend on having economic partners but lack time to sustain each other emotionally."[21]

Undoubtedly, couples have to tap all their ingenuity to maximize their time for *pleasurable and intimate contact*. Still, by creating these opportunities, mates automatically introduce novelty into their daily lives, lifting themselves out of rigidly defined roles and routines. Like the Slaters, they make a romantic adventure of their focusing, unleashing more passion in their lovemaking and in all their direct interactions.

COMPLICITIES OF FRAGMENTATION

Over time, however, a couple's unwavering decision to stop reproducing is likely to make them feel biologically useless and uncertain about what to do with the creativity they had previously directed toward bringing life into the world. Both mates are disturbed by the realization of having completed one of the most fruitful functions of their relationship. Their malaise is aggravated further as they discover their offspring no longer require as much care as they did during infancy and early childhood.

Naturally, these qualms coincide with all the threats of love that mates stir up in striving to attain the desirable objective for this stage. Ironically, their very progress in *focusing* much more on relating to one another—and much less on having and rearing children—severely exacerbates their fear of loving. As a defense, they devise complicities for curtailing their intimacy and *fragmenting* the loving core of their marriage.

Scott and Liz slowly undermined their marital happiness without seeming to realize why or how they were doing it. The first sign of their mutual subversion emerged in acute feelings of oppression during their luncheon meetings. Finding it almost impossible to carry on a conversation, they dreaded going to the cafeteria every day. Picking at their food, each wondered: "What *is* there to say—the same old gripes and gossip? Maybe I'm missing some fun or useful information by not sitting with other people." Still, they maintained their agitating ritual, which had been the joyous focal point of their days for the past 4 years. But they prayed silently for some kind of deliverance from their pain.

Their hopes appeared to be answered when Scott was asked to replace the retiring Chief of Physical Therapy, because they knew his extra duties would put an end to their togetherness at the hospital. In fact, the gulf between them widened swiftly following Scott's promotion. Since he had to remain at the hospital to do paperwork long after Liz was free to go home, he began taking his own car to work. He also used his lunch hours to discuss administrative issues with colleagues. In effect, the Slaters stopped seeing each other from breakfast until night. Yet both of them felt released from their emotional suffocation.

Months before Scott's offer came through, Liz had been selected to reorganize her town's training program for emergency medical technicians. The pay would be nominal, but she had all the qualifications, *plus* the personality, to expand the program. She'd been flattered by the town's request but hesitant to take it on.

After Scott's advancement, however, Liz decided to go for it. After all, she had no prospect of becoming head of *her* department. Surely, she deserved an ego boost as much as Scott did. As for the girls, they were now old enough to take care of themselves after school. So Liz went out several nights each week, speaking to groups of prospective trainees, conducting classes, and sometimes even going on calls with the ambulance crew.

The frenetic lifestyle of the Slaters led them to neglect their parental responsibilities. But they seemed neither to notice nor to be concerned about how they were relating to their children. Becky responded to their apparent indifference by failing to keep her room in order or to offer any help with the household chores. Liz and Scott would sometimes criticize her for being lazy, but they did not make the effort required to hold her to account consistently.

As a budding adolescent of 13, Becky spent a lot of time "hanging out" with teenagers in her school, thinking obsessively about her looks, how to keep up with other girls, *and* how to attract boys! She had many qualms and questions about dating and sex. But she was embarrassed to confide in Liz and Scott. Anyway, they always looked so tired. Somehow, it never seemed exactly right to approach them, and *they* never brought up any of the issues that were on her mind.

Meanwhile, Pam became envious of Becky's physical development—her aura of glamor and adultlike maturity. Pam also envied Becky for getting whatever she wanted: expensive clothes, dancing lessons, and permission to stay up late on Saturday nights. She nagged her parents for equivalent "goodies," insisting they enroll her in a gymnastics class, get her more books and records, and buy her every outfit in a doll wardrobe she saw advertised on television. If they objected to any of her demands, she erupted into a temper tantrum. Reluctant to cope with these hassles, Scott and Liz usually gave in to her, just as they indulged Becky.

To make matters worse, Scott started to work on Saturdays, leaving Liz to do most of the shopping and other chores. Although resentful about this change, she resigned herself to it. But her resignation turned into cheerful tolerance as Scott's busyness gave her time to become involved more romantically with Dr. Martin Wallace, a resident in her pediatrics unit. From the day he showed up on the service, Liz was impressed by his tender and gentle manner with the infants and children as well as their mothers. Unquestionably, he was more sensitive than the attending physicians who supervised him.

But *then* Liz let herself notice how good-looking he was—almost *too* handsome to be real! He was also younger than she. But that seemed to make no difference to them. Soon they established a powerful rapport, talking enthusiastically and agreeing on almost everything. What a contrast from her conversations with Scott! Yes, they did talk for a few minutes before falling asleep. But they spoke in lifeless monotones, mostly about the mechanics of their work and household.

She still had intercourse with Scott, although not often, and not with the passion of a man and a woman flaming with love for one another. On those nights Liz would lie awake after Scott fell asleep, musing about what it would be like to go to bed with Martin. Of course, they hadn't "done" very much—yet. Once, he was just about to kiss her in a supply room when they were interrupted by an approaching nurse. But his touch made her reel with giddiness. She knew he would be more than willing to "go all the way" with her, and they could easily arrange a rendezvous on any Saturday when Scott was at work. No, she was the reluctant one, already feeling guilty about what she was doing behind Scott's back. But she also had other qualms that froze her with fear.

Her apprehension arose after a visit to Martin's apartment, which he had personally decorated, skillfully combining objects of art, elegant antiques, and contemporary furnishings. Like himself, the place seemed almost *too* stylish and neat for a man. But wasn't his artistic flair something she admired most about him? What was wrong with that? Still, he had never married. God, what was she thinking? Maybe he just wanted to wait until finishing his residency. He couldn't be homosexual if he was so excited by her. But what about bisexuality? Wasn't that a real possibility? Hadn't she often seen him leave the hospital with a doctor who was openly gay?

Still, Liz never mentioned her concerns to Martin. How could she, after doing her best to seduce him? But they were closing in on *complete* intimacy. What if he's carrying the AIDS virus? Her terror was undeniable. Could using a condom *guarantee* protection against it? What the hell should she *do?*

Obsessed with strategies for "covering her tracks," Liz had begun to lie to Scott about her whereabouts when she was actually with Martin. She was just as secretive with the girls about her illicit liaison. Sometimes, however, her "explanations" about where she was going—and why—were a bit far-fetched and tinged with anxiety. She then worried that Becky could see she was lying.

Actually, the deceptions used by Liz dovetailed with Scott's own sneaky game of "affair." Like Liz, Scott had not yet gone fully over the line with the woman he had "on the side." But he often committed flagrant adultery with her inside his head.

Scott met Doris Maloney when she became his patient. Her husband had died in the driver's seat beside her after their car skidded off an icy road and smashed into a stone wall. Lucky to have survived, she sustained a fracture in her right arm, requiring orthopedic surgery. Subsequently, she was referred to Scott for extensive physical therapy. In addition to the usual treatments, he gave her a lot of psychological support in picking up the torn pieces of her life, including the parenting of a 6-year-old son. She thus eagerly anticipated her weekly appointments with him.

Doris had a pretty face with keen blue eyes and reddish hair. Her body was voluptuous and appealing, and she was a very warm person who *really* listened to everything Scott had to say. Given his stalemate with Liz, he had an exceptional need to talk to a receptive woman. He was also moved by her appreciation of his work and her diligence in following his instructions to exercise. Most of all, he admired her courage, her ability to face up to the terrible tragedy of her husband's death and to take over his real estate business.

Scott made an effort to be properly clinical in treating Doris. But as her therapy neared its end, he began to feel an unmistakably erotic sensation in his groin whenever he placed his hands on her. Her facial flush and soulful looks told him that she was getting the same kind of charge from his touch.

Both of them balked at saying a final goodbye. But Doris brought up the possibility of continuing to get together. Their first "date" was in her real estate office, early one evening, when they had the place to themselves. After a few stilted remarks, they fell into each other's arms, letting loose the impassioned yearnings they had been building up for months. Doris was ready to do anything Scott wanted. But he clutched up after their frenzied kiss. No, his head buzzed anxiously, not now, not tonight. It's too fast. I'm too mixed up about what's going on. He begged off with a fabrication about having to rush back to the hospital on an emergency case that had come in just as he was leaving his office to see her. But they ended the evening by making another appointment—and with an unspoken understanding that they would be getting into a full-fledged affair.

The Slaters illustrate how a couple may fragment their relationship to the brink of dissolution. Previously focusing on the intensification of their intimacy, Scott and Liz had been fulfilling all four promises of love in new ways. Indeed, they had become closer and happier than ever before as a pair of confidants, reliable helpmates and parents, social equals, and passionate lovers. However, the threats associated with these exceptional gratifications stirred their fear of loving to an extraordinary degree. Eventually, they yielded to this fear by contriving a fresh repertoire of complicities that culminated in the inclination to form loving relationships with other people.

Thus, the more threatened the Slaters felt by expanding the boundaries of their individuality, the more they undermined their unity and increased their competitiveness. When

Scott's promotion made stringent demands on his time and energy, Liz did not empathize with his efforts or applaud his achievements. Instead, she displayed her rivalrous feelings by extending the scope of her own egoistic pursuits. Reciprocally, Scott remained insensitive to the frustration Liz felt over having no opportunity to advance in her own department. Preoccupied with their separate ambitions, they withdrew from one another and no longer looked forward to being together. Often, they had the feeling of losing some personal advantage by not spending even more time relating to colleagues in their own specialties, and they became very reluctant to talk honestly about what was going on within and between them.

Other couples act out similar complicities by throwing themselves into separate hobbies and cultural endeavors or by taking on stressful and time-consuming positions in different community organizations. Some mates go all out in a final effort to make an exceptional mark on their lifelong fields of work, becoming more involved than ever before in their individual strivings. Or both husband and wife may attempt to act out unrealistic and futile fantasies of starting *entirely new* careers. Thus, as the Laswells point out, "Patterns of overactivity that keep couples apart . . . are not always the result of poor scheduling or of too many demands. Keeping too busy to spend time with a mate often is a way of avoiding intimacy."[22]

In reacting to the threat of their increasing interdependence, the Slaters began to behave less reliably, neglecting their practical household responsibilities as well as their daughters' needs for care, supervision, and guidance. Feeling extremely detached from each other, Liz and Scott became more and more untrustworthy as they began to "play around" with Martin and Doris.

Other couples react to the threat of increasing their interdependence with a devastating complicity that undermines their previous agreement to stop having children. They devise a "contraception charade" and become capricious about using their habitual method of birth control. Eventually, they have an "accidental" pregnancy.

Of course, having made a decision to stop procreation, a couple needs to use birth control reliably until the wife completes menopause—a stretch of time that may extend for 15 years or more. However, by helping one another to choose and maintain an effective form of contraception, mates benefit tremendously, increasing not only their interdependence but also their sexual pleasure.

Still, it is not unusual for couples at this stage of marital development to conceive—"accidentally on purpose"—after their first two children are already teenagers. When this occurs, some mates decide to have a *fourth* child, using the additional responsibilities of rearing a "second family" as an excuse for avoiding the intensification of their own relationship.

Threatened by transcending their gender differences, the Slaters retrenched on their previous level of social equality. Becoming more "macho," Scott acted as if the duties of his new job and status were far more important than anything Liz was doing, deserving his total involvement and the respect of the entire family. He stopped sharing the daily chores around the house and left Liz to pick up the slack. Playing her stereotyped part in this gender-role complicity, she took on these extra burdens and did not demand equal consideration for what she was doing. In other cases, couples may revert to sexist modes of childrearing when they feel threatened by advances in their own relational equality.

Finally, the Slaters responded to the threat of immersion in the pleasure of lovemaking by falling into a pattern of "going through the motions." Eventually, having turned off their sexual appetites, they rarely bothered to touch each other. Other mates may react defensively to this threat by developing specific sexual dysfunctions.

AN AFFAIR: THE ULTIMATE RESULT OF FRAGMENTATION

The misery of these all-encompassing complicities may feel so unbearable as to motivate many spouses, like Scott and Liz, to look outside of their own relationship for the love they are blocking from one another. Thus, various studies indicate that about 50% of husbands and 20–40% of wives have at least one extramarital sexual encounter.[23] A lot of research supports the association between marital unhappiness and participation in affairs. Several investigators conclude that spouses who report low marital satisfaction, infrequent sexual relations, and poor quality of intercourse are more susceptible to outside involvements.[24]

Concern over waning youth, attractiveness, and sexual potency also is associated with extramarital involvements through which each mate tries to prove his or her youthfulness, desirability, and virility. Certainly, the desire to feel young again seems to precipitate many adulterous encounters and bondings.[25] Indeed, an increasing number of women are beginning to have affairs in their late 30s and early 40s, just as Liz was tempted to do. In their 1977 *Redbook* survey, Carol Tavris and Susan Sadd found that 40% of women over 40 years of age—as compared to 20% of those under 25—engaged in extramarital intercourse.[26] In a more recent survey conducted by *Cosmopolitan* magazine, 50% of the women 18–34 years of age had at least one affair, but the rate jumped to 69% for women 35 or older.[27] This correlation between age and extramarital affairs is also found among men.[28]

On the other hand, there is some evidence that the incidence of extramarital relations may be leveling off, especially for women. The most recent *Redbook* survey, done by Rubenstein and Tavris in 1987, found that the percent of respondents of all ages who had extramarital involvements was actually down 3% from the results of their earlier survey in 1977.[29] Experts attribute this trend to the present AIDS epidemic. Liz is not the only woman who experienced anxiety about the possibility of getting this deadly disease. Until a preventative vaccine is discovered, or a cure, "The fear of contracting AIDS should constrain sexual activity outside of marriage for many couples."[30]

Nevertheless, many experts in marital relationships believe that an affair functions *primarily* as a vehicle for getting someone else into the couple system. Murray Bowen, for instance, originated the concept of "triangulation," the tendency of mates to introduce triangles in their marriage.[31] In his view a couple may involve a third person in their relationship in order to shift the locus of their interpersonal conflicts away from themselves. Mates also use that person as a scapegoat for their mutual aggression and anger—or to block their intimacy with one another.

Frequently, the person designated as the "third" by such couples is their own child. In the last chapter we showed how couples include an offspring in their complicities. Similarly, the Slaters illustrate how a couple uses their extramarital involvements as a way of fragmenting their own intimacy. Henry Spitz, another family therapist, agrees: "You detour through a third person, a lover, which is no different than detouring through a child or a thing, like alcohol."[32]

Supporting our view of extramarital involvements as part of a mutually agreed upon scenario, Francine Klagsbrun states: "Even though affairs are usually secret, sometimes a covert agreement exists on the part of the 'betrayed' partner, a kind of unacknowledged and unspoken acceptance of the affair because that partner is relieved, too, to have a barrier to closeness in the marriage."[33]

Maggie Scarf also emphasizes this function of an affair, describing it as "an emotional distance regulator." In her account, there are no "innocent victims" and "vile offenders." It is irrelevant to know which mate is the first to get involved with someone else. Actually, *both* members of the couple "are lusting in their hearts" or dreaming of other partners because *both* are feeling profoundly alienated.[34] According to a clinical psychologist she quotes, even if only one partner is having an outside relationship, the other has also been fantasizing about becoming involved with someone else. Thus, for Scarf an affair does not happen *to* a person, it happens *between both mates*. It is a symptom of a global marital disturbance—*not* the disturbance itself.

In our view this "global marital disturbance" stems from a couple's dread about continuing to fulfill all four promises of love. Thus, as we showed in the Slater's case, mates jointly react defensively to the fear of loving aroused by each of the threats that accompany those promises. Eventually, they feel so thoroughly alienated by their defensiveness that the only way out seems to be an escape into an affair with someone else.

Given this escapist motivation, it is no wonder that most affairs are characterized by an intense sharing of feelings between the lovers. However, these feelings are more a function of the conditions of the new and illicit relationship "than any

magical matching of the partners involved."[35] For most adulterous lovers there is a sense of what John Gagnon calls "psychological compression."[36] On any single occasion they can
only be together briefly, on time that is usually stolen from
their marriages. Like teenagers restricted by parents, adulterous lovers are implicitly restricted by commitments to their
mates and children.[37] However, just because their mutual access is limited, their liaisons seem very special. This specialness is reinforced by the fact that they tend to concentrate
their attention on one another with no concern for the host of
mundane matters that continually confront spouses. According to Gagnon, guilt may also heighten the mutuality of their
desire, intensifying the gratification of their sexual
relations.[38]

Of course, most mates regard an affair as a gross violation
of their commitment to fidelity. Thus, they fear that if they
were discovered by their spouses, a marital crisis would ensue,
and they become very secretive about their behavior. Yet this
very secrecy, like guilt, may also stimulate feelings of adventure, contributing to their heightened experience of pleasurable excitement.

Scott and Doris finally set up a secure plan to begin their
lovemaking. Privately, he still balked at going ahead with it.
But he had already seen her three times, and his enjoyment of
those secret encounters outweighed all the intrigue involved in
arranging them. It was mightily reassuring for him to feel desired by so sexy and competent a woman as Doris. Besides,
when they kissed, his body seemed to ache with unrequited
desire. He therefore went along with her suggestions for an
idyllic Saturday in the country. She would reserve a room at an
old inn located in the center of an historic village. They would
meet in the lobby at noon, go to a charming restaurant for a
leisurely lunch, and return to their canopied bed for a long,
long "siesta."

A rehabilitation conference in Hartford provided Scott
with a perfect excuse to get away from home for longer than
usual. With his mouth dry and his heart racing, he told Liz he
just *had* to attend. Although she accepted his lie without reacting to his evident discomfort in telling it to her, she did feel a

momentary twinge of apprehension. Why was he going on so about it?

Coincidentally, Becky and Pam had been invited to visit their grandparents on the same day. Left entirely on her own, Liz could easily have managed to be with Martin. In fact, she had a compelling urge to call him. But she resisted her temptation, knowing he would ask her, once again, to go to bed with him. He had been pressing her lately, pointing out how juvenile it was to go around holding hands in dark corners of the hospital. Why not stop these silly games and "make it"—like mature adults? She didn't want to keep on teasing him with coy and false rebuffs. But how could she reveal the *whole* truth of her resistance? Yet she really hated the idea of breaking up their relationship.

Liz decided instead to work off a little tension by doing some spring cleaning. Maybe staying in the house alone would help her to resolve herself about Martin. While dusting the furniture, however, she got a call to accompany her EMT group to a remote farm where several people were injured when the barn went up in flames. Dropping her rag, she sped off at once to join her trainees.

After handling all of that stress, Liz stopped off in the nearby village to relax. While lingering to admire the colonial houses and quaint shops, she suddenly saw Scott and Doris walking toward her, only a few yards away. Scott's eyes locked with hers in a stare of mutual astonishment. For a horrifying moment, both of them were paralyzed and speechless.

Then, with her voice cracking and shaking, Liz said she would be waiting at home to talk to him. Whirling around, she rushed to the car. As she went, she almost stopped breathing. "My God," she mused in a gathering panic, "what have we done to each other? Scott has been slipping away from me and I didn't even want to know about it. What a stupid fool I've been! Flirting like a schoolgirl with Martin—and acting as if he meant more to me than Scott. Thinking I could take Scott for granted no matter what I did behind his back."

Discovered so unexpectedly, a bolt of terror tore through Scott. He almost left Doris on the spot to comfort Liz and beg her forgiveness. He cursed himself for ever getting involved with Doris. No, he didn't want to lose Liz for *anything* in the world! But how could he make it up to her? Hadn't he violated her trust while she was being faithful to him—despite their unhappiness?

The Slaters were extraordinarily lucky. The horror they felt when Liz discovered Scott with Doris shocked them into realizing how much they valued their marriage. It also exposed how false they had been to themselves, one another, *and* the two people they had drawn into their vortex of fragmentation. Forced by circumstances into honesty, each admitted to having suspected the other on many occasions. They also saw how they had been agreeing tacitly to maintain their many lies of omission and commission.

Because they had not become sexually involved with Martin and Doris, the Slaters were plagued by fewer worries than afflict many other couples who "play around." Clearly, spouses who have intercourse with outside partners run the risks of getting a sexually transmitted disease and participating in an unwanted pregnancy. After adding these emotional burdens to their load of anxiety and guilt over being unfaithful, they may feel the resulting rift between them is too extensive to repair.

A study of 108 affairs revealed that 30% of the spouses did get divorced, although less than 4% of them planned to marry the person with whom they had the affair.[39] So, as these figures suggest, most affairs evidently are not intended to become direct replacements for a troubled marriage. Instead, the affair is a dramatic signal of marital difficulties that spouses have chosen to evade rather than to resolve. Indeed, from our point of view, the few adulterous lovers who do marry will inevitably create the same kind of complicities as blighted their discarded relationships. Likewise, in contrast to the intoxicating aura of escape from reality that surrounded and glamorized their affair, these spouses are soon saddled, once again, with the inescapable responsibilities of married life: children, work, and the maintenance of a household.

Consequently, a couple may regard the revelation of an affair as a new beginning—not as the end of their marriage.[40] Indeed, as Klagsbrun remarks, an affair can function as a beneficial crisis if it motivates spouses ". . . to turn back to the marriage and take a hard look at it."[41]

RESTORING MARITAL AND PARENTAL INTEGRITY

Responding insightfully to their crisis, Liz and Scott openly confessed they did not want to lose one another. In effect, this meant reuniting so profoundly that they would never again bring their marriage to the brink of disaster. Of course, they needed time to flush out all the debris of their mutual deceit and suspicion, and they suffered through many days and nights of wretched accusations and recriminations. But they ultimately succeeded—with unquestionable sincerity—in strengthening their loyalty and fidelity. Jointly renouncing the possibility of ever having another affair, they pledged to spare no effort in overcoming whatever problems emerged between them in the future.

Confronting the same situation as the Slaters, other spouses also reaffirm a mutual commitment to their marriage as a basic condition for remaining together. However, to *improve* their relationship they need to resume its constructive development, which they had brought to a halt during the time of their affairs.

Launching this improvement, a couple rebuilds their romance, focusing on a common dream that is inspiring, attainable, *and* appropriate for this stage of their marriage. By directing their previously fragmented energies toward the realization of this dream, they invigorate every aspect of their relationship.

As professionals in the field of health, Liz and Scott could readily construct a common dream of working together in providing care to patients. They might establish a service for pediatric rehabilitation, combining her expertise with his, in a hospital, an outpatient clinic, or a private practice of their own. This creative blending of their special skills would be intellectually stimulating while giving them a fresh outlook on their vocational future.

From a relational standpoint, implementing this project would challenge the Slaters to fulfill the promises of their love in new ways. Indeed, to become successful *and* satisfied as codirectors of a service to others, they would *have* to become more interdependent, socially equal, and communicative than ever before. Excited by the adventures of their collaboration, they would put more passion into their lovemaking and, thus, derive more pleasure from it.

Couples who work in disparate occupations could derive the same kind of gratifications by focusing on creating common dreams in other areas of their lives. For example, they might become serious coworkers in a cause to improve the environment or to house the homeless. Or they might buy that small cottage in the country they've been longing for—an affordable "handyman's special" they would take pleasure in remodeling together.

However, while resurrecting their romance, couples would also do well to review the complicities they had formed as a prelude to their affairs. By tracing these defense pacts to their origins in the four threats of love, mates could help each other to learn how to cope more quickly and effectively with the similar ones they will be contriving as their marriage progresses.

Still, these enriching relational measures do not automatically erase the damage couples had done to the quality of their parenting. While fragmenting their marriage to the vanishing point, adulterous mates also shred the fabric of their relations with their children. As they flagrantly exceed the beneficial restrictions of their own vows of fidelity and honesty, these mothers and fathers are in no condition to be truthful with their offspring or to set helpful limits on their behavior.

Typically, while in the midst of their extramarital excursions, couples act as if they are doing nothing underhanded or dangerous. Yet they are secretly developing relationships that could result in the breakup of their families. They collude before their children, pretending to be free of marital problems. Then, having silently agreed to lie to one another *and* to their offspring, both mates ignore the falseness and irresponsibility of their pretense.

However, sensitive and intelligent children, like Becky, pick up subtle signs of parental deceit and disaffection. They also perceive the indifference and indulgence their parents are displaying toward them. Reacting to such "benign" neglect, children are inclined to become more dishonest and unreliable in relating to their mothers and fathers, as Becky did with Liz and Scott. Meanwhile, having detected gross hypocrisy in their parents, these children lose a considerable degree of respect for them.

Thus, mates face the daunting task of regaining that esteem and reclaiming their legitimate parental authority. Obviously, they cannot achieve these goals by continuing their collusion. To win back their legitimacy, parents must earn it by proving the genuineness of their *credibility.*

In this respect, it is in the best interests of the entire family for errant mates to practice what they hope to teach by disclosing what had been going on inside and outside their marriage. To be sure, it is painfully embarrassing for a mother and father to admit an affair to their children. Yet this is an emotional price worth paying for the restoration of their former standing as truthful and trustworthy. Besides, in making themselves exceptionally vulnerable by "coming clean" to their offspring, mates greatly increase their own psychological strength. At the same time, they implicitly invite a reciprocal increase in candor on the part of their children, which also strengthens them.

However, after hearing such a confession, children need reassurance about how their parents feel about their *future* as a married couple. To address that concern, mates certainly need to affirm the mutuality of their love, their mutual pledge of loyalty, and their joint resolve to maintain the integrity of their marriage.

Of course, considering the couple's past machinations, their children may retain some lingering skepticism. However, spouses can offer no more convincing evidence of their credibility than by actually confessing what they had done. Indeed, by this confession they make amends for their previous falseness and irresponsibility, and, by putting so much faith and trust in their offspring, they demonstrate the sincerity of their parental love.

Now unshakably committed to refrain from violating the limitations of their marital fidelity, spouses have no conflict about re-establishing similarly helpful limits for their children. Because of their dependency, children know that they *need* parental protection and guidance. While often objecting to rules and regulations, they are quite prepared to accept limits when they see the benefits for their own growth and welfare. In fact, these rational restrictions provide children with emotional security *and* with a sense of parental concern for their well-being. So, loving parents can reinstate the trust and compliance of their offspring by explaining the advantages of the renunciations they now ask them to make.

A couple could best follow up on the disclosure of their marital transgression by bringing out its meanings for a love-centered relationship. In terms their children could understand, they could explain how the various threats of love led to their mutual defensiveness and subsequent adultery. Similarly, they could give detailed and concrete examples of how spouses grow in intimacy and harmony by being open and cooperative; dependable and trustworthy; social equals who accept each other's gender differences; *and* sensual lovers. This last point may be especially difficult for parents to raise. But making love has the highest priority among all the activities involved in a love-centered marriage. Accordingly, they would want to emphasize the importance of marital lovemaking to their children.

Naturally, extramarital liaisons are also highly erotic in nature. So, upon hearing about the affairs of their parents, children would be stimulated to question them about their sexual attitudes and values. These queries are most likely to be posed by prepubescent and adolescent children who are already wrestling with weighty dilemmas of their own and seeking clarification about all kinds of issues pertaining to sex.

In the Slaters' case, Pam might ask about her physical development. When, for example, will she be getting breasts? How will they feel? And what about menstruation? Will it hurt and be awful? Or will it make her feel like a grown woman? Likewise, Becky might voice her erotic longings and come forward with her apprehensions about making sexual contact with boys. She really likes some of them but what should she do about it? Kiss? Pet? What about oral sex and intercourse? How do these things feel?

Dealing with these nitty-gritty concerns, the Slaters might be mortified by the irony of their situation. For while Scott was torn with conflict about having intercourse with Doris and Liz was petrified about getting AIDS from Martin, they never even *thought* of talking to their own daughters about the facts and implications of a sexual relationship—much less about birth control and the prevention of sexually transmitted diseases.

Surely, parents do not have to participate in affairs to qualify as mentors for a child's education in sexual matters. On the contrary, consistently faithful mates have a much more secure emotional basis for initiating talks about sex with their children. Having no affairs to explain, their parental credibility—and authenticity as lovers—is not at stake.

As a result of such open discussions, a couple and their children become freer to progress in their diverging paths of development. Due to the greatly heightened sexual drive of puberty, adolescents naturally experience rearoused Oedipal attractions to their parents of the opposite sex. Meanwhile, anticipating the time when they will have to break their close familial ties and assume adult responsibility for their own lives, their separation anxiety is also aroused severely.

However, being given the opportunity to confront and discard the sexually tinged fantasies they may have about their mothers and fathers enables adolescents to loosen their unrealistic attachments to their parents and to stop clinging to them. Simultaneously, they are motivated to form closer attachments to peers with whom they can realistically hope to integrate the sexual and affectionate components of love. Moreover, guided by parental perspectives on love-centered relationships, these children would approach their sexual behavior with wisdom. Getting involved only with people for whom they have real affection, they would also be prudent about avoiding unwanted pregnancies and sexually transmitted diseases.

Similarly, the parental "instructors" liberate themselves from the coils of their own reverse Oedipal involvements and separation anxiety that are rekindled by the blossoming development of their adolescent children. This liberation allows mates at the focusing stage to funnel a far greater quantum of eroticism into their own relationship. As Warren Gadpaille asserts: "Puberty and adolescence constitute the most prolonged and intense pressure toward further parental . . . maturation."[42] Adolescent children ". . . demand explanations for the hypocrisy they perceive and insist that parents validate their positions. . . . For parents with the basic ego strength to reconsider and modify previously insufficiently explored value systems, it can be a mind-expanding experience."[43] Gadpaille goes on to say that, for spouses, ". . . development at this stage of life usually manifests itself in the integration of healthier reciprocity in sexual relations and in a broader acceptance of sexuality as a normal and good part of life."[44]

By jointly educating their children in this crucial area, a husband and wife also eliminate some of the stereotypical divisions in gender roles they had established during the earlier years of parenting. In taking equal responsibility for informing their children about sexuality, mates spend more time talking about sex with each other. These communications help them to transcend their own intrinsic differences in gender when they make love, improving their ability to express all the facets of personality that men and women have in common.

As they head toward the end of this marital stage, a couple has the cumulative familiarity to explore new areas of erotic enjoyment. If they had previously been wary of oral-genital contact, for example, they can confront their inhibitions in a spirit of comfortable camaraderie. After all, they are-"lifers" now. Why pretend there is anything too "heavy" for them to deal with, especially something that could only result in more fulfillment for both of them? Of course, they are likely to find that their long-standing sexual inhibitions stem from their common defensive reactions to the threat of immersion in the pleasure of lovemaking. But this very discovery would permit them to break yet another complicity that has impaired the sharing of their love.

Likewise, mates could verbalize erotic fantasies that have been obsessing or troubling them. Some of these fantasies may merely reflect sexual behavior, like oral-genital contact, that they had yearned for but had been afraid to engage in together. Other fantasies, however, may be symptomatic of relational frustrations that extend far beyond the erotic realm. Discussion of these kinds of fantasies may lead a couple to examine unbroken complicities they have ignored for years. By breaking these complicities, they improve their relationship in other respects as well as sexually.

Naturally, couples grow in pleasurable intimacy as they do all of these things. Indeed, they become more sufficient unto themselves during the very time their children are rapidly growing away from them. Thus, a husband and wife prepare each other for the actual separation that will occur when their "little" boys and girls leave home for college, marriage, and a career.

NOTES

1. Scanzoni, L. D., & Scanzoni, J. *Men, Women, and change: A sociology of marriage and family.* New York: McGraw-Hill, 1981, p. 531.
2. Knox, D. *Human sexuality: The search for understanding.* St. Paul: West, 1984, pp. 479–484.
3. Miller, W. B., & Godwin, R. K. *Psyche and demos: Individual psychology and the issues of population.* New York: Oxford University Press, 1977, p. 136.
4. Knox, op. cit., pp. 488–489.
5. Lasswell, M., & Lasswell, T. E. *Marriage and the family.* Lexington, Mass.: Heath, 1982, pp. 359–360.
6. Masnick, G., & Bane, M. J. *The nation's families 1960–1990.* Cambridge, Mass.: Joint Center for Urban Studies of M.I.T. and Harvard University, 1980.
7. Verbruge, L. M ., & Madans, J. H. Women's roles and health. *Marriage and Divorce Today Newsletter,* April 1985, pp. 3–4. See also Hall, H. A woman's place . . . despite the stress of doing it all, for most women the rewards of working outweigh the costs. *Psychology Today,* April 1988, pp. 28–29.
8. Coleman, J. C. *Intimate relationships, marriage, and family,* 2d ed. New York: Macmillan, 1988, p. 289.
9. Moore, K., & Sawhill, I. Implications of women's employment for home and family life. In J. Knaps (Ed.), *Women and the American economy: A look to the 1980s.* Englewood Cliffs, N.J.: Prentice-Hall, 1976, pp. 102–122.
10. Weingarten, K. Interdependence. In R. Rapoport & R. N. Rapoport (Eds.), *Working couples.* New York: Harper & Row, 1978, p. 156.
11. Ibid., p. 150.
12. Ibid., p. 155.
13. Ibid., p. 151.
14. Procaccini, J. "Parent Burnout": Latest sign of today's stresses. *U.S. News and World Report,* March 7, 1983, pp. 76–77.

15. Frank, E., & Anderson, C. The sexual stages of marriage. *Family Circle*, February 1980, p. 146.

16. Strong, B., & DeVault, C. *Understanding our sexuality*. St. Paul: West, 1988, p. 313.

17. Avery-Clark, C. Career women most likely to suffer from inhibited sexual desire. *Behavior Today Newsletter*, August 1985, pp. 4–6.

18. Lasswell and Lasswell, op. cit., p. 234.

19. Ibid.

20. Procaccini, op. cit.

21. Bozzi, V. Time and togetherness. *Psychology Today*, January 1988, p. 10.

22. Lasswell and Lasswell, op. cit., p. 234.

23. Hassett, J. But that would be wrong. *Psychology Today*, December 1981, pp. 34–53. See also Petersen, J. R., Kretchmer, A., Nellis, B., Lever, J., & Hertz, R. The *Playboy* readers' sex survey (Part 2). *Playboy*, March 1983.

24. Thompson, A. Extramarital sex: A review of the research literature. *Journal of Sex Research*, 1983, *19*, pp. 1–22.

25. Allgeier, E. R., & Allgeier, A. R. *Sexual interactions*, 2d ed. Lexington, Mass.: Heath, 1988, pp. 443–445. See also Klagsbrun, F. *Married people: Staying together in the age of divorce*. New York: Bantam, 1985, p. 128.

26. Tavris, C., & Sadd, S. *The Redbook report of female sexuality*. New York: Delacorte, 1977.

27. Wolfe, L. *The Cosmo report*. New York: Bantam, 1981.

28. Petersen et al., op. cit.

29. Rubenstein, C., & Tavris, C. Special survey results: 26,000 women reveal the secrets of intimacy. *Redbook*, September 1987, pp. 147–149.

30. Allgeier and Allgeier, op. cit., p. 443.

31. Bowen, M. *Family therapy in clinical practice*. New York: Jason Aronson, 1978.

32. Klagsbrun, op. cit., p. 123.

33. Ibid.

34. Scarf, *Intimate partners*, p. 132.

35. Knox, op. cit., p. 210.

36. Gagnon, J. *Human sexualities*. Glenview, Ill.: Scott, Foresman, 1977.

37. Knox, op. cit., p. 210.

38. Gagnon, op. cit.

39. Knox, op. cit., p. 218.

40. Vaughn, J., & Vaughn, P. *Beyond affairs.* Hilton Head, S.C.: Dialog Press, 1980.
41. Klagsbrun, op. cit., p. 130.
42. Gadpaille, *The cycles of sex,* p. 401.
43. Ibid., p. 404.
44. Ibid., p. 401.

12

RENEWING AND REGRESSING

It was Columbus Day in the Berkshires, and the foliage blazed against an azure sky. The air was crisp and bracing, filled with a musky scent of earth drying from the morning dew. Walking into the woods behind our house, we felt frisky as young deer. Laughing, we crunched the fallen leaves and kicked them into swirls of rusty orange and red. Entering a grove of beech trees, we paused to look up at the canopy of yellow leaves still clinging to the branches. The bright sun filtered through, casting a golden spell on our path. Delicate ferns swayed languidly around the trunks of towering maples. Emerald moss on ancient logs glowed under ethereal shafts of light. Awed and reverent, we moved deeper into the forest.

Heading toward the nearby river, we followed its course upstream until we found a clearing on the bank. The water gurgled over glistening rocks, and tiny minnows darted about in crystal pools. Unseen birds sang a chorus of celebration as we sat down to drench our senses in this little corner of Paradise. Holding hands, we remained absolutely silent, reluctant to disturb the ecstatic purity of our peacefulness.

Soon, however, a sharp wind came blowing down the river, ruffling the reflection of a pair of birches into icy plumes of silver. Sweeping across our faces, it roused us from our reverie. As we stood up to go home, an eerie shiver of dread crept over us. True, it was unexpectedly chilly. But we were in no danger of being trapped in a blizzard. Where did the coldness of our anxiety come from?

As we stepped on the lawn leading to our back door, we finally saw that the entire episode—our utter contentment and our acute distress—emerged from our mixture of emotions about entering this season of our lifelong relationship. Yes, the spring and summer of our marriage were gone forever. But we had not yet faced the fact that fall had arrived for us as a couple. By making vivid contact with the changes going on in nature, we had gotten in touch with analogous changes in ourselves. Calmed by this insight, we acknowledged how much we needed to assess where we were at in our collective existence. What had we gained in almost three decades of our marriage? What had we lost? What lay in store for us in the imminent future—and beyond? Only by answering these questions could we decide how to go on developing our loving relationship.

We began by counting our blessings—as we had done, unknowingly, in admiring the beauty of the woods during our walk. Yes, we agreed, this time of our lives was very beautiful. Mellowed by the richness of love fulfilled, we felt secure in our ability to gratify each other sexually and emotionally. We had repeatedly passed the test of standing up for our values in our work, our parenting, and our social relations. And we had confidence in our will to find mutually satisfactory solutions to whatever relational problems arose between us. Having put forth the effort to sprout the seeds of our relationship, we had ripened fruitfully. Now, we relished the prospect of merging even closer as mates. For we were fully convinced that our happiness had evolved from our willingness to set no limits on our intimacy.

Our marital autumn was also very bountiful. Our adult children, married and in households of their own, personified the crop we had reaped. One day, we imagined, they would have children, enriching the field of life and love we had been privileged to cultivate before them. But while cheerfully painting this mental picture, we were seized by the same wave of anxiety that had come over us at the river. There it was—the "down" side of autumn! For what follows in the wake of the abundant harvest if not the barren blasts of winter?

Yes, fall reminded us of death. We still felt vigorous and creatively alive. But with Sue past her menopause, we had, as a couple, lost our ability to create life itself. True, we had long ago renounced the possibility of conceiving more children than the son and daughter we were fortunate to have. Still, giving up the use of a potential is quite different from being deprived of the potential itself. Renunciation *willed* in the interest of a desired fulfillment is a positive affirmation of a couple's values. But when infertility is *imposed* on mates by the process of aging, they are likely to interpret it as a harrowing loss of virility and a gloomy herald of bodily deterioration.

Saddened by these thoughts, we sank into a dim view of our "empty nest." Certainly, we were glad to see our children out in the world and able to deal with it responsibly as adults. But when they left us, they took the bubbling vivacity of youth out of our daily lives. Never again would our living room be filled to overflowing with singing and dancing adolescents. Never again would we be energized by "partying" with the endless procession of friends our children brought home from high school and college. Never again would we feel so indispensably helpful to any human beings.

Feeling sorry for ourselves, it was easy for us to enumerate and visualize other grave losses. Some of our closest friends had already died from cancer and heart attacks. Others were chronically ill. Sue's mother and father were already dead, while Irv's parents were ailing and depressed. So, what did *we* have to look forward to by the time we were too debilitated to work? Or even to make love? How ghastly it was to contemplate spending day after day just rotting and waiting to die.

Having descended to the nadir of our funk, we started to laugh at ourselves. What crepehangers, acting as if we were already dead! No, we were still in good health and, with luck, could expect many years ahead of us. Rather than moaning about our deprivations, why not figure out how to use our time as fulfillingly as possible? And what had given us the most fulfillment in the past if not the sharing of our love? Yes, we *did* have a basic program for the next step into our future. Only now we were challenged to adapt it to the limitations and opportunities presented by this period in our married life.

Much later, while formulating our conception of relational

development, we drew on this incident in defining the desirable objective for the fifth stage of a love-centered marriage. Specifically, a couple has the goal of *renewing* the vitality of their relationship, taking into consideration the ramifications of two major losses that have occurred at about the same time: they no longer have children at home and they have lost their collective ability to procreate, while steadily declining in their overall physical prowess.

FROM AN EMPTY NEST TO A FULLER MARRIAGE

When all of their children grow up, a couple loses the daily satisfactions of parenting. Besides, without children around as a barrier to the intimacy of their relationship, mates feel at a loss, at least temporarily, about how to relate *exclusively* as husband and wife. Indeed, they may be haunted by a sense that something is missing in their relationship although, in reality, there is *more* going on between them in terms of direct and unmediated interaction.

Unfortunately, for numerous couples the end of childrearing is, in effect, the end of their marriage.[1] These husbands and wives failed to define or maintain their own loving relationship as their highest priority in living. Instead, on becoming parents they implicitly gave this supreme value to relationships with their children. In time they became more emotionally attached to their offspring than to one another. So, with no children left in their household, they find little comfort in their marital relationship, which seems like a hollow shell—devoid of substance and purpose. Eventually, such couples may get divorced, convinced there is nothing worthwhile in their marriage to renew.

Yet the departure of adult children actually opens channels of mutual gratification that had long been closed to all couples. The very emptiness of their nest *automatically* provides mates with a sanctuary from the accumulated strains of childrearing that peak as they shepherd their offspring through the stressful years of adolescence. Meanwhile, a husband and wife are becoming middle-aged, losing much of their former strength and patience. By the time their teenagers feel prepared to "fly away" into adulthood, mates may be equally ready to let them go.

In retrospective studies most couples report that their marital happiness rose after their nest became empty.[2] Both husbands and wives emphasize the liberating effects of this change: freedom from familial responsibilities; freedom to put financial resources, previously depleted by the obligatory expenses of childrearing, into travel and other activities of their own choice; and freedom from the constraints that parenting had placed on their joint participation in those activities.[3]

Even so, all couples experience some difficulty in returning to a situation of pristine privacy. Alone for the first time since becoming parents, mates are bound to feel a bit frightened by the process of renewing the exclusiveness of their couplehood. For a while they may reduce their uneasiness with a binge of shopping, tourism, and socializing with friends. Surely, mates may enjoy these activities, which they had to restrict with Spartan discipline while raising young children. Sooner or later, however, it is desirable for a love-centered couple to resume the development of their relationship through face to face interactions that have *no other objective* than a fuller sharing of their bodies and minds.

For mates who have always cherished each other's company above all else in life, this goal will be highly welcomed. Uninhibited by the presence of children, they more easily reveal the entire range of their feelings: the tender and the troubled, the silly and the serious. Without any audience at home to collude for, they are relieved of a large external prop to the maintenance of their complicities. More open in expressing their negative emotions, they give each other a less-censored view of how they are enacting their scenarios, and they have more privacy for going through the anguish involved in breaking their pacts of mutual defense.

Meanwhile, a couple has a chance to renew their romance. Previously, their common dream had included the rearing of a loving family. But now, with the children on their own, mates need to envision a dream for their future as an aging couple. To be sure, as people in their fifties, a husband and wife may be very vigorous and at the "top of their form" in their careers. Nevertheless, no matter how good they feel on entering this stage, their physical condition has slipped several notches downward since the previous period of their marriage, and it would be reasonable to expect this decline to accelerate over the next 10 to 20 years. Allowing for this eventuality, it behooves spouses to be as realistic as possible in constructing the common dream for this era in their lives. Of course, it may seem strange to include provisions for *renunciation* in the building of a romantic future. Yet mates will be unable to actualize—much less to enjoy—any dream that does not allow for an anticipated reduction in their levels of energy.

In considering how to deal with their remaining years at work, a husband and wife may discover that they want to stay in their present occupations until they approach their seventies. Accordingly, to uphold the priority of their relationship over their careers, they begin to ease up on their individual ambitions, avoid working overtime, and take more frequent vacations together. In addition, they could set an approximate time for *both of them* to shift from full-time to part-time employment. This "tapering off" enables each mate to give more to the other at a time when they may have less to give to anything at all.

Alternatively, some mates may agree on a date for leaving their separate jobs and establishing a joint venture, permitting them not only to be together in the same workplace but also to pursue common interests long held in abeyance. Still others may decide on when to quit working altogether. Living on a combination of savings, Social Security, and their pensions, they could participate as a couple in unpaid social or political action.

In discussing and visualizing these changes, spouses add adventure to their daily lives. Naturally, the question of *where* to implement their plans will arise. Many couples may want to stay put, regarding their familiar domicile as a comfortable and manageable base for the rest of their lives. Others may prefer a smaller place or one more convenient to relatives, friends, or the location where they hope to set up shop on their own. Those who anticipate total retirement in a different setting— city, country, or seashore—may wish to prepare for it in advance by setting down some roots in that area. They could buy an affordable house or apartment and use it enough to feel "at home" with neighbors and shopkeepers by the time they are ready to live in it for keeps.

A husband and wife expand the boundaries of their individuality by airing their thoughts and feelings on every detail of their new common dream. Through this communication they strengthen their relational unity and get on the same wave length for making the changes they have projected into the future. Similarly, in taking the concrete steps necessary to realize their dream, they greatly increase their interdependence. To carry out their plans each spouse must depend on the other to shoulder the risks involved and to come through on everything that needs to be done. Demonstrating their mutual reliability, they gain the confidence to cope effectively with whatever unforeseen complications accompany their transition. Each one also develops a greater sense of self-reliance and more competence to function independently if the other becomes severely ill or dies.

Meanwhile, as they grow older, mates have a powerful incentive to preserve their strength by transcending debilitating differences in their gender roles. They lighten their individual burdens by sharing any marital responsibilities they had been doing separately: relating to adult children and grandchildren, shopping, cooking, cleaning, and banking. Actually, researchers have found that middle-aged mates *are* converging toward social equality. Thus, the longer a couple is married, the more flexible they become about departing from habitual gender roles. Mates often resume the sharing of "provider and domestic" tasks as they did before their children were born.[4] Likewise, they overlap in socially learned differences in personality. Husbands become more sensitive and nurturant, revealing "expressive" traits conventionally regarded as "feminine." Simultaneously, wives display "masculine" or "instrumental" characteristics, experiencing less inhibition or guilt about being assertive and acting independently.[5]

LOVEMAKING AND MENOPAUSE

In this period of renewal, it is vitally important for mates to keep fulfilling the promise of immersion in the pleasure of lovemaking as the top priority in their relationship, for this holistic interpenetration permits them to merge more intimately—and to feel more romantic—than anything else they could do together. Happily, they now have the privacy to make love more frequently and leisurely than ever before, securing the fullest mutual gratification.

Still, the physical depletion of aging impinges on a couple's sexual relations. Most dramatically, they are affected by the wife's menopause, terminating her capacity for reproduction. Yet leading experts in human sexuality have shattered the myth that this "change of life" necessarily means the end of an erotic life for women and their mates. On the contrary, freed from the fear of unwanted pregnancy, the responsibilities of rearing young children, and the hassles of using contraception, most women eventually feel a tremendous sense of relief.[6] Sharing this freedom, a husband and wife can give spontaneous and uninterupted expression to their desires for making love. Surely, liberation from contraception leads them into a domain of pleasure from which they had been barred since first becoming lovers many years ago, except for brief periods while trying to conceive and during pregnancy.

However, women may suffer from a variety of impairments as they go through menopause. The stereotypical catalogue of "female troubles" includes hot flashes, headaches, fatigue, depression, and a lack of sexual responsivity. But although ". . . at least as many as 50 percent . . . of all women suffer some of these uncomfortable menopausal symptoms, only about 10 percent are severely affected, and a sizeable proportion—at least 10 percent and perhaps as many as 50 percent—display none of these symptoms."[7]

In the years following menopause, however, the walls of a woman's vagina gradually become thinner and less elastic, and there may be a lessening of her vaginal lubrication during sexual arousal. Thus, it may take a woman more time to become ready for penile penetration. Besides, if her vagina remains dry, penetration may be painful and lead to further irritation of the vaginal tissues. Fortunately, this condition can be remedied through the use of estrogen suppositories and creams or other kinds of lubricants.[8]

With the availability of these remedial measures, postmenopausal women can thoroughly enjoy intercourse. Moreover, as Masters and Johnson have reported, women who had always been sexually active, having intercourse once or twice a week, show no decline in vaginal lubrication.[9] Indeed, Helen Singer Kaplan states, "Women tend to want more sex rather than less as they approach middle-age and beyond."[10] Similarly, Lillian Rubin found that many women finally discover their full sexual capacity after having felt trapped by traditional female roles and inexperience earlier in their marriage. After their children left home, these wives began to take the initiative in sexual relations, no longer submitting passively to their mates.[11]

For their part, husbands are subject to gradual physical and hormonal changes that result in a decrease in stamina, a general "slowing down," and a reduced production of testosterone. While they never lose their capacity to sire children, these changes do pose sexual challenges for many men. A man's sexual responsiveness may diminish, and he may occasionally suffer from bouts of impotence. Generally, he requires more time and physical stimulation to get an erection that may not be as full and as hard as in the past.[12] Although these changes do not prevent a man from engaging in sexual intercourse, he may become self-conscious and worried about his sexual performance.[13]

A husband may also feel badly about the increased amount of time it takes to ejaculate and about his lengthening refractory period, often requiring 24 hours or more after ejaculation until he can have another. Yet the same man may now be able to "hold out" and extend the pleasures of foreplay, giving his wife all the stimulation she may need for a fulfilling climax. As Bernie Zilbergeld states, husbands can regard this slowing of ejaculatory response as a gift, "particularly those who were quick on the trigger when younger."[14]

Besides, as Gadpaille points out, husbands at this stage "may well possess advantages that can more than offset their slightly declining capacities." These men are not preoccupied with sex for its own sake or simply for their *own* gratification. "The relationship with a partner as a whole takes precedence over sex alone. They have sufficient experience to have more sensitively learned a woman's responses and . . . are able to achieve more pleasure for both of them."[15]

While renewing the pleasure of lovemaking, mates have a unique opportunity to progress in accepting—and thus in transcending—their *intrinsic* differences in gender. Although they are equally afflicted by alterations in their sexual functioning, they necessarily differ—as a man and a woman—in their symptoms. For example, an empathic husband cannot fail to become aware of the changes distressing his wife during and after menopause. Displaying kindness and care, he engages her in talks about her condition, which may be just as upsetting to him. Together, they confess a common feeling of loss over *their* inability to procreate. These discussions enable him to accept the inevitability of her menopause rather than to blame or resent her for it. In turn, his compassionate understanding permits the wife not only to express her anxiety and depression but also to sustain her morale and self-esteem.

A loving wife is just as sensitive to her husband's ongoing physiological changes and as sympathetic to his accompanying upsets. She helps him by starting conversations about what he is experiencing, giving him the psychological support to weather these changes without getting unduly depressed. At the same time, she extends her acceptance of his particular manifestations of sexual decline, alleviating his feeling of personal inadequacy and assuring him of her willingness to make the behavioral adjustments necessary for the continuation of their erotic satisfaction.

By contrast, Rubin found that some wives deceive their husbands by not asking for all the sexual contact they really want.[16] Meanwhile, it might be safely assumed these husbands do not ask their wives for whatever additional stimulation they need for sexual arousal and orgasmic release. Consequently, such couples may jointly weave their lies of omission into a complicity against immersion in the pleasure of lovemaking.

Surely, it is possible for mates to avoid lapsing from mutual consideration into mutual frustration. When a couple has the courage to reveal their sexual needs and desires, they work out the means to satisfy each other. By openly voicing the intensity of her erotic feelings, a wife admits how important it is for her to have frequent sexual interaction *with her husband.* Reciprocally, a husband can reassure his wife that he still finds her attractive despite her loss of youth and the changes in her bodily appearance. Together, they relax in the warmth of their truthfulness and resolve to help one another. By explaining to his wife exactly how to give him more effective stimulation, the husband gets a firmer and more lasting erection while she gets the degree of gratification she has been yearning for. Indeed, both mates receive a windfall of erotic "dividends" from what each gives to the other.

COMPLICITIES OF REGRESSION

In the fourth stage of relational development, mates began to worry about losing their youthfulness. However, with the emptying of their nest, the wife's menopause, and the husband's symptoms of aging, a couple knows that the most fertile and lively era in their lives is irretrievably behind them. In this context, mates may well dread the eventual loss of their ability to work as the final curtain to be dropped between themselves and their participation in "real life."

In this fifth stage, therefore, all couples are struck by an unprecedented degree of existential fear. This fearfulness renders them exceedingly vulnerable to all the threats of love they stir up while *renewing* their relationship in the ways we have spelled out. They experience a greater fear of loving than at any prior stage in their relational development. Typically, in defending against their common fear, they respond by *regressing*—acting far more immature and less insightful than they actually are.

Sabotaging and Salvaging Collaborative Work

We had been married for almost 30 years when we began to write our first book together. Long before, as a young couple, we had jointly developed some material for an illustrated story for preschool children. After encountering resistance to our proposal from a few publishers, we abandoned the project without finishing it.

Subsequently, we often toyed with the fantasy of doing creative work together. This possibility became especially alluring whenever we asked each other for help on problems we were tackling in our separate careers. On those occasions we let ourselves get totally "into" the process, temporarily setting aside all concerns about which one of us "possessed" the particular problem at hand. Nevertheless, after arriving at a common solution, we returned to our individual occupations. For we were still reluctant to give up the rewards of personal recognition we had gotten by doing different things.

However, we had become quite weary of being separated by our vocational activities. We knew how exciting and enjoyable interactive creativity could be for us—a psychological equivalent to lovemaking—if we could "get it together." We also shared the compelling intuition that taking on and completing a collaborative project would be a boon to our marriage, *requiring* us to resolve interpersonal conflicts we had evaded chronically. Besides, having pursued similar substantive interests, we sensed that whatever we produced together would be better than anything we could do separately.

By this time, Irv was firmly established in his academic career, having specialized in theory and research on personality. A tenured professor at New York University, he had written three books and many articles in his area of expertise. In addition, he had published several essays and a short story, reflecting an interest in more literary forms of expression. Meanwhile, She had switched from an earlier career as an artist to one in psychology and education. Sue was an adjunct instructor at LaGuardia Community College, teaching human development and psychology of the family.

For some time, Sue had been thinking of doing a book on sexual development in childhood and adolescence, using masturbation as the focal point of reference. Initially, she planned to do an anthology that she would edit alone. Discussing her ideas with Irv, she asked him for suggestions on her evolving format and organization. Irv was very enthused since he had recently begun to teach a course on the psychology of love. It soon became apparent to both of us that sexual development was integral to the development of a person's capacity to love. In fact, our intellectual "cross-fertilization" had already begun to germinate a joint creation. At that point, we agreed to become coauthors of an original work addressed to professionals and general readers.

Embarking on our new adventure, we created a common dream of how much fun we would have writing and about how innovative, cogent, and useful our book would be. We bubbled over with thoughts about what topics to include and what each of us could best contribute. Then we wrote with zeal and dedication. However, we quickly found it necessary to make compromises in order to combine what we produced individually. But to compromise was highly threatening to both of us, bringing home the reality of having to agree on a written merger of our identities. Terrified by this threat, we became completely *unyielding* over whose ideas and writing should prevail. Acting extremely competitive, we regressed back to our individualistic strivings. And our "coauthorship" became only the semblance of a cooperative effort.

In conferences about what we had written, Sue criticized Irv's work as being too philosophical and lyrical, and she insisted on including a more systematic and comprehensive presentation of the latest research findings. Conversely, he scoffed at her writing, deriding her for being too concrete and "texty," and he demanded that we brighten our theoretical exposition with artistically written case studies and personal vignettes.

Working in separate rooms, we frequently lapsed into private and egoistic daydreams. Instead of writing, we wasted many hours in what we later described as "mental masturbation," giving ourselves psychological "strokes" about the amazing impact "the book" would have on our individual reputations and careers. Irv harbored fantasies of promoting himself as a leading theorist and author on the psychology of love, and Sue imagined herself becoming famous for making a daring and original contribution to the field of human sexuality.

Over a long span of months, we deluded ourselves into believing we were making progress. Actually, we did produce a lot of interesting material. But we always regarded it as tentative, awaiting final revision. We deferred all decisions to blend our individual writings. Often, the rivalry between us was so disabling that we talked about scrapping our project. Obviously, we weren't having fun or deriving any of the other benefits we had sought.

However, we wouldn't take "no" for an answer. Rather, we pledged to keep the faith we had put in our collective ability to overcome the dilemma we had made for ourselves. Thus, even in the darkest depths of our despair, we persisted in struggling to make good on our commitment. Eventually, we succeeded in helping each other to understand the dynamics of our shared "writing block." This understanding freed us not only to go on working together but also to enjoy it as we had hoped to do.

Appropriately, our breakthrough came as we sought to clarify the reasons why mates avoid disclosure of their mastur- batory inclinations. This led us to originate our concept of com- plicity, which explained the basic meaning of *our own* self- concern and competitiveness. Subsequently, we became much more cooperative and finished our manuscript. Its publication led us to feel stronger as a couple *and* as individuals while also validating us as a creative team. The benefits of this experi- ence encouraged us to take additional steps toward centering our personal and professional lives on love. Thus, we renewed our relational intimacy, widening our collaboration—as mates and as professionals—in teaching together and by writing this book on marriage.

From Making Love to Making Trouble

In American society people are often viewed as having "run the course," sexually, by the time they reach middle age[17]; unfortunately, many spouses appear to confirm this neg- ative stereotype. True, at this stage both husband and wife have less of the sheer physical energy they once brought to their sexual coupling. He is no longer the Pounding Bull of the Pampas. Nor is she the Seething Tigress of the Serengeti. How- ever, since their mutual affection has grown over the years, they have a vastly enlarged ability to put themselves *emotion- ally* into their lovemaking. Now they are much more "there" for—and with—one another, injecting more energy into every physical expression of their affectionate feelings and creating a degree of sensually saturated intimacy they could not have done before.

Love-centered mates also draw on their cumulative famil- iarity and satisfaction, secure in the knowledge of the exact places to touch and to kiss; the best pace and positions for thrusting; the right timing for advancing the flow of their pas- sion. Guaranteed of these pleasures, they have confidence that a "fresh shipment" of desire for each other will always be arriving. So why hold anything back? Why not let all the "good times roll," no matter how strange or scary it feels to explore novel ways of tapping into levels of ecstasy they never believed were possible for "old-timers" like themselves?

Yet these exquisite discoveries *do* increase a couple's vulnerability to the threat of immersion in the pleasure of lovemaking. They are inclined to "clutch up" and form complicities in which they regress to previous means of avoiding opportunities for making love. For example, they may become engrossed, once again, in the strenuous sports they had relinquished during their years of childrearing. Returning with a vengeance to the tennis court or jogging track, these mates thoroughly sap their diminished strength. For them, "going to bed" means falling asleep, not falling into an embrace as an overture to intercourse.

Given their empty nest, such couples frequently devise scenarios for re-enacting the parental roles they had played while rearing young children. Usually, the most accessible persons for this regressive entanglement are members of their own extended family: adult sons and daughters who are single; married children and their spouses; their own aged parents; and grandsons and granddaughters. Naturally, husbands and wives initiate these *unsolicited* involvements as a pretext for destroying the time and privacy now available to them for making love. However, their defensiveness has a similarly undesirable impact on the sexual functioning of the people they include in their scenarios. Thus, they make trouble not only for themselves but also for others.

Al and Gina Conte directed this kind of troublemaking toward Maria, a sophomore at a university located 2 hours from their home, since their two older children were already married and living far away. Brilliant and balanced, Maria had received a full scholarship covering her tuition, room, and board. She also took a part-time job on campus to pay for her clothes, travel expenses, and other "extras." She was thus economically self-sufficient. Although still undecided about an eventual career, she was leaning heavily toward journalism. For about a year she had been romantically involved with Robert, a classmate at her university. They were now talking about getting married and were sleeping together quite regularly. Objectively, therefore, Maria was doing very well in assuming all the responsibilities of adulthood. A loving daughter, she wanted to maintain a good relationship with her parents, but she expressed no desire to be babied or relieved of anything she could do for herself.

However, Gina and Al started to treat Maria as if suddenly she had become incapable of handling everything she was actually doing so well. After all, they agreed, she's still just a youngster, isn't she? And isn't it our *duty* to help her, even if she doesn't ask for it? They decided it was absolutely essential to call her several nights during the week. Often, these calls caught Maria and Robert "in the act" or just before it. In either case the interruption not only "cooled them off" but kept them distressed for hours afterward. For the Contes invariably grilled her on all the minutiae of her daily life: her studies, her work, her health, her extracurricular activities, and, of course, her relationship with Robert. At the same time, they deluged her with offers of assistance. Didn't she need some money? Surely, she *had* to have more clothes than she could buy with her own earnings. What about her room? Couldn't she use a new set of drapes and a bedspread? Between these calls Al and Gina mulled over Maria's answers, evaluating her assurances, evasions, and contradictions. This analysis gave them plenty of material to talk about anxiously in bed—the better to turn *themselves* off erotically.

Besides, the Contes often felt it necessary to visit Maria on weekends to make sure she was *really* okay. First, they dragged her around on shopping trips for things she neither needed nor requested. Then, at night they took her and Robert out for dinner. But Gina and Al gave them indigestion with their "interviews" of Robert, questioning him about his background, attitudes, and vocational aspirations, and with their attempts to dissuade Maria from journalism, which they felt was too risky and demanding a field for women. Wouldn't something like social work be more practical? These evenings diverted Al and Gina from the possibility of becoming sexually intimate while leaving Maria and Robert too agitated and self-doubting to make love.

Finally, the Contes demanded that Maria reciprocate their

visits by coming home for weekends. Wouldn't the rest do her good? And Momma's cooking? Of course, Robert was welcome too. However, they "laid down the law." She could do whatever she wanted with Robert—somewhere else. "But not in *our* house!"

So, on these "homey" weekends Maria and Robert were forced to sleep in separate rooms, writhing in frustration and anger and hardly able to wait until they could escape on Sunday afternoon. Meanwhile, Al and Gina slept fitfully, waking periodically to listen for sounds of hanky-panky on the part of their daughter and her boyfriend.

Other middle-aged couples begin similarly troublesome interventions with married children and their mates. Like the Contes, they employ a variety of intrusive devices: an inordinate number of telephone calls, often at times when their "targets" are likely to be in bed; constant pressure to visit or be visited on weekends; and a flood of offers of assistance.

Clearly, parents have no moral justification to prevent married offspring and their mates from sleeping together while visiting them. Nevertheless, the "folks" often create an atmosphere in their home that is poisonous to lovemaking. Mom and Dad become so prim and serious as to imply that any thought or act connected with sexuality is a gross offense to their sensibilities. At night, the older couple may also keep the younger one on edge with searching inquiries about how they are living and long lectures on how to improve themselves. By the time the parents finish with them, the "kids" are too "heavied out" for sexual contact with each other.

If they were not locked in a complicity to undermine their own sexual relations, these parents would refrain from doing such "numbers" on their adult children. On the contrary, if a couple values the privacy and peace of mind for making love, they want their offspring to have the same psychological supports for their sexual activities. Such mates are considerate about when and how frequently to call their children on the telephone. They do not keep barging in on their lives with pretexts for pulling them away from erotic intimacy. Rather, knowing how important lovemaking is for themselves, a couple encourages their adult children to sustain it as the highest priority within their own loving relationships.

This encouragement does not require parents to be exhibitionistic or to flaunt their erotic prowess. Nor does it involve any prying into the sexual relations of their children. But it does rest on the couple's openness to whatever sexual issues adult children—and their lovers or mates—bring up for discussion and on their ability to foster mutual respect for each generation's sexual needs and desires. Ironically, ". . . older persons are often more comfortable about their sexuality than their children and grandchildren are about recognizing that the older couples are still sexually active."[18]

Thus, middle-aged parents who are comfortable and satisfied with their sexual interactions clearly indicate that sexual fulfillment for adult children and their partners in love is not only okay but also commendable. This forthright approach is a continuation of the candidness about sexual matters such couples displayed while rearing their sons and daughters. It is also consistent with the holistic perspective they gave their children about integrating the erotic and affectionate components of love.

Or course, all parents may sometimes upset their adult offspring by preaching to them or being overly solicitous. These lapses occur out of empathy with the suffering their children are bound to endure in taking on all the responsibilities of adulthood. Intergenerational conflict is often accentuated as children, like Maria, assert their full independence and establish the new priorities involved in forming loving relationships of their own.[19]

Given their greater experience, parents also feel they have much worldly wisdom to impart about how their children could maximize their happiness and steer clear of painful mistakes. In a context of mutual respect, children absorb this occasional preachment and solicitude as a passing annoyance, and they can always preserve their adult autonomy by gently chiding the parents about trying to take on problems that are no longer theirs to solve.

This does not mean that loving parents must "walk on eggshells" when conversing with a son or daughter. Rather, adult children *have the right* to hear their parents' honest opinions. Weighing and measuring that input as they would any other relevant information, children ultimately decide what to do, *not* because their parents "said so," but because they have responsibly decided what is best for their welfare.

However, children do face a trying task in fending off parental efforts to enlist their participation in the kinds of "anti-sex" complicities we have described. Still, as fully responsible adults, these designated "pawns" have the power to resist such enmeshment. True, they may have to go through many stressful confrontations with their parents before permanently establishing their autonomy. But they *do* have the option of remaining relatively unscathed by the sexual troubles their parents may try to make for them.

On the other hand, some married children and their mates may be "shopping around" for a complicity of their own to dampen the fear stimulated by the threat of immersion in the pleasure of lovemaking. They may seize on parental intrusions to construct a reciprocal scenario for themselves. Over time both couples become intermeshed, each pair feeding their own defensiveness on that of the other. In these complex interactions the younger couple is as persistent as the older one in initiating regressive interventions. Both couples use interactions and preoccupations with one another to ward off their own sexual relations, and neither couple complains since this is exactly what both of them are seeking in their common enmeshment.

Some middle-aged couples may even bring *grandchildren* into their antisex complicities. Of course, regardless of their marital problems, most couples feel good about having grandchildren, seeing in them heartening reaffirmations of the life they had created in conceiving their own children decades before. A grandchild also represents the continuation of a couple's "lifeline" far beyond their own demise, assuring them of a relatively lasting presence in the world as contributors to someone else's existence.[20] Besides, by actually helping even in a small way to rear grandchildren, mates put a coda on the theme of youthful parenting that once made them feel so virile and alive.

On the other hand, becoming grandparents confronts a couple with a stark reminder of their aging. Adding Gramps and Granny to the titles of Dad and Mom may make a husband and wife feel a million years older overnight. Certainly, this new status is archetypically associated with a passing of the "generational guard"—the grandparents marching a giant step closer to the grave. So, couples generally experience a fair degree of ambivalence while adapting to the reality of grandparenthood.[21]

Yet, quite soon, with a grandchild sitting on their laps and smiling happily at them, they usually "bond" with him or her in a relationship of mutual love. Then, Grandma and Grandpa give the child more concentrated indulgence—more "fun and games" and fewer disciplinary restrictions—than Mommy and Daddy. Consequently, grandchildren often feel a unique sense of freedom and unconditional acceptance in the company of their grandparents.[22]

Reciprocally, the grandparents feel free to get down on their hands and knees to play with the "kiddies" and to inbibe their childishly wondrous reactions to everyone and everything. This kind of regressiveness exerts no negative impact on a child. Quite the contrary. By consciously and temporarily descending to the child's emotional level, grandparents help him or her to build a bridge of enjoyable contact with them. In turn, this contact gives the child an incentive to reach up to adults, furthering his or her own communicative abilities.

However, by involving a grandson or granddaughter in a complicity of sexual alienation between them, mates may exert undesirable effects on the child's sexual development. Often, this occurs when a couple uses babysitting as the nexus of their scenario. Having a toddler in their home all day and night is enough to exhaust the energies and destroy the privacy of any middle-aged couple. But for grandparents who are defensively aiming to keep themselves too "wasted" for sexual activity, an occasional day or night of babysitting is not sufficient. Rather, these mates *plead* with married children to let them look after young grandchildren for days—or even weeks—on end.

Some of these grandparents virtually usurp the roles of the parents themselves; indeed, the grandchildren scarcely discern any distinction between their own mother and father and their grandparents. Obviously, for middle-aged couples such "taking over" is a regressive substitute for the childrearing they completed years before. The "taken-over" child may look forward to the coddling he or she receives from doting grandparents, but the child may also become torn in emotional loyalty between them and his or her parents, and very confused by the conflicting standards of one set of caretakers versus the other.

These grandparents may also give a child very mixed signals about what is permissible sexually. For example, one couple told us that their 2-year-old grandson always has difficulty sleeping through the night on his frequent and extensive visits to their home. They explained that he quickly falls asleep in a room adjacent to theirs. However, they chuckle, he awakens after they are asleep, demanding to be taken into their bed. They permit him to climb in and wedge himself between them. Then his Granny lets him snuggle up close, with his arms around her, until morning, implicitly treating him more as a consort than her own husband. Meanwhile, Grandpa displays benign tolerance, rolling over to his side of the bed and sleeping without any disturbance or complaint.

This same couple, however, is strict in imposing taboos on the boy's masturbatory inclinations. Although they let him go around naked whenever he wishes to do so, they forbid him from touching his genitals. The child therefore is caught in a double bind between expressing and suppressing his erotic desires. If fondling and embracing Grandma in bed all night is permissible, why can't he rub his own "wee-wee?" These grandparents have the same kind of influence described in our chapter on nurturing and negating, where we showed how a couple's complicity to avoid immersion in the pleasure of lovemaking leads them to communicate negative attitudes toward a child's sexual self-stimulation.

Finally, some mates regress by becoming inappropriately involved with their *own elderly parents*. These meddlers frequently mask their mischief under a pose of unassailable righteousness. How could we not call the folks several times a day? Or drop in on them at least two or three times a week? Or talk them into staying with us? Sure, they can still take care of themselves. But who knows for how long?

The most regressive reattachment to the "old folks" occurs when a husband and wife invite them to live in their home rather than encouraging and helping them to manage a household for themselves. While this invitation appears to be an act of selfless generosity, it is actually an emotional booby trap for the aged parents. If they accept, they expose themselves to harmful doses of daily stress, for they are likely to become extremely guilty about being a burden to their children—draining their energy, preempting their time, constraining their freedom of movement, and inhibiting their communication. At the same time, the older couple is deprived of the privacy *they* need to deepen their own intimacy and the erotic fulfillments of their lifelong marriage.

Naturally, if their venerable parents are in genuine need of help, it is appropriate for a loving husband and wife to come to their aid—just as they assist adult children and grandchildren who are stricken with a debilitating illness. However, many couples create unnecessary difficulty for themselves by seeking involvement with their aged parents for their *own defensive purposes*. These couples regress by resurrecting childish ties with their parents. Indeed, they may include the older and the younger generations in an elaborate complicity to keep themselves from renewing the pleasures of their own lovemaking.

RELIABILITY AND RENUNCIATION

No matter how strongly mates renew their relationship, they become much weaker *as individuals* on their biological passage through middle age. Indeed, a large segment of the population over the age of 65 suffers from a chronic ailment that limits their activities. A much more ominous warning for couples is contained in the actuarial fact that men of this vintage have an average of 14 more years of life. The comparable figure of 19 years for women, while higher, is far from infinite.[23] Thus, husbands die considerably sooner, on the average, than their wives. Nevertheless, from the standpoint of *a couple*, the demise of either spouse forever ends their loving relationship.

Given these sobering statistics, mates can consider themselves exceedingly fortunate if they are still alive and in good health by the time they reach the age of 65. Consequently, they would want to be reliable in helping each other to remain healthy and to live as long as possible. This means taking advantage of *every day* to build their interdependence and to waste no time in changing their lifestyle in whatever way is necessary to avoid undue stress. Often, this reliability requires the *renunciation* of involvements in work and other activities that jeopardize their physical well-being or even their continued survival.

Joe and Ellen Berk were very pleased that their two daughters were finally married. Now approaching their mid-sixties with considerably reduced expenses, they could ease up on their money making and begin to take better care of themselves. Joe's blood pressure had always been quite elevated and Ellen's arthritis had been getting worse. They knew it would be wise to work less and relax more. However, while giving lip service to the importance of their health, they refused to pass up *any* opportunity for increasing their income. Joe continued to push himself in expanding his insurance agency. Meanwhile, Ellen, an interior decorator, took on more and more customers. Disregarding all inner promptings for rest, the Berks seemed oblivious to the strains mounting in their bodies.

It took a common medical crisis for them to face the realities of their age and physical condition. Joe's blood pressure had shot up to an alarming level and Ellen had become wracked by excruciating pain in her hip. Their doctor sternly warned that Joe was in danger of having a stroke or heart attack and that Ellen might wind up unable to walk or require a hip replacement. The Berks then admitted how horrible it would be if either of them became severely incapacitated—or even died!

With a renewed appreciation of how much they loved and valued each other, Joe and Ellen modified their daily routines. Assuming joint responsibility for safeguarding their lives, they diligently monitored their schedules. Ellen made sure that Joe left his office by four in the afternoon, allowing him to unwind before dinner. They also installed an answering machine on their telephone to keep him from being bothered by business calls when he was at home. Besides, he stopped taking on any new clients, referring all of them to younger associates. Ellen made a similar reduction in her load, accepting no additional job until she finished an ongoing one. Neither of them brought home any work at night or on weekends.

For 6 months Joe and Ellen were conscientious about sticking to the restrictions they had set for themselves, and their mutual reliability paid off in a stabilization of their physical conditions. However, their increased interdependence made them feel more and more hemmed in. Becoming unbearably restless, they devised a complicity for sliding back into their past negligence. Little by little, Joe remained longer at his office. When he got home, he often "forgot" to turn on the answering machine. So he dealt with upsetting calls until late in the night, and he began to keep many new clients for himself.

Ellen also widened the scope of her services. How could she turn down all the people recommended by her staunch customers and friends? Who else was good enough to send them to? She ran around much more to furniture showrooms, antique shops, and fabric stores, standing on her feet for hours and putting extreme pressure on her hip. Frequently, she also arranged to consult with customers in their homes at night.

Thus, the Berks abandoned all the renunciations they had made to stave off a worsening of their ailments. Eventually, they clung more tenaciously than ever before to their old occupational pursuits; in this regression they brought back their original symptoms in full force.

Other couples design scenarios similar to the Berks' for retaining outworn roles and routines. They hold on to dreary jobs even though they already have the financial resources for a comfortable retirement, and they resist innovations in the content or method of their work. They may also shun the possibility of moving into a more manageable home or remodeling their old one to suit their present and future needs. Indeed, many couples refuse to change *any* feature of their lives. Like frightened toddlers clinging to security blankets, they settle for the dullness of habituation, even though it may endanger their happiness and longevity.

Some couples regress in exactly the opposite manner. Instead of refusing to renounce an old and harmful lifestyle, they balk at renouncing the illusion of eternal youth. Thus, they pretend to be newlyweds and to start their married life all over again. Impulsively, they quit their jobs, sell their house, and sever contacts with children, parents, and friends. Then, like adolescents during the counterculture of the 1960s, they "hit the road" to seek adventure by traveling randomly to nowhere in particular. Alternatively, couples may keep on the run by going on endless cruises and trips abroad or by moving from one housing arrangement to another, searching for an unattainable rejuvenation.

While their son and daughter were growing into adulthood, Peg and Dan Olson had created a fantasy about throwing over all the restraints of their work, getting rid of their big house, and "taking off" for an early retirement in the South. However, with their children married and living in the vicinity, they were no longer so sure about "kicking it." Now in their early sixties, they still liked their work more than they had been willing to admit. Didn't Dan, a lawyer, "light up" in the courtroom, harnessing all of his wit and verbal skill in defense of his clients? And didn't Peg positively glow with an outpouring of energy as she taught her first-graders how to read? Besides, wouldn't it be best to stay in their spacious house rather than cramp themselves in an apartment?

But the Olsons has been plugging away for almost 30 years, and they often felt more than a little burnt out. True, they were as used to their house as to old slippers. But wasn't it really *too* roomy? And wouldn't it soon become too burdensome to them? Aware of their mixed feelings about leaving, neither Peg nor Dan wanted to make a precipitous move. They agreed to "stay in the saddle" until they cleared up their doubts about retiring.

Nevertheless, after tolerating their ambivalence for about a year, the Olsons cracked. Their mutual reliance in assessing the pros and cons of their common dilemma became too threatening, and they devised a complicity to scuttle their growing interdependence. After all, they had a nest egg large enough to maintain their customary standards of living. So why go on knocking their brains out? Wouldn't it be better to have some *real* fun in the good years left to them?

Thus, in a virtual fit of impatience, Peg and Dan brushed aside all of their qualms. Denying how much they enjoyed being near their children, they bought a "condo" in Florida. For several months, they felt delightfully warmed by the "sunshine state" that compared so favorably to the northern winters they had always grumbled against. In this climate the diversions of their adult community seemed truly liberating. After dawdling over morning coffee on their patio, they devoted one pleasant day after another to golfing, playing tennis, and doing "laps" in the Olympic-sized pool. Then, feeling trim and invigorated, they went out for a night of dancing at the clubhouse. Soon, they began to shun responsibility for planning their own activities, giving themselves over to the events arranged by the social director. Their days and nights were so full, they didn't have a moment to think. It was wonderful, just like all the summers they spent in camp as young kids!

However, these carefree recreations soon turned out to be confining rituals in which they, and everyone else, felt *compelled* to participate. In fact, the Olsons discovered that the "community" was actually split into tightly knit cliques, each with its own "crowd" and each competing against and gossiping about the others. Sitting around the pool or in the clubhouse, they could hear the buzz of comments people made about each other. Look at that *awful* outfit she's wearing. Do you think he *dyes* his hair? Hasn't she gained a *lot* of weight lately? Don't they both look so *old,* all of a sudden? Is Mrs. White having an *affair* with Mr. Green? And what about the Browns, is *their* marriage on the ropes?

Peg and Dan grew to resent having to "be on their toes" every time they stepped out of their door. Feeling continually observed and compared to their neighbors, they worried about becoming paranoid. One night, to their utter dismay, they found themselves regretting the change they had made. What the hell had happened to them? Why had they done such a foolish thing? Could they ever trust each other again after opting for such a meaningless and empty way of life? Did they have to resign themselves to being stuck in this mindless birdcage for the rest of their lives? To becoming soft in the head from all the superficial chatter they encountered everywhere? But what *could* they do now, after burning their bridges behind them?

Slowly, the Olsons lifted themselves out of their paralytic despair. No, they couldn't go on pretending, like pathetic clowns, to be younger than their age: pretending to be interested in the drivel of the local newsletter or intellectually satisfied with the inane discussions other people wanted to have with them; pretending not to miss their loved ones; pretending they could hide from the harsh realities of the world and shed their social consciences completely, after devoting themselves for years to worthwhile causes.

Eventually, the honesty of these insights restored the faith Peg and Dan had lost in their judgment. Ceasing their bitter recriminations about who was to blame for their situation, they forgave each other for their irresponsible impulse to buy a "new life." Making careful plans for a realistic return to their "old life," they sold their condo and bought a small house in the town where they used to reside. Now, having gotten a taste of unencumbered leisure, they had no desire to resume their professions on a full-time basis. But they did decide to keep their minds "oiled" and make a social contribution by working part time as volunteers: Peg as a tutor to children who needed special help in reading and Dan as an attorney for the Legal Aid Society, giving free counsel to those who could not afford to pay for it. At the same time, they renewed their relationships with their married children, eagerly anticipating the arrival of grandchildren.

In similar circumstances other couples could also "cut their losses" by communicating about how to get out of whatever mess they have jointly made. However, to secure *any* decision that is *enduring* in its satisfaction, mates need to give themselves unfettered time for discussion and reflection. Yet some husbands and wives acquire the habit of pressing each other for a "quick fix" to every problem, just as they rush through lovemaking to attain a Big O. In their mindless speed, however, they overlook many productive ideas, just as they miss many opportunities for erotic enjoyment. They often arrive at half-baked solutions and at orgasms that are far from big.

By contrast, it is most gratifying for mates to linger over the special sensuality of their foreplay, gathering up their energy for an optimal orgasmic release. Likewise, they can "get into" decision making as a pleasurable process, drawing out their deliberations until *both* of them have thoroughly explored all the relevant issues and plumbed their truest feelings. Then they are ready to "let go" and experience what Eugene

Gendlin has called a "felt sense" of closure, an ineffable feeling of "rightness" that permeates their beings.[24]

On their way to this holistic sense of completion, mates may change their minds repeatedly as they contemplate each alternative in the light of others they think of subsequently. Some people mistakenly condemn such tentativeness and prolonged exploration as "neurotic." However, it is crucially important for spouses to express every nuance of their uncertainty, anxiety, and ambivalence. This uncensored ventilation permits them to "touch bottom" on their feelings and to achieve an unequivocal agreement *before* implementing any plan for changing their lives. Thus, while increasing their interdependence, a couple evolves a most satisfying course of action and rectifies, as far as is humanly possible, a past and poorly considered decision.

NOTES

1. Coleman, *Intimate relationships, marriage, and family*, 2d ed., pp. 363–364. See also Lasswell and Lasswell, *Marriage and the family*, p. 453.
2. Glenn, N. D. Psychological well-being in the post-parental stage: Some evidence from national surveys. *Journal of Marriage and the Family*, 1975, *37*, pp. 105–110.
3. Aldous, *Family careers*, p. 186.
4. Albrecht, S., Bahr, H., & Chadwick, B. Changing family and sex roles: An assessment of age difference. *Journal of Marriage and Family*, February 1979, *41*, pp. 41–50.
5. Neugarten, B. L., & Gutman, D. Age-sex roles and personality in middle age: A thematic apperception study. In B. Neugarten (Ed.), *Middle age and aging*. Chicago: University of Chicago Press, 1968, pp. 58–71. See also Eichorn, D. H., Clausen, J. A., et al. *Present and past in middle life*. New York: Academic Press, 1981; and Livson, F. B. Gender identity: A life-span view of sex role development. In R. B. Weg (Ed.), *Roles and behavior*. New York: Academic Press, 1983, pp. 105–127.
6. Gadpaille, *The cycles of sex*, pp. 420, 424. See also Notman, M. T. Changing roles for women at midlife. In W. H. Norman & T. J. Scaramella (Eds.), *Midlife: Developmental and clinical issues*. New York: Brunner/Mazel, 1981, pp. 85–109; and Eastman, P. Life after menopause 'liberating,' women say: Researchers find

attitudes upbeat. *AARP News Bulletin*, July/August 1988, *29*, pp. 4–5.

7. Hyde, *Understanding human sexuality*, p. 106.
8. Allgeier and Allgeier, *Sexual interactions*, 2d ed., p. 458.
9. Masters and Johnson, *Human sexual response*.
10. Kaplan, H . S. *The new sex therapy*. New York: Brunner/Mazel, 1974, p. 113.
11. Rubin, L. B. *Women of a certain age: The midlife search for self*. New York: Harper & Row, 1979.
12. Zilbergeld, B. *Male sexuality*. Boston: Little, Brown, 1978. See also Hyde, op. cit., p. 337.
13. Zilbergeld, op. cit.
14. Ibid., p. 333.
15. Gadpaille, op. cit., p. 421.
16. Rubin, op. cit.
17. Allgeier and Allgeier, op. cit., pp. 456–457. See also Offir, C. W. *Human sexuality*. New York: Harcourt Brace Jovanovich, 1982, p. 352.
18. Lasswell and Lasswell, *Marriage and the family*, p. 472.
19. Aldous, op. cit., p. 285.
20. Benedek, T. Parenthood through the life cycle. In E. J. Anthony & T. Benedek (Eds.), *Parenthood: It's psychology and psychopathology*. Boston: Little, Brown, 1970, pp. 185–206.
21. Aldous, op. cit., p. 288. See also Lasswell and Lasswell, op. cit., pp. 457–458.
22. Aldous, op. cit., p. 290. See also Bengtson, V. L. Diversity and symbolism in grandparental roles. In V. L. Bengtson & J. F. Robertson (Eds.), *Grandparenting*. Beverly Hills, Calif.: Sage, 1985, pp. 11–25.
23. Garrett, W. R. *Seasons of marriage and family life*. New York: Holt, Rinehart & Winston, 1982, p. 441.
24. Gendlin, E. T. *Focusing*. New York: Everest House, 1978.

13

DEEPENING AND DRIFTING

In a materialistic society, participation in the economy is the measure and meaning of everything human. Upon meeting for the first time, American adults usually feel obliged to ask each other what they "do." Everyone knows that this "doing" refers to the performance of a function in the production of goods and services that people consider valuable enough to pay for. If one has a well-paid job, he or she is thought to be "doing well." Even if poorly paid, however, every employed man or woman is at least a "somebody." On the other hand, if unemployed or retired, people are regarded as "doing nothing"—in effect, as having no socially legitimate claim on personhood. Of course, such an individual may be loving, creative, and helpful to others. Still, by the criteria of the marketplace, he or she is a "nobody."

Similarly, employment marks the course of aging in America. Adolescence ends and adulthood begins when people finish formal schooling and go to work on a full-time basis. Much later, their entrance into old age is defined by retirement. In 1993, however, mandatory retirement will be legally abolished.[1] The responsibility then for deciding whether and when to retire will be entirely in the hands of employees. Then, too, their decisions will hinge largely on how much they have adopted society's standards for defining themselves and their goals in living. Thus, many conventional couples may recoil in horror from the double jeopardy of becoming old *and* "nobody" simply by *choosing* to leave their jobs. These husbands and wives thus may continue working until they literally drop dead "with their boots on."

Dying in the saddle of one's lifelong occupation has been advocated by some gerontologists, particularly for people who do intrinsically interesting work. In his book *A Good Age*, Alex Comfort offers many vignettes of famous individuals who went on working productively throughout their seventies and eighties. Moreover, he regards engagement with useful work as a crucial contributor to an aged person's morale.[2]

Undoubtedly, it is inspiring to know what people are capable of accomplishing in their old age given sufficient health, will, and talent. It is also true that men and women of *any* age thrive on doing things they enjoy and find consonant with the actualization of their potentials. Yet Comfort and other authorities on aging tend to view the subject from the standpoint of an *achieving individual*. These specialists generally fail to consider that a *loving relationship* is not only a most worthy achievement but also a collective one. Accordingly, they do not emphasize the fact that absorption in *solitary* work *detracts from* the ability of elderly mates to maximize their *mutual fulfillment in love*.

By contrast, love-centered mates are *primarily* committed to achieve the lifelong development of their marital relationship. Even while young and energetic, they make sure not to let work become their highest priority. Indeed, they make whatever adjustments are necessary to keep their jobs subordinate to and supportive of their marriage—the "main event" in their lives.

Of course, many spouses will have retired by their midsixties. But those who are still working face yet another adjustment to ensure their relational progress. Now, they *know* how much more a day's work takes out of them than it did a year ago. They do not need a Federal statute to inform them that they are "old." As fit and as nimble as they may be, they cannot deny that "until death do us part," while still their pledge, is also a prediction that will come to pass all too soon.

When either of them reach the age of 70, therefore, mates

have sufficient incentive for meeting the sixth and final objective of a love-centered marriage: to go on deepening the gratifications of their relationship, even in the face of severe debilitation and the imminence of death. This objective calls on them to make whatever changes in their lives that will permit them *to be together in everything they do*. Consequently, by retiring from work, mates create the ideal circumstances for culminating their lifelong romance with the common dream of loving each other as deeply as humanly possible by the time either of them dies.

However, at this age a husband and wife are peaking in their involuntary fear of dying, magnifying their fear of loving to its maximum extent. So, they are more threatened by *deepening* their relationship than they ever were about meeting the desirable objectives of the previous stages in their marriage. Facing the end of their own lives *and* the ambiguity of not knowing which of them will die first, they shrink away from admitting that their individual well-being—and even their survival—is contingent on their merging to the utmost. Assailed by self-concern, they devise mutual defenses for *drifting* apart well before they must be separated by death.

TOWARD A MORE PERFECT UNION

Upon reaching this stage of marriage, many spouses have been employed for four decades or more. Leaving their home for 5 days a week, they got involved in different tasks and related to different people. If the wife stayed at home for a few or all of those years, the couple was just as divided, mentally and socially.

Naturally, some couples were always careful to minimize these barriers. Still, it was impossible to prevent all the divisive effects of work on their relationship. Precious moments they yearned to extend were irretrievably shortened by occupational demands. Conversations started late at night had to be postponed—and never were resumed in their original intimacy and meaningfulness. Even seemingly long vacations were actually taken under strict temporal constraints that sometimes impeded the couple's relational unity. Thus, after having begun to delve into a relational problem, they had to stop because their holiday was over. Returning to their work, they may have been required to wait a long time before they could re-create the interpersonal atmosphere conducive to the depth of communication they had put "on hold."

For love-centered mates, however, "better late than never" is a most appropriate adage. By voluntarily retiring from their individual jobs, they finally become the constant companions they had longed to be since first creating their marital romance. Now, in the same place at the same time, they experience their daily life *as a couple*. Instantly, they are able to communicate any thought or feeling that occurs to them and to carry on every discussion in unbroken continuity until conclusively resolving the issue under consideration.

By coordinating their exit from work, couples enter the last stage of marriage with maximum unity. Accordingly, as some experts agree, it is desirable for dual-career mates to retire *simultaneously*.[3] Understandably, this "double" retirement already is quite popular,[4] for it permits spouses to remain "in synch" while making the transition from their old and divided routines to a new and united pattern for living out their lives.

Of course, some couples may have previously formulated a detailed plan for their postretirement years. Others eschewed such planning, preferring to "play it by ear" and give themselves a chance to see how it actually feels to be retired. These mates may travel extensively or simply putter about their homes until crystallizing a "gut feeling" about the activities they want to take up on a regular basis.

Eventually, however, it is beneficial for mates to participate jointly in activities that keep them mentally alert and emotionally responsive; that give them a means to deepen their relationship by stimulating their interpersonal creativity; and that reflect their humane values. Surely, it is not advisable for couples to sequester themselves in a Floridian playpen as the Olsons tried to do, vainly seeking fulfillment through one form of consumption or another. Rather, mates facilitate their mutual satisfaction and personal growth by deciding how best to combine their interests, skills, and talents. In fact, they expand the boundaries of their individuality by honesty exploring their options. Then they increase this expansion by cooperating to implement their collective decision.

A husband and wife may wind up doing something similar to what either of them had done before retiring. Or they may choose an activity that is novel to both of them. The essential point, however, is to be *together* in whatever they finally do. In this respect, couples like the Olsons could deepen their relationship if they were willing to unify their participation in part-time and unpaid work by switching from separate pursuits to a common one.

But while spouses are furthering their relational unity in these ways, they are sorely afflicted by feelings of personal loss over the occupational identities they have given up. Moreover, at this age they worry a lot about their own longevity *and* about which one will be the first "to go." Nevertheless, they become much closer by talking about these concerns. Each acquires greater empathy for the other by disclosing the anguish of losing whatever "strokes" of respect, admiration, or recognition he and she had received while working. One of them may feel more cruelly bereft of such psychological rewards than the other, depending on the differentials in their salaries, status, and power. Thus, it may take them quite a while to dispel those feelings and to consolidate their sense of self more completely around their *collective* identity.

Mates hasten this consolidation by reminding each other of how meaningless the occupational props to their egos had actually become in the light of their advanced age. Really and truly, would they have wanted to pass up the final opportunity to develop and enjoy their loving relationship in favor of getting a few more flattering comments from supervisors or colleagues? What further raises or promotions could compensate for the *personal losses* they would have incurred by *staying* on their jobs instead of retiring to deepen their love? Didn't pushing themselves separately to be a "this" or "that" only result in diminishing their strength? And didn't they always energize themselves the most by interacting as a unified couple?

It is far more difficult, however, for mates to flush out their anticipations about dying. For in their imaginings about death they are projecting themselves into new hazards of an unknowable future rather than discarding the stale crumbs of a well-known past. Still, by openly discussing their ultimate fate as aged mortals, mates forge an immensely strong emotional bond. In such exchanges they expose their greatest dreads and most self-centered preoccupations; by peering into the bleakest pits of their human commonality, they attain new depths of compassion for each other.

Thus, it is essential for mates to confront the twin terrors of being the first to die *and* the one who is "left behind." Talking about these macabre prospects, a husband may point out that women usually outlive men. Upset by the truth of this statistical fact, the wife may dispute its applicability to their case in an attempt to comfort him. Yet each one harbors the secret wish of living as long as possible, even if that means surviving after the other's death. This natural ambivalence draws mates into an uneasy and unacknowledged contest. Surely, it is difficult for either of them to admit that, after sharing so many years of marital intimacy, they are worried about saving their own skins.

On the other hand, the possibility of surviving may be as secretly feared as dying before one's spouse. Indeed, the survivor will have to endure the loss of the mate *and* the end of the marital relationship. In memory, of course, a widow or widower keeps the deceased mate vicariously alive. Mentally, too, he or she perpetuates the essence of their lifelong relationship. In reality, however, there is no one with whom to go on fulfilling the promises of love. In addition, the survivor loses the *spousal identity* linked to an ongoing marriage.

For love-centered mates this loss is especially devastating to contemplate. Having consciously dedicated their individual lives primarily to the development of their relationship, they defined their adult selves mainly in terms of functioning as a husband and a wife. A key feature of each one's personal identity is obliterated by the death of a mate. However, in developing their relationship, love-centered mates have also developed the personal strengths that would maximize their ability to function effectively as a widow or widower. Still, in anticipating the other's death, neither mate is likely to reflect so objectively on the future. Rather, each privately fears that he or she may be deprived of the very selfhood needed for subsequent survival.

It is extraordinarily wrenching for mates to uncover these horrifying thoughts and eventualities. Yet as Robert Butler and

Myrna Lewis state, "A conception of personal death must become consciously realized. At first this can be frightening and painful, but if favorably resolved, a mature resignation frees the person from fear. . . . old age can then be enjoyed but with a full awareness of death, which lies beyond."[5] Of course, for a *couple* to enjoy old age together, *both mates* must confront this fear. In mutually disclosing themselves, they interpenetrate the most guarded recesses of each other's minds, and each releases the energy tied up in being "on guard." Thus, both of them take enormous strides in becoming more lovingly honest despite their fearful tendencies toward evasiveness and secrecy.

Still, the actual loss of a lifelong occupation and the expected loss of life itself combine to threaten a husband and wife to the utmost about continuing to expand the boundaries of their individuality, and they experience a similarly extreme increase in their fear of loving. In mutually defensive reactions, even quite courageous spouses drift away from each other, bringing the development of their relational unity to a standstill. Transforming their fear of loving into rivalry and greed, they enact those negative emotions in competitive complicities that reflect their dire apprehensions.

For years Fred and Sandy Blair had entertained the fantasy of opening an "antique boutique" in the barn of their house in the country. They pictured this venture as a perfect combination of their fondness for beautiful things. Fred had devoted his career to industrial design, and Sandy was an assistant editor of home furnishings for a women's magazine. Now, he was nearing 70 and she had just turned 67. Claiming to be "sick and tired" of occupational pressures, they also complained about the pollution of their urban environment and the strain of keeping up two residences. They kept telling each other the time had come to leave the city and start their "fun business" in the rural setting they loved so much.

Eventually, they set a date for their "double" retirement. However, while talking about when and how to give notice to their employers, each of them secretly worried about what they would be giving up in personal satisfaction. Sandy's name would no longer be on the masthead of her magazine. Unable to have exciting lunches with writers, she would be buried in the woods. Instead of being sought out for advice by members of her staff, she would be dusting dead bric-a-brac. Fred's mind was also awhirl with his imagined deprivations. Where would he get the praise his boss and colleagues always lavished on his work? How could sitting around as a clerk in their barn compare with the excitement of coming up with a design that would knock the eyes out of the leading professionals in his field?

Stricken by these qualms, the Blairs silently agreed on a hidden agenda to undermine their plans for retirement. So, when "R-Day" arrived, they let it pass without a word, each suddenly becoming busier at their work than they had been for months. Soon, however, they had to recognize the fact that neither of them had quit. Sandy attributed her resistance to the differences in their careers. After all, she had taken years off from *her* job to stay home and raise their children, while Fred had gone all out in *his* work. She greedily asserted that she should have a chance to make up for lost time. Besides, she *was* about three years younger. Didn't *that* mean a lot at their stage of life?

Fred did not argue with her rationale. Rather, he admitted to being less energetic than she. But he didn't want to crap around in the country like an old fart. He had plenty of talent left in him. In fact, as she knew, he had often thought of doing some painting and drawing. Why couldn't *he* develop himself as a *creative* artist instead of just grinding out designs for toasters and radios? Meanwhile, he mused privately, look at what Grandma Moses accomplished in her old age.

Elaborating their complicity, the Blairs contrived an arrangement in which Fred retired while Sandy remained at her job. That way, they falsely told each other, he could slow down and they could go to the country whenever it was convenient for her to get away. Thus, they started the "second act" of the scenario to shatter the common dream of their old age.

At first, they did take long weekends together. However, to compress 5 days into 4, Sandy had to work late every evening. Fred started to paint in a loft he rented near their apartment. Often, he wasn't home when she returned from her office. Working such long hours, Sandy soon felt too tired to make the weekend trip to the country. Going up there alone,

Fred decided that the barn was ideal for his work. So why waste money for a studio in the city? Gradually, the Blairs got totally out of synch, spending more time apart than together.

When she did join him in the country, Sandy acted as if she enjoyed her work more than ever—and had everything under control. But she was inwardly disturbed about how much she was actually "slipping." Beginning to forget important details, she also found it harder to make the quick decisions required by her job. Although never telling it to Fred, she hated coming home to an empty apartment, and without him in bed with her, she had trouble falling asleep.

Fred put on an equally false front, regaling Sandy with stories about the interesting artists he was meeting and the excellent response he was getting to his paintings. But *he* knew how agitated and driven he felt. Often staying up half the night to work, he neglected his health and his appearance. He also felt very embarrassed going around to galleries, trying to be taken seriously as a "new talent" at his age.

Meanwhile, Sandy found it more and more difficult to handle her job. Frustrated and tense all night, she was depressed during the day. Making elementary errors in judgment, she was sharply criticized by her boss. Besides, she had to go alone to all the office parties. She tried to convince Fred to come into the city to join her, but he consistently refused, saying he was too involved in his own work. Having to answer questions from her colleagues about him, she could not avoid the pain of feeling how far they had drifted from one another.

Fred finally got a show in a local gallery, but he got far less than rave reviews and sold only one drawing. It was now Sandy's turn to get one up on him by refusing to attend the opening of his exhibit. He sat there numbly, compelled to watch a handful of people make inane comments and stare blankly at the pictures he had slaved to produce.

Thus, the Blairs found no rewards commensurate with the efforts they had put into their separate strivings. On the contrary, each achieved a Pyrrhic victory over the other, since their unbridled competition corroded their relational unity. Exhausted and demoralized, they felt totally disoriented about how to pick up the pieces of their marriage.

Of course, even if they retire at the same time, mates may

put themselves out of synch by forming complicities in which
they get involved separately in egoistic pursuits. A wife may
relentlessly strive to be the leader of a civic group, while her
husband does the same in another organization. Ultimately,
they become more concerned about staying in touch with their
associates than with each other. Similarly, after retiring together spouses may scuttle their freshly deepened unity by returning to separate jobs with different hours.

However, even when no individual activities separate
them, aged mates do not escape from the fact that either of
them could be snuffed out at any moment. Obsessed with
worry about this possibility, many couples devise a "sour
grapes" complicity in which they reject the benefits of uniting
any further. In these ghastly scenarios, each mate acts as if the
other were already dead. What's the point of talking to a
corpse? Tuning out each other, they drift into separate rever-
ies, rewriting their personal pasts or inventing fantasies for an
unattainable future. While lying side by side in the sun or sitting in the same room day after day, husband and wife essentially are out of contact with each other. Although their attention is not distracted by any individual project or job, they
could just as well be on different planets.

Having tied themselves into any of these complicities, elderly mates may feel too weary to make the effort to liberate
each other. Besides, they composed such taxing scenarios because they were too frightened to go on building their collective unity. However, the emotional cost of this defensiveness is
even more frightening, for they have condemned themselves
to a living death, an unremitting misery that is far worse to
bear than any fear they would have to tolerate in breaking a
complicity. Facing this horror, they have everything to gain and
nothing to lose by disclosing whatever fantasies they have
been harboring *and* anything else that bothers them, including
their most disturbing thoughts and feelings about themselves
and their relationship.

This candid disclosure enables a couple to be much more
efficient in enhancing their unity. Instead of wasting their energies and stressing themselves by competing, they can *collaborate* in expressing their interests. According to many experts,
people are capable of learning at *any* age.[6] With good health,

adequate education, and intellectual stimulation, the amount of decline in mental ability with aging is not as great as was thought previously. While there is some reduction in speed and reaction time, abilities such as judgment, accuracy, and general knowledge actually increase.[7]

Adult education offers many vehicles for couples to develop old interests and sample new ones together. The Elderhostel, a year-round residential college program for people over 65, offers courses taught by the regular faculty at 800 different campuses throughout the nation. Other programs, conducted by voluntary group leaders in community settings, integrate the arts and humanities with local issues and concerns.[8]

In addition, couples could participate in programs aimed at providing elderly people with the ability to help themselves and others of their age. Courses set up for this practical purpose focus on issues of health, stress management, and exercise. Some programs also recruit and train peer counselors to work with people in emotional crises.[9] Given this type of education, mates may construct a new and productive role for themselves after retiring from the conventional marketplace.

MAKING LOVE FOR A LIFETIME

About 40 years ago Kinsey and his coinvestigators discovered a couple whose sexual vigor was as awesome as their longevity. The husband of 103 and the wife of 90 were having intercourse regularly with mutual orgasm.[10] Those mates may have set the American record for erotic performance in old age. However, since Kinsey's time, researchers have found that spouses who were always sexually active tend to remain so in the latter years of their marriage. According to the Duke Longitudinal Study, men and women aged 66–71 who had maintained an interest in sex expressed *more* interest in it than they had between the ages of 46–50.[11]

This finding is very good news for love-centered mates. Having sustained lovemaking as their top relational priority in the past, they are properly prepared to go on making love in old age. They may also find encouragement in the fact that lovemaking is positively associated with both health and lon-

gevity. Of course, this correlation can be interpreted as showing that healthy and long-lived mates have a greater ability to
make love than do ill and short-lived ones. Nevertheless, a
number of experts have emphasized the importance of sexual
gratification as a causal factor in the preservation of psychophysical well-being among the elderly. Making love is described as a desirable form of muscular activity that "stimulates the adrenal glands and sympathetic and parasympathetic
nerves." Like an aerobic exercise, it "helps maintain fitness by
raising heart and breathing rates." Orgasm is also beneficial to
the genitalia of both sexes, facilitating the continuation of sexual responsiveness.[12] Besides, sexual activity has been associated with reduced insomnia.[13]

On the other hand, prolonged sexual abstinence may induce all kinds of psychosomatic illnesses[14] and severe depression.[15] Moreover, as Comfort cautions elderly readers, ". . . if
you drop your regular sexual activity for any length of time,
you may have difficulty and need treatment to restart."[16]

However, love-centered mates require no medical induce-
ments for engaging in what has always been their greatest pleasure. Having cut the binds of working on a rigid schedule, they
are in a position to create the ideal conditions for whatever
rhythm of sexual interaction they desire. They may choose to
make love in the morning—when they feel most refreshed—
rather than having to wait, as they once did, until their day's
work was done. Similarly, they can loll about in bed—before,
during, and after making love—without worrying about missing
an appointment, attending a meeting, or doing anything else
demanded by their preretirement occupations.

This freedom also permits mates to be optimally flexible
about *how* to express their mutual love in sexual terms. Of
course, there is no equivalent for the interpenetration of intercourse, which is the acme of intimacy and which, with its pelvic thrusting, affords each mate the fullest possible orgasmic
release.[17] But an aged husband and wife may often wish to
dally in the delights of foreplay, even to the extent of snuggling
and talking for *hours* without moving toward a climax. Moreover, they may even stop for a time before proceeding with the
leisurely assurance developed over decades of success in every
facet of erotic satisfaction.

On the other hand, aged lovers may be forced increasingly to forego intercourse by either chronic or acute illnesses. Still, even in those dreadful circumstances, they are frequently capable of making sexual contact to the point of orgasm via mutual masturbation or oral-genital stimulation. Obviously, these options are not open to them during a period of hospitalization. In the privacy of their own home, however, they can restore the basic integrity of their sexual relations—as the wedding vow says—"in sickness as in health."

Lifelong mates also are challenged to overcome adverse *emotional* reactions to changes in their own and in each other's appearance. Both husband and wife will be marked indelibly by wrinkles, sagging skin, bent posture, and many other stigmata of the aging process. While normal and unavoidable, these cosmetic blights are troublesome, especially in a youth-oriented culture, so they may view themselves as less attractive in one another's eyes.

However, having never suspended their lovemaking, mates readily adapt to these alterations. Regular sexual gratification also reinforces the feeling of irreplaceable preciousness each has about the other. With whom else could they experience the sublime enjoyments they have created over the years as a couple? When they share a gaze of passionate desire, they banish those years as if by magic. To each mate the other becomes *exactly* the person he and she knew as newlyweds. Simultaneously, their beings coursing with the imperishable vitality of loving, they feel themselves to be those persons. Thus, aging lovers retain a changeless quality of youthfulness for as long as they live.

Nevertheless, liberation from external constraints to lovemaking poses a degree of threat mates *never* experienced before. Now they can actually stay in bed—day after day—with *no* social obligations to pull them away from the ecstasies of lovemaking. This possibility is menacing precisely because they are extremely tempted by it. As we have noted, mates may happily yield to this temptation for hours at a stretch. Yet this yielding is bound to stir mortal apprehension in both of them. What if they lost *all* control of themselves and did *nothing* but indulge their erotic desires *day and night?* Wouldn't they lose their minds in a spinning kaleidoscope of pleasure? What about their ability to handle the essentials of survival? And isn't their survival a constant and growing concern now that they are so old? Rattled by these profound anxieties, mates form complicities to reduce or terminate their lovemaking. Instead of remaining in the warmth of sensual enjoyment, they drift away from each other in a cold wasteland of mutual defense.

Sam and Ethel Martin exemplify this unfortunate tendency. When they retired, he was 72 and she was 70. He had been an accountant in business for himself and she had worked as an assistant manager for a supermarket. They had been frugal, paying off the mortgage on their house and accumulating the financial resources to feel secure about their future. Their children were comfortably settled with families of their own. Thus, the Martins were able to travel extensively for the first time in their married life. Shortly after leaving their jobs, they booked a berth on the cruise of their dreams—a worldwide tour to sample the wonders of the five continents.

Fortunately, they were in very good health for their age, so they could take all the side trips the tour sponsored at its ports of call. True, Ethel had arthritis in her back, impairing her ability to scramble up steep inclines. Although remarkably agile, Sam had an enlarged prostate gland that made it necessary for him to get out of bed to urinate several times each night. However, they were so turned on by fulfilling their romantic dream that neither of them "felt any pain." Indeed, rather than sleep separately in the bunk beds of their stateroom, they cuddled together in the lower bunk, and they made love one or two nights a week.

Before the cruise was over, Sam and Ethel decided how to spend their retirement years. They would go on several shorter trips every year. Between these jaunts they would devote themselves to volunteer work in their suburban community, advising other elderly people on ways of managing their finances and filing their income taxes.

Upon returning home, the Martins implemented this plan. They kept their schedule very loose, changing it to accommodate other things they liked to do together. Accustomed to a lifetime of lovemaking in the evening hours, they waited until after dinner before getting into their queen-sized bed. Then they tapped into the erotic momentum generated on their voyage. After making love they imagined themselves rocking gently to the soothing waves of a ship, sailing off to sleep in a tender embrace.

However, their erotic enjoyment soon became *too* good, too threatening for them to tolerate. They then hit upon a very "rational" way of lessening it. In their complicity the Martins greatly magnified their ailments, using their differing symptoms as a pretext for discontinuing their sexual pleasure. They decided that Sam's nightly visits to the bathroom were an unbearable hindrance to Ethel's sleep. At the same time, they agreed that her arthritis had become an equally bothersome impediment to him. Acting as if she had become exceptionally fragile, she groaned loudly at the slightest bodily contact between them. She kept Sam up as often and as jarringly as she claimed he was awakening her.

After many weeks of mutual complaint, they arrived at a "solution" to their "sudden" problem. They would switch to twin beds. Thereafter, they became very inhibited about making sexual advances to each other. Wouldn't that mean sleeping together again, which, they had already concluded, deprived both of them of a night's rest? Even if they crawled back into their separate beds after making love, wouldn't intercourse be excruciatingly painful to Ethel and thus emotionally abhorrent to Sam? Given these negative expectations, the Martins eventually stopped their sexual relations, resigning themselves to chronic frustration.

Paradoxically, Sam and Ethel also deprived themselves of the specific benefits sexual intercourse provides for the very ailments they used as their reason for becoming celibate. Actually, the relaxation that follows orgasm brings relief from the pain of arthritis.[18] Thus, because of their abstinence, Ethel exposed herself to *more* pain, not less. Similarly, ejaculation keeps the prostate gland from getting congested. Having no orgasmic release, Sam became a candidate for prostatitis, which he never had before.[19]

As this case demonstrates, it is vitally important for elderly mates to sustain the regularity of their sexual relations. Surely, they may be prey to all sorts of aches and pains that interfere with the sheer mechanics of intercourse. But it is in their best interest—physically and emotionally—to avoid incorporating those difficulties into a complicity for drifting into abstinence.

Certainly, as either spouse becomes "old-old," a category that gerontologists say begins at age 75,[20] *both* of them must be more diligent about setting aside the time and energy for lovemaking. They can no longer serenely count on *any* future as lovers. As Irv's father, Nathan, who lived to be 91, used to say: "Life is a long story with a short ending." So it might seem to someone who is very old, very sick, and very tired, hardly able to move and feeling Death as a palpable presence crouched heavily on his or her stooped shoulders, waiting for an opportune moment to pounce. In such a harrowing condition, many aged people have been known to wish for a speedy end to their lives, regarding any further extensions of their "long story" as unmitigated suffering for themselves, their mates, and their children.

Yet a *fully lived* moment of love is a blissful experience at *any time* in a person's live, lifting him or her beyond all concerns with illness or mortality. Undoubtedly, it is difficult for ailing mates to put themselves totally into such moments and to string together a timeless strand of pleasure. But even if the ravages of their flesh prevent them from having sexual intercourse, a husband and wife can immerse themselves in the most intimate forms of erotic interaction still feasible for expressing their affection: fondling, hugging, kissing, and mutual masturbation. As Herant Katchadourian has observed, "Awareness of the approaching sunset of life . . . can impart a special poignancy to each act of love."[21] Even if every sexual avenue of loving communication is permanently closed to them, lifelong mates still can engage in spiritual lovemaking, attaining a fulfillment akin to orgasm just by holding hands and looking into each other's eyes with complete surrender to their mutual love.

ENDING "SPITE WARS" BETWEEN THE SEXES

From the beginning of their marriage, love-centered mates strove to express their essential similarity as human beings, for they regarded the transcendence of their gender differences as a basic promise of their love. In fulfilling that promise, both of them broadened the repertoire of their individual skills and interests while enriching the range and quality of their inner experiences. Meanwhile, as a couple they enhanced their social equality.

Surely, in this last marital stage mates would not wish to discontinue this major aspect of loving. Indeed, they may actually help to keep each other alive by becoming even more flexible about their roles. A husband with an infirm wife may be faced with the challenge of learning to do household tasks that both of them once considered "feminine." Moreover, he may have to bathe and dress her, or even assist her with toileting functions. On the other hand, if a husband is the one who becomes incapacitated, the wife may be required to do all the driving, make household repairs, and manage the couple's finances—"masculine" activities they had relegated entirely to him.

But this flexibility is also enjoyably liberating for a husband and wife. No longer bound by occupational roles, retired mates are free to think, feel, and act in whatever ways are most pleasing to them. In fact, their *common* status as retirees induces them to *redefine* the roles they want to play in society and in relating to each other.

Yet that very freedom places a fresh burden of responsibility on both of them. Despite their past efforts to equalize their relationship, they *did* spend decades playing socially prescribed and differing parts in the workplace. Their self-concepts as male and female have been strongly conditioned to the specifics of that role playing. If they drop those familiar and stereotypical parts, won't they lose their gender identities? But gender identity is a core element in each one's sense of individuality, and if they tamper with *that*, wouldn't they be risking psychological annihilation?

As we have seen, with death coming ever closer, elderly mates become desperately fearful of losing their separate identities, and they feel mortally menaced by anything that appears to hasten such a loss. Often, they strenuously resist the possibility of changing in any way that alters their perceptions of themselves as masculine and feminine. So, they fail to take advantage of the unique opportunities this stage offers for their relational and personal growth.

This type of failure has been widely reported among retired couples.[22] Typically, a wife complains that her husband is underfoot all day, not knowing what to do with himself and interfering with her housework. Reciprocally, he resents her ability to keep busy at the household routines she has maintained since the earliest days of their marriage, and he is bitter about being pushed aside and sent on errands by her. Soon, these mates may drift away from each other and get involved in various activities with members of their own sex.

After a rocky start, other retired couples temporarily succeed in sharing all their roles. But the threat of transcending their gender differences eventually mounts and acutely stirs their fear of loving, which they transform into envy and spite. They act out these negative emotions in a "spite war"—a combative complicity in which they draw firm battle lines around themselves and burrow into separate foxholes of relational inequality.

When the Coopers retired, Ralph was 73 and Betty was 70. He had been a civil engineer and she had taught biology in high school. While still working, they had started a garden in the backyard of their suburban home. Betty specialized in small vegetables, and Ralph did some gourmet cooking with their own produce. Before leaving their jobs, they decided to pool their interests and skills in the business of growing and marketing herbs.

In the first fall of their retirement, the Coopers remodeled their basement, setting up an indoor space to get their seedlings started for the coming spring. They worked together, installing shelves, trays, and grow-lights. They also turned a spare room into a studio for making their packages and labels. With Ralph's advice and encouragement, Betty quickly acquired proficiency in basic carpentry and electrical work. She learned how to order lumber and other supplies, shopping carefully for the best bargains.

Meanwhile, she assisted him in designing their logo, labels, and packages, often voicing admiration for the style of his drawings and calligraphy. At the end of the summer, Ralph tried out exotic recipes that they planned to include with their products, featuring the herbs Betty had planted, tended, and harvested with his help. With tips and knowledge from her years of experience in the kitchen, he began to relieve her of most of the cooking, letting her focus on the gardening.

After about a year, the Coopers were ready to "go public" with their enterprise. They went around soliciting business in food stores throughout the area, taking turns with their sales pitch. As a steady stream of orders came in, they cheerfully delivered their wares from the back of an old station wagon. Their commercial success also symbolized the attainment of a greatly increased level of relational equality, which was what they had supposedly wanted as a couple. Yet they felt severely threatened by it.

Ralph became extremely disturbed by Betty's ability to take on the difficult physical and technical jobs he had performed exclusively. Despite the pleasure he took in his new culinary and artistic work, he broke into a cold sweat over the thought of becoming too soft and ineffectual as a result of those "womanly" activities. Betty found it just as threatening to see how well Ralph was doing "her" jobs around the house. Maybe it was foolish to let him spend so much time cooking and making delicate drawings while she hammered, sawed, and hoisted heavy trays of plants. Wouldn't she become too tough and lose her femininity?

Reacting defensively to these common feelings of threat, the Coopers devised a complicity to cancel the progress they had made. In their scenario they became mutually critical, spitefully complaining about how poorly each was doing the work formerly done only by the other. While Ralph had initially admired the confidence Betty brought to their project, he now condemned her certitude as overbearing. He also displayed envy over the fact that, although she had retired, she still retained a definite role and identity as a homemaker, simply because she was a woman. But for *him* retirement meant losing his *sole source* of status and power. Now experiencing that loss as a tremendous blow to his "masculinity," he began to "put her in her place." If he found *any* imperfection in her work, he immediately jumped on her. Feeling she had become "too big for her britches," he also made snide and embarrassing remarks about her in front of other people, especially when they were negotiating with customers.

While stung by Ralph's comments, Betty became just as bossy and biting. She lacerated him for being a "pushover" when it came to getting a good price, and she acted as if everything she did was *perfect*. Yet she secretly envied him for his mastery of tasks she was still learning to do. Although she frequently wanted to get his advice, she spitefully let things slide rather than give Ralph the satisfaction of asking for his help.

Besides, she became the testy monitor of his work as a homemaker. When he took the trouble to prepare a delicious meal, she complained it was too spicy, bland, or fattening. If he made a suggestion for arranging the furniture more attractively, she accused him of bad taste and went out of her way to find dusty corners he missed in vacuuming a room. Instead of standing up to her, Ralph passively absorbed Betty's abuse. Quietly defiant, however, he became inept and careless under her scrutiny, spitefully antagonizing her by breaking some of their best china or ruining a meal by not taking it out of the oven on time. On those occasions she let loose a salvo of invectives, questioning his ability to do *anything* right.

Soon the Coopers felt very nervous when they were together. Since neither of them gave any ground, they drove each other into a tormenting stalemate. Feeling mutually defeated, they began to talk about giving up their business. Maybe it had been foolhardy to start it at their age. Why should they put up with any more fighting? Wouldn't it be better for both of them to get involved in different hobbies or part-time work? But Betty burst into tears whenever she went into the basement to tend the little green shoots sprouting from the flats they had already started for next summer's crop. What a pity and a waste! Did they *really* have to call it quits? Ralph felt just as wretched as he wandered aimlessly around their studio. How *could* they give up all they had accomplished? Sure, they were going through hell, but what about their wonderful times?

As they continued their enmity and procrastination, new orders kept coming in, and old ones had to be met. When and how were they going to tell customers of their intention to go out of business? In confronting this crucial question, they arrived at their moment of truth. Sheepishly and shakily, both of them admitted they did *not* want to scrap their project. It meant too much to them, despite all the humiliations they had inflicted on each other. Besides, what would be their alternatives? Would Betty be happy to join other women in the local gardening club? Would Ralph like to go back to a mostly male environment as a consultant to an engineering firm?

No. They had thrived too much on teaming up as husband and wife, on the novelty of exchanging their know-how and experiences. Yes, they had been venomously hostile in disparaging each other. But wasn't that to be expected after so many years of doing a "man's" and a "woman's" work? Couldn't they be open about their resentments as they came up instead of nursing them spitefully? Of course, they might still snipe at each other. But they could deal with those situations on the spot. Maybe they could even have a few laughs in seeing people of their age getting so upset over whether the wife is being too "macho" or the husband too "femme."

As the Coopers' case illustrates, it *is* possible for a couple to make peace after launching a "spite war." They do not have to blast each other back into the separate "territories" from which they had begun to venture. In fact, whenever mates become worried about what activities are "his" or "hers," they can regard this concern as a symptom of their common threat about becoming more equal. The same principle applies when they find themselves thinking about joining groups that are segregated along gender lines.

Of course, many adult communities, condominiums, and centers for senior citizens contain suborganizations that formally divide men and women into different clubs. Thus, a husband and a wife who want to participate as a couple in all activities often feel under social pressure to go into separate groups. Consequently, even in old age, love-centered mates affirm their egalitarian values by resisting those pressures and by participating only in groups that welcome members of both sexes. Thus, they strengthen their own relational equality and give implicit support to elderly peers who also are opposed to the conventional forms of sexism.

Finally, by avoiding the constrictions of stereotypical role playing, retired mates derive maximum enjoyment in relating to their grandchildren. A grandfather can feel just as relaxed going shopping and baking bread with his grandson as he does playing baseball and chopping wood with his granddaughter. Likewise, a grandmother is free to engage in the same full range of activities with grandchildren of both sexes. And, since neither mate has a monopoly on wisdom, each of them shares nuggets of it with this upcoming generation. At the same time, they encourage nonsexist attitudes and behavior on the part of their grandsons and granddaughters. In turn, the couple remains educable to what their grandchildren spontaneously teach them about the latest cultural trends and technological innovations.

GOING THE DISTANCE HAND IN HAND

Although freed from occupational demands, elderly mates cannot retire from life. As long as both of them remain alive, they have to deal with all the other realities impinging upon them. Now, however, each one is likely to be suffering from a chronic ailment. Generally, too, retired couples must live on far less income than they had while working.[23] For the sake of their health and economic security, therefore, they must become more adaptive and ingenious in old age than ever before.

Rising to this challenge, love-centered mates add an exciting element to their lifelong romance. By resolving to retain full responsibility for their common well-being, they continue to fulfill the vital promise of interdependence. At the same time, they grow as dependable and trusting individuals and sustain their morale throughout their final years together.

Certainly, spouses feel reassured when both of them know they are doing their utmost to care for their marital and personal welfare. By coming through in this thoroughly reliable manner, they maintain their confidence *and* their competence. In exercising their physical and mental abilities, they keep optimally fit to handle their own affairs. Likewise, by doing whatever needs to be done, they strengthen their motivation to act in their own behalf. Thus, active interdependence and effective functioning are mutually reinforcing, setting up a beneficial cycle that encourages an aged couple to prevail over their adversities.

On a daily basis, mates enact their own reliability by adhering to whatever regimens of diet, exercise, rest, and medication are desirable for their optimal health. Of course, they may need to call for assistance from doctors, nurses, repair people, relatives, and neighbors. Still, they further their relational reliability by discussing why, when, and with whom to solicit such assistance and by stating their most considered judgments before making any decisions or taking any actions.

Couples usually are obliged to be just as wise about using their monetary resources. In particular, mates of this age have to avoid becoming either too spendthrift or too miserly. To achieve this balance they consult each other about their expenditures and assets; if necessary, one mate can correct faulty assumptions or rash suggestions on the part of the other.

However, the majority of elderly couples face a losing battle in attempting to preserve their preretirement standard of living. Inflation steadily erodes the spending power of their fixed and greatly reduced income. In addition, the possibility of being wiped out by a catastrophic illness is omnipresent. Although they may be very judicious in managing their money, aged mates have good reason to feel economically insecure.

This very unpleasant feeling may drive some couples back to full-time or part-time work although they may endanger their health by returning to occupational pressures. Thus, they are damned either by the inadequate income of their retirement or the excessive stresses of working to earn more money.

It is outrageous for the wealthiest nation on earth to treat its elders in such a heartless fashion. True, the Social Security System was set up to ease the financial burdens of retirees. But pension payments scarcely meet the regular expenses of retired people. Indeed, 40% of the elderly population is required to subsist near the poverty level.[24] Moreover, medical benefits from Social Security do not cover many costly contingencies, such as dental care and long periods of hospitalization.

In keeping with their social values, therefore, love-centered mates could help themselves and others by supporting legislation to expand federal funds for the aged. They realize that the effectiveness of their own marital interdependence is at least partially contingent on the material resources the society is willing to make available to *all* senior citizens. Consequently, they benefit by participating in a collective effort of political interdependence with people in a similar predicament.

The Gray Panthers, the American Association of Retired Persons, and other organizations offer channels for this kind of action.

However, at this stage, becoming more interdependent is also uniquely threatening to mates. Having been highly dependable for a long lifetime, each may feel suffocated by the prospect of continuing to be consistently helpful to the other, who is becoming more and more in need of this steadfastness. Since both mates are showing dramatic signs of enfeeblement, each begins to quake inwardly at the mere thought of having to spend the rest of his or her days caring for a grossly incapacitated spouse. Conversely, as both spouses succumb to troublesome or debilitating illnesses, each becomes leery of depending on the other. Thus, each worries about having to put himself or herself into the hands of a mate who is patently "losing it"— physically or mentally—at the same time.

In reacting to these sources of threat, aged mates convert their resulting fear of loving into the negative emotions of detachment and distrust. They then form complicities to enact those feelings. In a widespread scenario the husband and wife tacitly agree to let each other drift into a quagmire of despondency. Claiming to be hopelessly depressed about their individual ailments, each cements a wall of dreary detachment about himself and herself. Simultaneously, in keeping with their mutual distrust, each refuses to accept helpful advice or assistance from the other. Rather, both mates drift into an abyss of seemingly inconsolable self-pity.

In one case the husband suffers from diabetes that he has under only erratic control. He could stabilize his condition if he were less obese. Whenever he looks into a mirror, he feels very bad, seeing himself as a blimp about to explode. Yet he continues eating far too much, and too many sugary foods. His wife had offered to make special meals for him, but he spurned her offer, castigating her for not knowing how hard it is for someone with his constitution to lose weight. So she let the matter drop.

At the same time, she has been getting hard of hearing. For a while she scarcely noticed this impairment. Eventually, however, her husband had to raise his voice louder and louder to communicate with her. When he suggested that she go to a specialist for an examination, she resisted the idea, accusing him of exaggerating her hearing loss. Besides, even if she has a tiny problem, why bother with one of those *awful* hearing aids? It would make her look *much* older and uglier. Thus rebuffed, the husband withdraws and concentrates on feeling sorry for himself. Likewise, having decided to do nothing in her own behalf, the wife sinks into her own misery, relentlessly cursing her fate for being impaired.

Consequently, both mates act as if they had *no choice* but to become helplessly resigned to their own and each other's afflictions, and they cast a funereal pall over the atmosphere in their home. Moreover, unless they confront their complicity and break it, they may turn the rest of their years into a slow-moving cortege.

Of course, no couple can avoid periods of depression. But they do not have to incorporate their depressed states into a complicity that becomes a blight on their lives. Rather, by understanding the psychological meaning of depression, mates can help each other to shake it off promptly and to go on enjoying their good fortune about still being alive *and* together.

Depression is a natural human reaction to loss. It is not surprising that it is *the* most prevalent emotional disturbance among the elderly. As we have pointed out, people lose their occupational statuses and roles, as well as the identity, income, and social relations connected with their employment. Simultaneously, the aging process is depriving them rapidly of their psychophysical abilities. Moreover, they are besieged by shattered illusions about all the things they once hoped to accomplish but did not. They may also grieve the failure of their children to turn out exactly as they wished them to be. Finally, nearing death, they increasingly anticipate losing life itself.

While absorbing this procession of losses, mates may sometimes feel that the whole of their existence has been for naught. Enraged by the implacable limitations of the human condition, they stew in the juices of their inability to be invulnerable and immortal. At the same time, they feel an irrational sense of guilt for not having been perfect in everything they tried to do. Their depressed moods reflect their existential wrath and self-blame for their imperfections.

However, even after the death of a beloved person, the

depression of survivors need not last forever. In successful mourning, people amply express their grief and restore their emotional equilibrium within 6 months to a year.[25] Similarly, aged mates would do well to dredge up and air their bleakest feelings about whatever losses are giving rise to their bouts of depression. Such a joint catharsis permits them to lighten the load of their discontents. Accordingly, they express their interdependence in a most therapeutic manner by taking the initiative to confront each other whenever either of them gives *any* indication of settling into a depressive state.

Robert Butler has suggested it would be good for elderly people to conduct a "life review," deliberately reminiscing about their entire past.[26] Naturally, in compiling such an experiential inventory, a couple exposes the very sore points about which they are depressed. However, those wounds are precisely the ones they need to face and heal together in order to purge themselves of festering sorrows and regrets.

On the other hand, love-centered mates will be gratified to recount how much they have benefited at every stage in their lifelong relationship. It would *not* be Pollyannish of them to recall exactly what they have *gained* over their years together. Through these positive reminders, they retain a realistic perspective on the value of their past, and they can honestly rejoice in the fact that, for them, the cup of life has been more full than empty. After all, they *created* their contentment. For a lifetime they have struggled to preserve their love against the obstacles posed by society and their own human nature, and they have also made purposeful changes in their lives to develop their loving relationship.

However, it is maladaptive for mates to lull each other into complacency. To remain contented in their old-old age, they need to persist in this constancy of struggle and change. For now they are shadowed by the nearly total eclipse of their time on earth. Indeed, it takes all the will they can mobilize to make sure they will die as contentedly as they have lived. In addition to reviewing their past, they help each other by looking diligently into their fleeting present and their foreshortened future.

Taking Care of Unfinished Business

Unfortunately, many husbands and wives avoid this prudent scrutiny, bringing misery to each other and their loved ones. One poignant but popular complicity is exemplified by Ben and Molly Fisher, who had lived in Philadelphia for over 70 years. When he was 74 and she was 71, they decided to spend their remaining years in Arizona. The Fishers adapted surprisingly well to these new surroundings, furnishing their small house, making friends, and doing some voluntary work at the hospital in their community. From the beginning of their move, they maintained regular telephone contact with their four children who reside in various parts of the Northeast. Each child arranged to visit Ben and Molly once during the year, and the entire family also had an annual reunion.

When Ben reached the age of 83, his cataracts began to cloud his vision, especially at night. In fact, while driving after dark, he had two minor accidents within a few weeks. Greatly alarmed by this news, the children begged him to call a taxi whenever he and Molly went out for the evening. Appeasing them on the telephone, Ben promised to take their advice, but he had no intention of keeping his word. Molly also raised doubts about his visual acuity. Bristling with distrust, however, he chastised her for presuming to get inside his eyes and to tell him how well *he* could see. While remaining suspicious of Ben, she was also reluctant to give up the convenience of his driving. By continuing to ride beside him at night, she acted just as unreliably as he did.

Meanwhile, Molly began to feel the destructive effects of arteriosclerosis. First, it hit her in transient moments of dizziness. Soon, her symptoms worsened and she started to fall—once in the kitchen and once in the bathtub—bruising her head badly each time. Terrified after the second episode, Ben urged her to see a doctor immediately. Distrusting him, she laughed off his alarm and dismissed her falls as "little nothings." While ridiculing him, however, she ruminated anxiously about what might be happening to her. Although he did not trust her ability to diagnose herself, Ben was just as untrustworthy, drifting away into silence about the matter.

Upon hearing of Molly's falling, the children pleaded with

her to go to the doctor. On the telephone, as Ben had done, she promised to follow their suggestion. But as soon as she hung up the receiver, Molly laughed hollowly, remarking on what "big shots" their children were trying to be by telling her what to do. No, *she* saw no need for a medical opinion and she would *not* get one.

The Fishers had also become blatantly slack about their housework. On a yearly visit one of their daughters saw their place littered with dust and piles of old newspapers. Subsequently, a son found dirty dishes in the oven instead of in the dishwasher. Yet on the telephone Ben and Molly had repeatedly assured the children they were keeping their place spotlessly clean, even without a cleaning service.

Upon returning home, these children alerted their siblings to what was going on. All of them quickly got together to discuss what they could do for their parents, who were clearly approaching a crisis. Although it was difficult for the four of them to achieve a consensus, they finally decided on an excellent plan. They would ask their parents to return to Philadelphia, where the oldest daughter lived. She would get an apartment and hire help for them. Afterward, she would supervise their arrangement on a daily basis. The other children would take turns on weekends, visiting and providing whatever assistance was necessary. In addition, all the children would contribute the extra funds required to pay the person who did the cleaning, shopping, and cooking for their parents.

After accepting this generous and considerate offer, the Fishers suddenly called their children and indignantly berated them for ganging up to take control of their lives. By this time Ben and Molly were involved deeply in their complicity to be mutually unreliable in assessing the reality and implications of their differing ailments. In line with their scenario, Ben continued to disavow responsibility for his own visual impairment and for helping his wife to get medical attention for her dizziness and falling. She displayed the same irresponsibility about her own difficulties and his. They also pretended not to notice how negligent they had become about their housekeeping. Besides, they colluded in relating to the children, insisting they had no problems warranting their intervention.

Given the degree of distrust between them, Ben and Molly

were not disposed to trust their own family. Instead, they spent many hours searching for the shoddy motives the children might have in proposing their return to Philadelphia. Perhaps the kids hoped they would die in the harsh winters—the quicker to get their inheritance. Perhaps they wanted to enslave them as babysitters for the grandchildren. Or maybe the children were covetous, unable to tolerate the thought of their parents having such a good life in the sun.

The Fishers took no measures to protect their safety or to improve the conditions of their household. Instead, they acted out their mutual detachment by blandly watching each other suffer, as if from afar. One night, however, Ben ran their car into a telephone pole, fracturing his skull, but surviving. While also coming out alive, Molly had several broken vertebrae in her upper back.

Summoned by the hospital, two of the children rushed to Arizona. Now thoroughly traumatized and obviously unable to function on their own, Ben and Molly had no alternative but to let themselves be flown to Philadelphia. In this disabled condition and with no prearranged apartment waiting for them, they also had to accept the only housing their children could get to meet the emergency: a room in a health-related facility for senior citizens. Thus, by undermining their interdependence, the Fishers brought tragedy to themselves and their children.

To be sure, mates need not "go gentle into that good night"—in the sense of abjectly submitting to death without making every effort to live as long as possible. But this determination does not necessarily require them to "Rage, rage against the dying of the light"[27] as cantankerous and pigheaded people. For love-centered spouses, by contrast, the most philosophically congenial reaction to impending death is an unequivocal willingness to take care of their unfinished business in living.

Of course, mutually reliable mates attend to the material aspects of their ultimate demise while they are still relatively sound in mind and body. Even before becoming "young-old" at the age of 65, they write their last will and testament. They also specify the other details of their bequest. If they own real estate, they see to it that the deed and other important documents are on hand and known to their designated heirs. The same is true of all their bank accounts and other investments. Likewise, they decide which heirs get what items of personal property, such as jewelry and mementos. They also make realistic appraisals of the living arrangements that would be best for each of them if the other is the first to die.

But it is far more challenging for mates to set their "interpersonal house" in order. Surely, love-centered couples would want to perpetuate the trust they had built not only within their own relationship but also between them and their children. Responsible about monitoring their failing health, they are prepared to admit when "enough is enough." Then they are ready to entrust themselves to the kind of care their children believe is best for them. In contrast to the Fishers, such a couple demonstrates what Myrna Lewis calls "responsible dependency." They realistically evaluate the necessity of getting help from others, and they accept that assistance "with dignity and cooperativeness, rather than denying the need or abusing the opportunity to be dependent."[28]

In addition, mates maximize their harmony and spread it to others by taking the initiative to resolve any conflicts or misunderstandings they still sense with adult children and their mates, as well as with siblings, other relatives, and friends. Of course, a couple may not attain this resolution with everyone. Some people may resist their attempts to go beyond whatever level of distrust had prevailed among all concerned. Yet both mates will have practiced what they preach until their last breath, exemplars of trust for the entire family. Thus, they die serene in the knowledge of having fulfilled their chosen pathway in life, and they leave behind a legacy of relational development that remains an inspiration to their loved ones.

NOTES

1. *Public law 99–592. Age discrimination in employment amendments of 1986.* United States Congress, October 31, 1986.
2. Comfort, A. *A good age.* New York: Crown, 1976, p. 30.
3. Tryban, G. M. Effects of work and retirement within long-term marital relationships. *Lifestyles: A Journal of Changing Patterns,* Summer 1985, 7, pp. 207–222.

4. Parker, S. *Work and retirement.* London: Allen & Unwin, 1982, p. 120.

5. Butler, R. N., & Lewis, M. I. *Aging and mental health: Positive psychosocial and biomedical approaches.* St. Louis: Mosby, 1982, p. 39.

6. Moody, H. R. Education as a lifelong process. In A. Pifer & L. Bronte (Eds.), *Our aging society.* New York: Norton, pp. 199–217.

7. Butler and Lewis, op. cit., p. 29.

8. Moody, op. cit., pp. 209–211.

9. Ibid., pp. 211–212.

10. Cited in Comfort, A. *The biology of senescence.* New York: Elsevier, 1979, p. 169.

11. Weeks, J. R. *Aging: Concepts and social issues.* Belmont, Calif.: Wadsworth, 1984, p. 77.

12. Nass, Libby, and Fisher, *Sexual choices*, p. 320.

13. Allgeier and Allgeier, *Sexual interactions*, 2d ed., p. 483.

14. Baker, E. F. *Man in the trap.* New York: Avon, 1967, Chapter 14.

15. Comfort, op. cit., p. 195.

16. Ibid.

17. Lowen, A. *Love and orgasm.* New York: Signet, 1965, p. 196.

18. Nass, G. D., & Fisher, M. P. *Sexuality today.* Boston: Jones & Bartlett, 1988, p. 212.

19. Strong, B., & Reynolds, R. *Understanding our sexuality.* St. Paul: West, 1982, p. 238.

20. Weeks, op. cit., p. 54.

21. Katchadourian, *Fundamentals of human sexuality*, p. 387.

22. Parker, op. cit., pp. 120–121. See also Butler and Lewis, op. cit., pp. 44–45.

23. Weeks, op. cit., p. 159.

24. Ibid., p. 173.

25. Ibid., p. 280.

26. Butler and Lewis, op. cit., p. 326.

27. Thomas, D. Do not go gentle into that good night. *The collected poems of Dylan Thomas.* New York: New Directions, 1957, p. 128.

28. Butler and Lewis, op. cit., p. 58.

NAME INDEX

SUBJECT INDEX

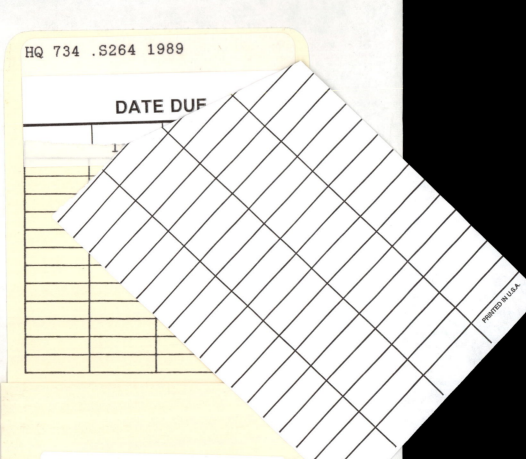

HQ 734 .S264 1989

DATE DUE

PRINTED IN U.S.A.